Heroes from the Attic

Heroes from the Attic

A Gripping True Story of Triumph

Herman I Neuman

Writers Club Press
New York Lincoln Shanghai

Heroes from the Attic

Writers Club Press
an imprint of iUniverse, Inc.

For information address:
iUniverse, Inc.
2021 Pine Lake Road, Suite 100
Lincoln, NE 68512
www.iuniverse.com

This is a true story and all of the people are real. However, I have changed the names of most of them to protect the innocent and, very reluctantly, also some of the guilty, for reasons that can be learned herein. The sarcasm and satirical humor reflect solely on the characters and are definitely not intended to be a reproof or criticism of any particular group, faith or dogma.
The Author

A 425-page edition of this memoir is also published by iUniverse.com, Inc. under the title of
"Bastards, Bitches, and Heroes," Copyright 2001.

ISBN: 0-595-22314-1

Printed in the United States of America

To all *heroes*,
young and old,
forgotten in *attics,*
may you triumph too!

Contents

Acknowledgements

My dear wife of many years helped in various ways during the creation of this memoir, especially in taking over some of my other work, thus enabling me to spend more time writing. She is also a most efficient assistant and I thank her deeply for her great and prolonged efforts.

I also give hearty thanks to the many readers of the first edition of this book who have inspired me with overwhelming enthusiasm and support.

The centered verses quoted in italics throughout this memoir are the last lines of each stanza of the poem, *September 1, 1939,* from W.H. AUDEN COLLECTED POEMS by W.H. Auden. Copyright (c) 1940 by W.H. Auden. Reprinted by permission of Random House, Inc. Also published and copyrighted (c) in 1977 by W.H. Auden in THE ENGLISH AUDEN. Reprinted by permission of Faber and Faber, Ltd.

Preface

I never did give anybody hell. I just told the truth and they thought it was hell.

—*Harry S. Truman*

If I tell the truth, will others suffer hell?

◆　　◆　　◆

Although I have overcome many incredible adversities, I never wanted to write this memoir, mainly because I felt that I would not have the emotional stamina to think about our past. I thought I'd short out the keyboard with my tears. But it was not that way because something changed in me. I could do it now because I have learned a lot about other people and myself, have banished most of the ghosts from my soul, and, together with my wife, have built a fantastic life.

Inadvertently my friend, my horse, encouraged me to write. His girlfriend was neighing for him from a distant corral, while I stood before him, restraining him with a halter rope. Frustrated, with the saddle hanging under his belly, he reared up, jumped forward and bounced me off his chest, crashing me to the ground. I cannot blame him, because I would have done the same had my wife called me. Then he bucked, kicked and bounced over the top of me lengthwise, yee-haaa, but never touched me.

However, my impact with the ground tore loose one of my collar-bones. With my right arm tied to my chest, I had a lot of spare time to peck out a short personal history with my left and eventually expanded it into this book. So far I had suppressed many memories of our early years and had to search for them like pieces of a puzzle in one of the holes in my head. The more I searched, the more questions I raised; there were so many riddles to be solved. Because my early experiences had been traumatic, I began to research my family's enigma only in brief sessions. But as time went by my agony changed to self-respect, and I became obsessed with completing my story as quickly as possible.

My brother Siggi and I existed, at times, at a subhuman level for about two decades before we managed to claw ourselves out from under our sweet relatives and to the starting line of life. We kept up the momentum of our rise from the abyss to soar into high orbit. Ironically we are remaining there, while sadly, seemingly ever more people are destroying their own lives and those of others, wittingly or out of ignorance.

While reflecting on our existence, I wondered how had we survived? How many people could endure such exciting turmoil for so many years without reacting violently? Why were we not killed? Why did we not kill? Why did we not wither into drunken wastrels? We are the opposite; we're full of zest and very much alive. I delight in the smallest to the biggest, from the ants and flowers to the sun and stars in the sky.

I did not embellish our story, except for balancing the intensity of our drama with satire and corrosive humor. My kind of humor. Embellishment would detract from the experience that had been so unusual and overwhelming by itself. Even though no words can adequately describe it, I did not want to distort the truth because it might trivialize our sufferings.

I learned much of our early history from hundreds of letters which our parents had written over the years. Ma had saved them and I had saved the ones she had written to me, some of which I have quoted herein. These also confirmed some of my recollections from early childhood. She was not schooled and wrote in very long sentences, in the "old style," as she called it, but I edited them to make them easier to read and tried not to change her ideas and feelings.

My musings in this memoir, concurrent and belated, are written in *italics*. Too often I did not have many useful thoughts during my early years because they hid from my consciousness. They vanished like cockroaches when exposed to the bright light of our grim reality, allowing me to be mostly only an elementary creature that did not want to be destroyed or driven insane by people and the ghosts that they had created.

If it had not been for some events before Siggi and I were born, our lives might have been quite different. Without them this book might not have been written, because there might not have been much to report. Our grandfather spanked our mother and "bounced her off the furniture when she was a baby." He dented our mother's head, literally, but I only learned this in my late fifties. Such experiences may have customized her personality. Her dented personality and the "I need fun immediately" attitude of our father greatly contributed to the protracted destruction of our family.

Or did Ma become lazy, domineering and eccentric because so many other people had also mistreated her when she was a child? From personal experiences I know that it is as Pat Conroy wrote in *The Prince of Tides,* "There is no fixing a damaged childhood. The best you can hope for is to make the sucker float." Was this true for our mother as it was for my brother and me?

Regardless of what might have caused those tribulations, they would not have lasted nearly so long, nor would have been so severe, if our lawyers, judges and others had embraced justice. But because they had not, humans attacked us like jackals, and our parents murdered our family by tearing chunks from our souls. Fortunately, after many years of unrelenting steadfastness, we grew strong enough to gain freedom and independence.

We finally triumphed, Siggi and I. We earned our ways through college and traveled the world. Some of my globetrotting adventures with my wife are also recounted herein.

THE AGONIES

○ ○

Whom the gods would destroy, first they make mad.

—Ancient Greek proverb

With artistic calligraphy our father wrote for his wedding:

"OUR PRAYER!"

"...How does a sinner dare to step before Thy countenance to thank Thee for the goodness and happiness that Thou has given to me in the form of a dear woman, who is everything to me and always will be...Unite us both in a perfect exemplary marriage and give us Thy blessings therefor.

"Amen!

"This prayer sprang from my inner being. It shall close for us both the day with the most inner feeling of thanks.

"Your unforgettable Herbert."

1

THE BIG WAR

Our father prayed for an exemplary marriage. Why did we become dirty slaves, Siggi and I?

◆　　　◆　　　◆

I was born six weeks after Hitler invaded Poland, six weeks after September 1, 1939. Ma wrote me that she had begun squeezing me out at eight in the morning and was done by eight twenty. I could not wait to conquer the world, so I lowered my little head in order to attack quickly. She nicknamed me Ami, "friend" in French, and was so delirious about her squeezings that by ten she wrote her mother of the result. The result was I, a very hairy big baby. Years later she wrote that for the next eighteen months I pulled her bosom out of shape and because of that I'm **again** in super shape today. Thank you, dear Ma, for feeding me the real stuff and not questionable substitutes.

Siggi joined me in the center of the universe, the Thousand-Year *Reich.* He arrived two years later and two years into the bigger war after the big war that was to "end all wars." Sensible people don't make wars, or babies during wars, but the *Fuehrer* paid to produce, to produce cannon fodder. Pa needed relief; the *Fuehrer* needed fodder. That's why we have Siggi.

Our family lived with Mr. Doebele in his apartment in Rheinfelden, Germany. It was the top floor of one of the four-story rowhouses that ringed the Adolf Hitler Square. Mr. Doebele suffered such severe tuberculosis that the hospital dismissed him because like so many in this land, he had become hopeless. The Square was the center of the city, the hub from which five streets radiated like the spokes of a wheel. Our rowhouse was located on a corner where a spoke joined this hub. It was built of concrete and clay blocks and was finished with stucco like all the others. Its Mansard roof faced south and west to absorb the sun's rays to boil us during the summer. But I cooked too slowly, so Ma placed my crib on the metal sill of the open window and leaned it against the hot roof tiles. With me in it. High above the Square, I burned and blistered so well that Ma wrote me years later:

"...people said 'look at that brown baby,'" and

"'...he looks like a high-mountain babe.'"

Strangely, I suffered a heatstroke. My first stroke of luck in life. Ma carried me to a nearby doctor who saved my life. I don't remember and didn't ask her, but she also would write me in another letter that she heard our neighbors say:

"Katje walks around the city with a dead baby."

That's what she wrote me. She wrote me that she walked around town with a dead baby. That dead baby was I. Maybe I'm weird, but I would not have told this to anyone and certainly not to the "dead baby."

I was cooked, nearly a goner.

Ma was inventive. She also hung me from the ceiling in a shopping net, such as abnormal people used for toting groceries. I cured like a ham, and while I cured I dripped a lot of stuff. Cleverly she placed newspapers on the floor to catch my droppings and squirtings because she thought that I was a big squirter. You should be impressed by this because while enhancing the political propaganda in the papers I invented disposable diapers. I accomplished this even though I was only a baby.

In our apartment Mr. Doebele was counting his days because his illness had reduced him to a skeleton. He was in great pain and could not sleep at night. Neither could he sleep during the day. It was hot and

Siggi and I also disturbed him with our joie-de-vivre because it was a screaming lot of fun to be there. Since Mr. Doebele insisted that we leave during the daytime so he could rest, Ma had to store us in a kindergarten.

Pa wrote Ma after the war, when he did not love her anymore, about her extortion to get him to resign from the church. He also mentioned something about diapers in an aluminum cook pot, and that she left the same unwashed dishes in the kitchen sink. For weeks she licked them, when she should have washed them, and food stuck to them for days. They discovered that they were not compatible because he did not like the same licked dishes in the sink, while she did not mind having these dishes in the sink. Since he did not like to lick or wash them either, they could not resolve this intolerable situation.

They also seemed to have had trouble resolving what to do with Siggi and me.

Ma wrote to me:

"I dressed you in the little pants I had. Siggi was one and one-half years old (!) and I walked with you to see Sister Annie at the kindergarten at the Evangelical Church. I begged her to let you stay outside in the garden if there were no room for you. Heartlessly, that woman turned us away. I cried until we got back home."

Maybe there was no room for us because Ma had coerced her sparring partner, Herbert, who also happened to be our father, Siggi's and mine, to cancel our church membership early in their marriage.

She further wrote:

"At that time I was still stupid and had a prejudice against the Catholics. I believe they would have let you stay in their kindergarten."

In desperation she took us to the NSV, a Nazi organization which took us in, and would take us as well. Its kindergarten was furthest from the aluminum and dynamite factories, and Ma reasoned that since the war was rumbling closer we could become *collateral damage* during imminent bombings that can be quite destructive to little children. In this kindergarten I became hot, raspberry red and began to boil again. So Ma kept me home from this toddlers' warehouse, much to the annoyance of Mr. Doebele. In sympathy, Pa, with awe-inspiring self-restraint, did not dally in a cat house.

Ma wrote me:

"...Old Dr. Bork was in charge of the kindergarten. I asked him every day, for eight days, to examine you. Every day he said that tomorrow Ami will be able to return to the kindergarten and that my thermometer was defective. Every day I told him that this was false and I finally used Mr. Doebele's thermometer to prove it. You had *Nesselsucht* (nettle craze or rash) and kept clutching your ear. I asked him to sign you over to the hospital, which he finally did eight days later."

And eight weeks too late?

Ma could not muster someone with a car until late that evening to drive us to the hospital in Loerrach because our *Fuehrer* had confiscated many private vehicles to help enlarge, or to destroy, his *Reich*. At the junction of two highways a Nazi guard stopped us. Fear and paranoia permeated the Fatherland; blood covered the street, Dr. Wehrle's blood. He had passed through this checkpoint several times that day and each time had shown his identification card. On his last trip through he sped past the sentry without doing so in order to help with the birth of another cannonball baby. Dutifully protecting his Fatherland, a guard had shot him.

Now the sentry would not let us pass, but Ma insisted that I was very ill. He searched our vehicle, babies must be checked, they could be enemy agents. Ma became hysterical and handed him her fiery red offspring, which convinced the astute soldier that I was indeed very ill, so he let us pass. She then delivered me to the hospital and spent a sleepless night waiting.

I continued to pull my right ear but it did not come off. My screaming pain would not leave me.

Dr. Heineman informed Ma that there was gooey decay near my brain. Since my goo was only separated from my brain by eggshell-thin bone, he had to operate immediately or in a day or two I would be dead. Yippee! Had I foreseen the next two dozen years of my life, I would have insisted on that option, gladly have forgone my first stroke of luck in life.

Ma wanted to take me to the hospital in Freiburg because of its reputation, but Dr. Heineman had to carve on me immediately. He did so and removed the goo and everything that was beyond repair, including part of my skull, leaving a shrivelly deep hole behind a customized ear. To scoop and sculpt me the doctor used a saw, knife, needle and pliers. Even so, I still could be an egghead because he didn't crack my eggshell.

I was too young to realize that I was now different and not just a run-of-the-mill production like other people. Now that I was defective my life was at risk, because Nazis, National Socialists, sooner or later destroyed imperfect bodies and imperfect minds. And perfect bodies and perfect minds if they disagreed with Nazi doctrines. Euthanasia was common under the Hitler regime. It was one reason why people were afraid to speak out or were in denial that this was possible.

Many, many years later, our aunt and uncle, Mathilde and Hermann, sent me a history book of the village of Boennigheim. There is a sidebar with the following description about the *Euthanasie-programm:*

"…Through chance we know somewhat more about one of these victims. He was first taken to an institution. After some time he was delivered back dead to Boennigheim. A neighbor invited the driver to eat and drink with them. He then drank too much and told everything he had had to do. He said that he was 'with the vehicles of destruction,' the so-called 'gas wagons,' and that with these vehicles the exhaust gases were piped into the loading room. He also reported that not only mentally handicapped people, but also old and infirm ones, who did not have any next of kin, were also destroyed in this manner. The neighbors, an older couple who served him dinner, thereafter had great fear that this could happen to them also.

"The victims individually:

Elise Spathe, 1911–1941   Walter Bark, 1920–1940

Karl Pantle, 1911–1944   Willi Bailer, 1913–1940

Wilhelm Mann, 1878–1943   Otto Waegerle, 1897–1944.

"It cannot be determined today which one of these persons died of natural causes or was killed in a psychiatric hospital or in a camp. A further victim of the Nazi regime was also Karl Hofmann, born July 6, 1911. He sold his identification card to a Jew. This one was caught, and Karl Hofmann was thereupon sentenced and also killed in a concentration camp on September 16, 1943."

In this book is also a photograph of the main street of this village showing long Nazi flags hanging from every building. Some of its lengthy caption reads:

"…In any case one cannot draw the conclusion from the display of the flags that the Boennigheim people went over to National Socialism with 'waving flags.' The hoisting of the flags by the people living on this street was an obvious duty. Every deviation from this requirement could have meant danger to their lives and families."

In other words, this was a wonderful time and a wonderful place for Siggi and me to arrive on this earth, to be among a wonderful people. But we were too young to know this yet.

"The unmentionable odour of death
Offends the September night."

◆   ◆   ◆

After Operation Scoop the Goo, to prevent **my** odorous death, Dr. Heineman could not guarantee my life nor give Ma much hope. Siggi, craving attention in the sibling rivalry game, followed my leadership to infect an ear or two and joined me in the hospital. Ma worried so much that she turned yellow with jaundice and joined us to help build a more colorful family. My little brother remained there for three weeks while I lingered for more than six. Probably because of allergic reactions, my body sprouted ornamental sores everywhere. Ma told me years later that I became moist and yellow and looked as if I had been rolled in one of those big German pancakes. But I did not like to be pancake filling so I recovered, although without one ear.

Toward the end of my stay in the hospital, a girl with exotic manners in the bed next to me contorted her face into various idiotic expressions. I watched her with great interest and imitated her. Or maybe I became an authentic exotic also. We proudly played our faces to impress big people who worried that my latest character building had damaged my brain.

Ma wrote me that Dr. Heineman reinforced this by telling her:

"When I picked up Ami this morning, to stand him up, he fell over. There is something wrong with him. And always will be."

His prognosis kept her in a state of hysteria and caused her to shed many a tear. She told the doctor:

"I want to have my Ami back, even if I have to carry him in my arms for the rest of my life."

Ma's worries caused her to shrink a lot of fat cells, and she frequently weaved across the street to visit Siggi and me. She wrote that she cried so much that she would not have a tear left if I would die as Dr. Heineman had warned her.

She did not pray.

Pa was having too much fun to pray.

I lost one ear and received more damage to my already sun-scorched soul. No one knew if I actually had become mentally or physically more defective from this latest episode, but after weeks of rehabilitation I learned to walk again and began to act normally, although sluggishly.

After we recovered we returned home to Mr. Doebele's apartment. Later, under the threat of bullets and other high-speed objects, Ma bicycled to Saeckingen, to the district office of the NSV to claim a reward for my damaged head. They told her that there was insurance for cases such as mine and that I could receive payments until I died. I could have become a socialist on the *entitlement* side, but Pa forbade Ma to make such a claim on my behalf. Like everyone in the Fatherland he was afraid of Nazi programs. One almost devoured him while he nursed glasses of wine in a café, where he carelessly proclaimed that he did not like the designs of Adolf Hitler who aspired to be an amateur architect. Pa's assessment conflicted with the Do Not Criticize Your *Fuehrer* Law, so the Gestapo came to lock him up overnight to teach him respect for his leader.

Ma reminded Pa later in a letter:

"…before it was too late I wanted to sue the NSV and you *Angsthase,* scared rabbit, could not bear this. Ami would have surely received a good sum for the loss of his ear but today it is too late."

And don't forget about the lifelong rot in my head, Mama.

Ma wanted to know if I'd be able to go swimming. Could water in my ear cause infections in my brain? Instead of trying it out by pouring a liter or so into my head, to see what bubbled out, she bicycled to Dr. Heineman in Loerrach with Siggi and me. Siggi sat in front and I on the luggage rack behind her behind.

She asked the doctor: "Can Ami go swimming?"

"I do not know," she wrote me he said.

This could have been the trip that someone from Loerrach would tell me about years later. They said that we had stopped at their house to warm up, and that they had thought that our mother was crazy because Siggi and I were shivering and blue. Even so, blue is still my favorite color and I still love the outdoors, the sun and high places.

◆   ◆   ◆

Although Pa was not visiting the brothels, he kept his wedding ring in his billfold and carried abortion medicine for emergencies whenever he traveled. Ma reminded him in a letter:

"A person, who goes on trips with *Dr. Lippel's Rezepten,* and remembers and dreams about miscarriages by the railroad embankment, can never stay calm...

"...if you knew about the efforts I made to change the lock, so they could not get in! But you with your frivolous friendship with the baker's daughters have made a mess and I am supposed to take it."

When I asked Ma years later about our father's fornicating habits, she wrote back:

"One of the baker's daughters was on a train and had to pull the emergency brake so she could get off. She then had a miscarriage by the railroad track, by him, as he explained it to me himself."

Pa was not only afraid of creating pregnancies and acquiring infections but also of being drafted into the military. Naturally he was inducted and *served* for fourteen months. After he survived the raid on Dieppe, he feigned an illness that could not be verified with certainty. Wisely he told Ma that it was better to live for his country than to die for it. Suffering from severe *Hexenschuss* (shot by a witch), lumbago, he was delivered to a military hospital where he was bundled in cotton blankets to ease his phantom pain. While there, he yearned for his years in technical college with its free-flowing women, wine and beer. He had been known there as the "Racing Pencil" because he had developed and drafted designs faster than anyone else. He had managed this even though, or because, he'd show up in his classes pickled with alcohol. His professor had asked him how he could be so talented when he was always plastered.

While in the hospital, Pa learned of an opportunity that he thought would keep him out of further battles. As an architectural engineer he could help rebuild conquered France and avoid encounters with Ivan, Tommy and Ami, i.e., the Russians, English and Americans. He applied at the Organization Todt and was appointed Chief of Reconstruction for Alsace-Lorraine, the area west of the Black Forest across the Rhine River that had been a historical bouncing ball between the French and the Germans.

Now his important position kept him out of the midst of war and his staff car gave him great mobility. He frequented French cafés and resumed his pursuit of hedonism by gorging, drinking, smoking and bouncing on girls. Since he was in a war away from home, Ma condoned his dallying and insisted that he wear condoms. Foreign girls might be dirty. She advised him how to avoid infections because she did not want to catch one when she cured his swellings herself. She even asked him to be examined for diseases before she would treat him personally. And after visiting her, he usually returned to France with goodies, such as foodstuffs and clothing.

Do Siggi and I have brothers and sisters in France?

While Pa was playing with girls in France, Ma played horse and rider with me. She wrote me and confirmed my memories:

"When we were alone, we had it so wonderful together. I put on my longest skirt and sat you on my lap. I bopped you up and down while we sang together this little rhyme (roughly translated as follows):

'Giddyup, giddyup rider,
When he falls he cries then,
When he falls into the ditch
He is devoured by ravens,
Falls he into the swamp,
The rider goes plop.'

"When we sang 'plop,' I let you fall into my skirt, holding you with both hands. You found it to be such great fun that you shortened the song and called 'plop, plop,' so you'd fall more quickly. We played this game every evening."

Pa was transferred to Regensburg to work with the Messerschmidt factories. We moved there also and shortly thereafter to neighboring Regenstauf. But not long after that our apartment was bombed, so we moved to the village of Diesenbach where we resided in the dance hall of a beergarden restaurant. Allied bombings were causing a severe housing shortage, even though there weren't as many live people as before. The restaurant owner, Mr. Pirzer, was an excellent cook, and this was the first time that Siggi and I ate hot meals because Ma never cooked. "Cooking destroys vitamins," she told people for years. Mr. Pirzer's delicious food made such an impression that I still remember some of it. I have not had these dishes since we moved away from Bavaria in 1945: *Knoedel,* tasty salty balls of grated potatoes; *Maultaschen,* pasta pouches with mouth-watering fillings.

We joined the Pirzers in their kitchen at meal times. In one corner was a built-in bench and table of the same dark wood as the wainscot on the wall behind it. Under a crucifix in the corner was a place setting, complete with plate, fork, knife and wineglass. But I could see no one sitting there. After Mr. Pirzer asked the blessing I asked him about the empty place setting.

He explained: "That place is reserved for Jesus. He's always with us."

I did not know anyone named Jesus and could not imagine anyone to be invisible.

After everyone finished eating, as if on cue, each person held his plate squarely in front of his face to lick it clean, to waste nothing. These had been the only standard and cooked meals for Siggi and me, and maybe that's why I remember them so well, because years of uniquely rotten diets were to follow.

◆   ◆   ◆

The war was fully upon us.

Whenever an air raid warning sounded, and the bombs did not hail down immediately, we ran into a beer cellar cave in Regenstauf and remained there for the duration of the bombing. A heavy door, like a castle gate, protected its entrance. But when the attack was immediate, we fled to the cellar of our restaurant, because there were no bomb shelters in Diesenbach. I still remember our defense equipment in the hallways: tubs and buckets with sand and water, shovels and hand pumps, and two kinds of gas masks, one for adults and one for children. Siggi and I would breathe vigorously into our masks to cause their rubber nose valves to snore like giants.

Someone explained that the sand was to be used to smother fires from the incendiary bombs. If these were doused with water, the fire would spread with the water instead of extinguishing it. This was our entire defense arsenal when the bombs rained into the city: sand and water to save buildings, masks and bunkers to save bodies, desperate prayers to save souls.

The bombings became ever more frequent and destructive, that is, effective. Nightly, at the wail of sirens, Ma and Pa scrambled over the masonry rubble littering the streets. They carried Siggi and me in their arms to the protection underground. Droning airplanes showered us with bombs that shook our world and everything in it in order to liberate the people huddling in bunkers, caves and basements. When the sirens announced the end of the rain of terror from the sky upon the reign of terror on the ground, we ventured out to find the city in flames and bodies in rubble.

In the corner of the yellow stucco walls of Pirzers' restaurant I created my own flames, when I lit some matches. Therefore Ma showed me off by baring my butt in public, did not wash me, but licked me instead with a length of electrical cord. I was hot, full of pain and expertly licked. Maybe that's why I remember this so well because years of whipping were to follow. Everyone else seemed to be allowed to burn whole cities, but I was not allowed to make my own little fire. I could not understand this. *Did the mothers spank their children after they rained fire from the sky?*

I remember hurrying to a bomb shelter with Ma, and only with Ma. Someone must have dragged Siggi off into another hole in the ground. Or he was forgotten. Pa was not there. Running through the siren-titillated air, we passed a big house whence a woman scurried carrying two blooming flowerpots. She screamed: "A fire-bomb hit my house." We did not care that much about flowers and kept running to beat her into our hellhole underground.

When the sirens told us that it was safe to come back out, we returned to a conflagration in which the flowerpot-less house was also burning down. Two men were pulling stacked firewood away from its wall, to save it for making fires when it got cold and there would be nothing left to burn.

◆   ◆   ◆

Whenever I heard air raid sirens, but always only from my left, I started screaming. They announced the beginning of joy, or the beginning of terror, depending if one were flying high, or scurrying on the ground. It could be a religious experience in either place. I preferred to have it in the sky and just had to wait for someone to send me there. In the meantime, I had to settle for the underground sensation instead. With Dante in Hades.

One day, after the sirens wailed the end of such an experience, Ma, Siggi and I emerged from the earth and walked back to our dance hall home. A single plane appeared over the trees and swooped down on us. Ma wrote me years later that she had screamed: "Run, scatter, run!" She wanted us to disperse so we would not present a single target. Forgetting Siggi and Ma, I ran to a steel bridge where invisible objects zinged off its structure, and I didn't know whence they came. Fortunately the big buzzing insect in the sky disappeared as quickly as it had arrived and all was quiet again. *Who wanted to liberate us?*

Our thrills did not only come from the sky but also from the ground, mostly as unfriendly and sometimes as *friendly fire*. As I played across the street from the beergarden, two men walked by and one of them said to me:

"Come here. Let me cut off your ears!"

He pulled out a pocketknife, folded out a blade, tested its edge with an expert thumb, and glanced at me with an evilly fiery eye. I froze in place, trembling, stammering: "Dddddd…ddd…ddon't…" I felt that I was already earless enough and could not let him make a silk purse out of me. Courageously screaming with angst in my soul and pee in my pants, the little ham I was, I dashed away, leaving hideous laughter behind, to bury my snout in Ma's skirt where I drew comfort from the familiar scent therein.

◆   ◆   ◆

In January of 1945, near the climax of the war in Germany when the big *Fuehrer* courageously moved into an underground bunker, little Siggi and I courageously moved into the aboveground children's clinic in Regensburg. Because we grew leather. In our throats. Hordes of bacilli formed *diphthera,* Greek for "leather," making it difficult for us to breathe. These bacterial games, called diphtheria, also produced powerful toxins that could damage hearts, nerves and kidneys. And kill people. This winter was cold, but we kept warm with high fever. During our microbial tournament, Siggi and I stoked hot fires within us to burn up bacteria. We burned for twenty-six days and enjoyed the adrenaline-gushing excitement around us from the comfort of our hospital beds without joysticks or remote controls. Even so, this hospital was a much safer place to be than at home; that's when our apartment blew up, or burned down, amidst the inferno, thunder and screaming around us. I still have two invoices for our hospital stay that prove that a deathly illness might have saved us from fiery death, little Siggi's and mine. But while we fought to keep our lives, our withering underground leader would soon blow away his own.

I was eating a rolled-up pancake filled with applesauce, sweet applesauce. Suddenly the air raid sirens began to scream, advertising another ripple on our river of life. Applesauce. There was terror in applesauce. I didn't know what it was, the flavor or the texture. It was definitely not apples per se because I like apples, apple juice and apple pie. My liking of apple pie would even help me become a good American.

I could not gag down applesauce again until I forced myself a few years ago. Whenever I tasted it, I became sad and shivered. I could not eat it, even though this would insult hostesses who would serve it to me over the years. I would eat everything else, from fresh guts retrieved from fresh manure to stale cattle feed with stale rodent doodoo, because such food would help keep me alive for many years, but not applesauce.

My mayhem ghost caused me to develop abnormally in that I cannot enjoy watching war movies. I find exploding humans and screaming sirens deeply saddening, instead of uplifting and fulfilling as they seem to be for normal people. They splatter guts onto their TV screens, stare at them by the millions and participate in such games on video.

*Do they want ghosts in their souls? Are today's children deprived because they can only watch virtual mayhem on glass screens? Why do these screens depict so little **real-time** mayhem when reporting real wars?*

Hard as I've tried, I have not always been able to avoid this mayhem ghost which would torture me at unexpected times. For example, my wife and I would one day visit a theater to see *Not Without My Daughter*. I had not met my mayhem ghost since my first war and forgot that it existed. This movie was based on the true story about an American girl who married an Iranian boy, and I did not expect to be instilled with the terror of air raid sirens. This invited my mayhem ghost. Nor did it occur to me up to this time that after so many years the siren's wail would still bother me. Now the devil's howl caused such an intense agony in my heart and soul that I wanted to cower under the seats, but I was stuck in the middle of the crowded theater. I forced myself to remain there to discover how intense this sensation could get and try to slay this ghost. I had to convince myself that it was only a ghost, and that I had nothing to fear, because it was not the devil, but only a distant memory of him.

Upon leaving the theater I burst out sobbing uncontrollably. A fist gripped my heart, but I wanted to rip it out myself so it would not hurt anymore. Squirting tears, gasping for air, I tried to explain to my worried wife that I was all right.

"I'm OK, sob, FlowerBear, sob, I'm just entertaining these people. Baahhhh. In case they found the movie boring. Bahhh."

That is what I would have told her, my FlowerBear, had my joking brain cells not been switched off by this disturbing episode.

◆   ◆   ◆

Before our liberators marched into Diesenbach, everyone removed the creepy Nazi flags from their buildings and hoisted white flags, sheets and towels everywhere, voluntarily and with great relief. Several American soldiers walked up to the fence around the restaurant garden where Siggi and I were playing. One of them, with the whitest teeth gleaming in the blackest face, gave Siggi and me each an orange. Three-year old Siggi burst forth with a baahhh while running into the restaurant.

We are all pure Aryans, you know!

Was this soldier charred in the siren fires? Did Siggi run in to check his face in the mirror? Can I find this man so I can hug him?

These soldiers introduced us to chewing gum, food that we could feast on forever. This was good because I became fixated in the oral stage. Since these brave soldiers ended our *Fuehrer's* reign of terror and also gave us candy, Siggi and I developed a liking for Americans. And so did Ma and Pa but also for other reasons. Pa wanted to get rid of Ma and Ma wanted to get rid of Pa, but not his financial support. A few years hence, Pa wrote to his lawyer that he thought that he had found a legal basis for divorce when he surprised Ma, his sparring partner, at two in the morning being squeezed in the arms of an "American bull." Instead of rescuing her from his grip, Pa was delighted and hoped that she might marry this bull and move with him to America, taking Siggi and me.

◆   ◆   ◆

The end of World War II in Europe began a long and bizarre sequence of events for our family. Now that Ma and Pa were together again full time, they eased from the agonies of the war to the tranquility of peace by bombarding each other with mouth grenades and accusations. They discovered that they did not like each other anymore and, therefore, began another war, their private little Progenitors' War.

Let the games begin!

Ma told Pa that she wanted to escape the post-war chaos in Germany, the destruction of almost everything. Demolished were the factories, housing and currency; there was starvation and homelessness. If people did not starve to death, they froze to death, and in addition to these miseries the Russians also terrified them. They were feeding refugees to the fish in the Baltic Sea by sinking their ships fleeing to the West, and Ma and Pa were afraid that the Soviets would move into Regensburg to terrorize us as well.

To relieve his worries, and since Ma refused to do housework, Pa told Ma he wanted to adopt a young medical student. She could clean and cook, and he promised not to have sex with her. He had self-discipline. His promise is documented by the many letters that our parents wrote each other after they separated, and which I would exhume years later from their elaborately and uniquely decorated tomb, our mother's apartment.

Ma presented Pa with the following proposal:

"Stine Brackler has a brother who is single and has been in America for eighteen years. He spent a lot of time with Helene (Ma's sister). He should fetch the boys and me…

"…this means for us to get divorced and for me to marry the American. Then I'll divorce him and marry you again. Or should we wait until we can emigrate. The Russians will be here by then."

◆   ◆   ◆

The intense discord with her husband and the socio-economic dis-locations caused Ma to leave Bavaria and return to the place of her birth, to live with her mother and sister in north Germany. Pa stayed behind, lonely with only a maid and lots of women. At this time he was employed to inventory the remains of the Messerschmidt factories.

Several months after the official end of World War II in Europe, on the tenth of September, 1945, the three of us sat by the railroad track for many hours with hundreds of people, waiting for a train to arrive. There were no train schedules because of track damage and personnel, fuel and equipment shortages. Pa was not there to see us off, to tell us that he loved us, to squeeze and hug us, to assure us that he'd soon join us again.

When a train finally arrived, Ma, carrying Siggi in her arms, pushed me through the horde that was part of the twelve million people fleeing from the east to roam the west searching for new homelands. It was pulled by a huge steam locomotive and consisted mainly of first-class boxcars and open, second-class coal cars, all sooty black to befit the mood of the country. Ma lifted us into a boxcar and climbed on her-self. When it became jammed with people, who sat down on the straw-covered floor, two men pulled our door shut and locked it. I remember people pounding and shouting on the outside for us to open up again, while others scrambled to the opposite side of our train and tried to get in from there. But someone informed them that our box was full of children to be reunited with their parents. The ones that didn't get caught, the ones that didn't get killed, and the ones that did not hide. He then pulled this door shut also, making it very dark for us.

Ours was similar to the railroad scene from the movie, *Schindler's List*.

We were lucky to get on this train. Laws had been passed that refu-gees were not allowed to stay in some communities for more than so many days if they could not find employment or did not have friends or relatives to take them in. Many could not find such because the economy had collapsed and many had perished. The main industries of armament, persecution and destruction were now passé. Consequently people roamed about western Germany, carrying their few belongings with them while searching for places to settle, places where they could root for truffles and other delicacies.

Our route mostly followed the Rhine River to the North Sea. We traveled most of our thousand-kilometer journey in crowded boxcars, where people survived on what little food they brought with them. They peed into pots and they peed into pans, and when Siggi and I had to pee, Ma held up our dented aluminum can. I was old enough to be embarrassed exposing my tender organ of the pubic to the public. To avoid this, I squeezed my muscles to hold back the flow. I squirmed around to postpone the inevitable, often until it was too late. When to my great relief and humiliation, soothing warm moisture spread about my pants, I hid behind Ma.

Whenever our train stopped, sometimes to take on coal and water for the locomotive, the travelers disposed of gallons of urine. Some of them hurried off to find private places for further hygiene and to fill their containers with water for drinking. They bought or bartered items being hawked on the station platform, and this was the usual routine during most of our stops. Along the way we changed to another train, a mostly empty one going to the Saar region to haul more coal back to Bavaria. Ma asked a one-legged stranger on crutches to help transfer our ninety-kilo wicker trunk across several tracks.

While sitting on our trunk, we were able to see over the sides of our coal car. We were alone here but were far less comfortable than before because the sooty smoke and coal dust from our steam engine now buffeted us, burning our eyes and choking our lungs.

◆   ◆   ◆

At the ages of three and five, Siggi and I did not realize that we had spent all of our lives in a war, the most devastating war in history. Traveling through Germany in open-air cars gave us a close-up view of its destruction. Whole cities had been bombed and burned into black, jagged gravestones rising from masonry rubble, grim reminders of our recent past to be remembered forever. Or to be forgotten.

We had been terrified in Diesenbach watching a train across the river explode from one end to the other. Ma wrote me years later, confirming my memories, that she had thought that this had been an unadvertised air raid and therefore ran with Siggi and me to the nearby forest for cover. Along the way, soldiers standing in a doorway had informed us that this was not a bombing raid but a sabotaged munitions train.

A long column of giant tanks had roared into Diesenbach, separating Siggi and me on opposite sides of the road. I could see him scream. I felt my body scream because we thought we'd never be able to get together again. One of these monsters had then chased me, and since I was certain that it would squash me, I had jumped into a ditch.

Everything and everybody seemed to chase, bite, beat, or attempt to kill us. We had lunged for cover under a tree when an airplane swooped down on us. A goose in Unterhut, where we also briefly lived, had torn at my britches. In Herten, whence we also had fled, I spotted a fat Zeppelin in the sky and thought that it was going to make loud thunder and roaring fires. To escape from this, I had run home but when I found the door locked, I beat it with my fists while screaming my guts out.

Siggi and I were too young to understand the reasons for the violence and destruction around us, to comprehend the purpose of our frequent moving from here to there, from city to city and back. We stayed tethered to Ma and barely let her out of our sight because she was our only comfort. Often we clung to her legs, hiding in her skirt like a brood of baby birds gathered under the wings of their mother. We never chirped, but she sometimes cackled.

During the few times that we had been with our father I felt uneasy with him. He had taken me bathing naked in the Regen River and tried to dip me under. I was screaming and Pa evidently found this amusing because he had a smirk on his face. So often he would have that smirk and I did not like it. I stopped screaming momentarily when I saw a partial man struggle out of the water before us. Both of his arms were more or less missing and one leg had departed as well. Now I was certain that it was dangerous to go swimming and continued to scream until I could draw no more air.

Another time Pa had taken me out on the river in his foldboat. He carried it there and did not want to return home to fetch the oars. On the way we passed a flatbed wagon that was loaded with a precisely-shaped, peaked manure pile. Pa stole this farmer's manure paddle, which must have frustrated him greatly because no self-respecting farmer ever drove through the village with a messy wagon.

Since this paddle was not made to beat water but to pound manure, Pa lost control of his craft out on the river, and we hit a sandbar that ripped a gash in the boat's skin. Forgetting about the partial man in the river, I promptly jumped overboard because I did not want to sink.

No, Pa could not be trusted. Once he walked with me into the forest to look at an anti-aircraft cannon that had been blown apart by the Allies. There were big holes in the ground and bodies, and parts of bodies, were hanging in trees and were strewn all around.

"Don't cry, Ami," Pa soothed me, "They can't hurt you. They're all dead now."

◆   ◆   ◆

When this war finally ended, much of Europe was full of holes and in ashes, therefore...

Life can only get better!

2

THE STARVATION

○ ○
I have been driven many times upon my knees by the overwhelming conviction that I had nowhere to go. My own wisdom, and that of all about me, seemed insufficient for that
day.

—Abraham Lincoln

So far our lives had been a little difficult. Had it been so for others?

◆　　　◆　　　◆

Ma, Siggi and I reached Simonswolde in East Frisia, east of Holland, seven days after leaving Bavaria. In normal times this trip would
take at most a day and a half. A few dozen red brick houses bordered
the brick road that wound from village to village and was barely wide
enough for two vehicles to pass. These were horse and ox-drawn wagons and an occasional motorcar. Sometimes a truck fueled by wood gas
generated in a furnace behind the driver also sputtered loudly through
the silence.

Drainage ditches paralleled both sides of this road. After lots of rain,
horse-drawn heavy sleds churned the mud in the lane that bordered the
brick pavement. Clay tiles or thick thatch covered the roofs of the
homes, as well as the farmhouses located at the edge of this village. A

few Holstein cows resided all winter in the barns that were attached to the front of the farmhouses, contributing heat and the freshest of aromas to these human-animal shelters. Cubic manure piles adorned their front yards, growing bigger throughout winter, while chickens foraged about them.

Inside each barn was a bench with a hole in it. It stank. To answer a call, one walked, preferably not in slippers, past the rear of the cows to make deposits there. At least one did not have to go outside when it was cold, or into swarms of mosquitoes when it was hot. Flies hatched in the piles and the holes; mosquitoes hatched in the moors, puddles and ponds. And there were many. In the spring, to really season the country air the farmers spread the fertilizer from the piles and the holes over the fields surrounding this village.

Outside of each house was a well. People drew water by dipping a bucket, which was hooked to the end of a pole, into it. A few of the homes had pumps inside where several up and down strokes with the iron levers delivered non-chlorinated water for drinking, cooking and bathing.

◆   ◆   ◆

Since the war had ended, Simonswolde was serene to the point of boredom. It was so peaceful that there'd be no resident peacekeeper here for years to come. Occasionally a policeman visited on his bicycle from the neighboring village a few kilometers away, and a shiny silver medallion on his helmet dazzled us children.

The flat, mostly treeless landscape around Simonswolde added to its humdrum. Long ago this land was claimed from the North Sea and, like Holland, was protected by dikes, ribboned with canals and dotted with windmills. Numerous ditches also crisscrossed this land for us children to play on, play in and sometimes drown in.

We moved into a small house near the center of Simonswolde where Aunt Adele and our grandmother were already living. Our aunt was in her early thirties and was still single. Oma, with snow-white hair pulled into a tiny knot, was widowed. Ma's prayers had been answered when grandpa hung himself. Even though it was not part of a farm, this house had a four-cow barn attached to its back, but since we had no cows we stored peat, coal and junk there, as did the other resident families.

Our new home was owned by an old woman, Mrs. Heddens, who lived in a room by herself. Bluish, transparent skin draped her skeleton, and I could almost see her insides. On her left cheek a sore was always oozing pus. Her insides were dripping out, and whenever a greenish bead formed there, she'd wipe it off with a twiggy finger. I knew this because I once surprised her harvesting her pus in our common vestibule when our kitchen door stood ajar, casting a dim light into it. Its light bulb had been removed years before, so this was a good place to do our boring, wiping and smearing, although I was reluctant to touch anything in the areas that we shared with Mrs. Heddens. Her pus was disgusting and she looked quite empty.

I worried. *Will her goo ever stop flowing? Do people die when they're empty?*

I worried because I too was oozing pus and it seemed to match hers in color.

I was too young to know what people had running out of their heads, and at this time I began to realize that I was not symmetrical. There was a deep dent behind my ear. But I did not question Ma about it because I did not know that this was not the way I was born. I had better things to worry about than a pit in my head. I also became slowly aware that you hear with your left ear, rotate your head to find the direction of the sound, and cock your ear in that direction to improve your reception. No one has to teach you this because you do it automatically.

You oozed from the other ear.

I worried about becoming empty too because Operation Scoop the Goo did not stop my chronic infection. Millions of germs in my head produced runny, well-aged Limburger-cheese-like-smelling crud. I habitually scooped it out with my finger, sniffed it. *No. Still stinks!* And as usual, I smeared it off on my clothes and other convenient places. It was normal to ooze and smear; Mrs. Heddens was doing it too.

My microbes were more peace loving than hers and established a relatively stable social order in my head. This meant, at least for the time being, that they fed mostly on ear wax, dead skin and such, and attacked my body only infrequently. In the meantime, Ma could not take me to a doctor because there was no doctor, and we had no money to travel to or to pay for one.

Mrs. Heddens' microbes were more vicious than mine. Like tiny piranhas they attacked her flesh and bones, slowly devouring her. But mine dwelled nearer to a brain, my brain, than hers near hers. Whenever our microbial tribes invaded each other's territory they fought each other for dominance, but these battles remained our secret since the First Biological War, BWI, has never been publicized.

Even though we never invited them, we also provided our kind hospitality to other types of microbes. For some time I provided room and board to the Rotten Tooth Gum Tribe. Ma keenly observed in a letter to Pa:

"…Ami pulled six of his own teeth, some of them during class. Five new ones are growing again, but the gums are red and infected in three places. He also has 39.5 centigrade (103.1 degrees Fahrenheit) fever and has been in bed for three days. The nurse said he has mouth rot…"

Now I had mouth rot as well as ear rot.

Hurrah, the tooth rot fairy came to visit me! But she did not leave me any money. My second set of teeth arrived, but instead of my canine teeth falling out to be replaced by new ones, they doubled up, new ones on top of old ones, double-decker style. Meanwhile my gums oozed pus, culinary pus, until I was able to spit out the offending teeth. We had no money for a dentist, no matter, for there was no dentist. But I did not have to worry that I would become empty from this body leak because I swallowed the suppuration. It tasted salty but needed some pepper since I like my food spicy. Sucking pus from my gums, squeezing and probing with my tongue, gave me something to do during my dreamy school hours. Gum, the chewing kind, was not featured in the village store; however, we did receive some Wrigley's in our packages from America. *To entice us to come over, Siggi and me?*

◆   ◆   ◆

Because we were so young and Pa visited us in Simonswolde only about once a year, a few days at a time to spar with his wife and sister-in-law, Siggi and I did not realize that our parents differed as day from night. Their interests were not the same. Ma had only an eighth-grade education; he graduated from a technical college. She descended from Frisians in the flat lowlands; his ancestors came from the mountains of the Black Forest. She was a teetotaler who constantly nagged him about the dangers of alcohol. He never listened to her.

Pa claimed that while he fluffed the goose down blanket up and down with Ma, she read a newspaper, maybe because she wanted to enhance her thrill by seething about the politics of man. He could not suppress his pride about his wife's torrid response, so he showed off her forte by reporting this to his lawyer when he would file for divorce. Nevertheless, Pa desired a less curious partner, so he attempted to fornicate with Aunt Adele to discover her actions or reactions to sex. *Will Siggi and I get a couster, sissin, brothsin or someone like that?*

Ma was extremely stubborn, domineering and thrifty. Pa was a spendthrift, bent on making up for lost time and lost mind in the war. The only reason they had married was because they were born on the same day of the same year, and they called themselves twins. And this seemed to be the only thing that they had in common, other than engaging in the most basic functions for survival. Ma was very intelligent, or so I would hear people say over the years, and her purpose in life was to give advice. Never did she accept such from anyone else, and her face belied her overbearing personality. It was round with a soft double chin, and on occasion when she smiled, her face became angelic. But she rarely smiled because humans had hardened her soul. When she was fourteen she walked out of church, saying:

"I don't believe there are angels, and that they can move through walls."

Whenever Pa did visit us, Siggi and I always wanted to play with him. But he rarely allowed it, and when we wanted his attention he usually sent us out of the house. He kept far away from us. We never connected, and I did not know why this was so. He was a stranger and normally went to bed at noon to nap. Siggi and I always had to be quiet during this hour, even when we played outside and Pa was not with us, because this was the time when adults always slept. *What did they do at night? Did they plant children or did they fight?*

Once I went upstairs during noon to enjoy a few golden moments with Pa. But he was asleep and a cigarette was burning in his ashtray. I took it, tiptoed back down and sucked a cautious puff.

"Ami, did you take my cigarette?" an angry voice came from above.

"Yeah," I coughed, *"but I didn't inhale,"* I added shamefully, but presidentially.

"You cannot smoke, bring it back," he ordered me grimly because he did not want to share his pleasures.

Dutifully I took it back to him, afraid that he'd spank me, but he never did. Not once in his life would he spank Siggi and me, except once, many years hence, he would slap Siggi so hard that he knocked him to the ground after he had reported to Ma what Pa had said about her to our relatives in Southern Germany. But someday Pa would do much, much more to us than just batter us and it would be in such a unique fashion.

◆　　　◆　　　◆

I enrolled in grade school. On the first day Ma walked me there. And left me there. I did not want to be there because I was often frightened without Ma. Ghosts in my soul. But after two hours in class the teacher gave us children some candy to entice us to come back again. The next day I walked to school by myself to get my candy, but we received no more. Instead, we had to sit patiently on hard wooden benches and pay close attention to the teacher for boring hours.

All children carried their school supplies in leather satchels on their backs. These contained a slate with a sponge tethered to it that swayed to the rhythm of our steps, a chalk-like stylus for writing, a dog-eared book or two, and sandwiches wrapped in newspaper. Since no one could afford to buy pencils or paper, and there were few such items for sale in the store anyway, we did all of our schoolwork on these slates.

During recess we drank water from an old steel drum which sat in front of the school. We dipped from it with a chipped porcelain cup, and since we had little chance to drink during forenoons, I sometimes filled up more than I should have. At times my bladder responded urgently before noon, the end of our school day, when our class had to stand up to pray. One time, just before such a prayer, I waved my hand for permission to run out to the pee trough. Our teacher saw me dance and wave, but began to pray, and while we prayed I soaked my pants, and my prayer was answered.

Two years after I started, Siggi also began school. We walked there together, often clickety-clopping like ponies prancing on the brick pavement, because we wore *Klumpen,* Dutch wooden clogs, tiny boats with pointed bows and rounded sterns. We flung them into the air with swift kicks forward. If shoes could be boats, they might as well be airplanes, and when they crashed they sometimes split. We moored them outside the classrooms in precise rows. The teachers did not like them hammering the hardwood sea. Sometimes when our new *Klumpen* were too big, we put straw in them, to cushion our steps, to move stealthily like the lion we had seen in Uncle Heini's Zoo.

After school we plodded home again, to eat lunch prepared by Aunt Adele. Lunch was not hotdogs or pizza with pop. Often it was un-skimmed milk and moldy bread with rancid lard; it was sour whey and shriveled carrots. *Was this more nutritious than the food so many people feast on today, since we did not become fat or fade away?* Siggi and I always had to finish every meal to make us grow strong and were admonished to "think about the starving millions in Germany." Then after lunch we always had to finish our homework, first under the guard of Aunt Adele or Ma and her whip, before we were allowed to play.

Homework was not easy for me, and the threat of punishment always filled the air. This intimidated me to the point that my mind was shut down, but no one realized this. Not even I because my mind was shut down. I was simply dumb. For years Siggi and I learned everything under duress and would still learn that way in slavery many years later. Aunt Adele, whom we called Murmerele behind her back, was always nearby and ready to pinch an arm or pull an ear for any mistakes we made. At times I'd fill my entire slate with homework, then she'd erase it all because of one error, and I would have to do it all over again. Only after we finished it to her satisfaction were we allowed to go out and play, away from the threatening adults who were always grumpy because they were crowded into a small house and were always hungry.

◆   ◆   ◆

We played in the fields and jumped over and into ditches. We kicked soccer balls, rolled wheel rims down the street and played marbles. We flew homemade kites and tossed boiled eggs back and forth on the pastures at Easter time. Because the ground was soggy, we could throw them far and high numerous times before they would break. We also aimed at the power lines and sometimes hit them, and when the eggs broke we ate them.

We floated our *Klumpen* on the canals and ditches. We earned wet-foot whippings from Ma, who always kept her training whip pinned to her waist with a shiny safety pin. She had several such training devices, and her favorite one, my least favorite one, was a half-meter long electrical cord that was covered with bluish-green fabric. At one time it had been part of a 220-volt appliance cable that now electrified Siggi and me. She probably liked this one the best because when she vigorously whipped our bare-naked cheeks, it embedded streaks of matching color in our pure white bottoms.

I will always remember our mother with a stylish wire strap dangling from her waist. For her it was such a simple device, yet seemingly much more effective than armies of experts theorizing and agonizing how to herd children toward proper adulthood. One of the few times when I really earned her memorable after-the-deed-was-done training was when I created my own little heat. I forgot that Ma had illuminated me in Diesenbach that I was not allowed to burn down cities, and I lit a newspaper in the upstairs bedroom. When it flared up, it became a hot news flash, so I opened the window to deliver it to the world. Just then someone blasted this still evening: "Mrs. Neuman! Ami is playing with fire." This caused me to drop the fire on the cabinet instead and beat it with my bare hands to extinguish it, but not before it scorched a permanent mark on the counter. Ma did not hear this fire call, never found out, but wondered how long that dark blemish had been on the white marble vanity top.

However, her spankings could not keep us dry because water was as abundant as earth, and our *Klumpen* were too small to carry us on water. There was so much water in Frisia that the windowsills had grooves to catch the condensation flowing from the windowpanes. It drained into metal drawers under the sills, where it grew mold and rust, and during winter translucent frosty flowers formed on the glass. Siggi and I scratched and breathed on them, and when they melted, they gathered into streams that also flowed into this moldy rust.

Water was everywhere, including in our beds. I peed in my sleep and dried it with my body. It was there even if I didn't because everything absorbed the moisture from the sodden air. On the coldest days before going to bed, we warmed them with hot coal in an iron bowl inside a wicker basket that we placed under the goose down blankets. Even so, I sometimes sweated so much that my sheets would stick to me.

When we had colds Ma put hot water bottles on our feet and wet, hot compresses around our necks. She advised us that: *"Das sind die Folgen vom Nichtfolgen,"* these are the consequences of not obeying. We could not avoid water and cold feet, and it was our fault that God had created microbes that liked to live with us.

For years she also warned everyone about draft because exposure to moving air could beget many illnesses. Outside, the wind was harmless; inside it was an evil spirit that spawned earaches, tonsillitis and tuberculosis.

◆   ◆   ◆

Because we had few toys, we played hide and seek, climbed trees, went swimming and sometimes walked to a nearby village to explore. We entertained ourselves and were not programmed, coached, nor supervised by adults whenever we were outdoors. We were free spirits and babysitters were unheard of. All of the children usually behaved well because they did not like to be punished. One time our friend Marten misbehaved while on our premises, so Aunt Adele caught him and whipped him. Justice was that simple. He fell to the floor, bawling, while she continued to wire him. Afterwards he did not tell his mother because he knew that he had deserved his unpleasant reward and she might compound it further.

We experimented, interacted, fought, destroyed and created. The absence of coaching and boredom stimulated our creativity. The development of our imaginations was not dwarfed by zapping electronics or rooms full of toys made of plastic, and so we were always roaming, always investigating, always inventing our own entertainment.

Over the years we occasionally did have a few toys that came from a store. One was a metal ocean liner that was painted in great detail and could be wound up to drive a propeller. We received a tinker toy set from our relatives in America. During the dreary winter days we assembled it and also drew crayon designs on thin plywood and cut them out with a toy-like handsaw. We spent hours assembling cranes, bridges and castles with an erector set which we also received from them. On one of his visits Pa brought us a little steam engine that actually worked. A lump of burning paraffin under the boiler brought it to whistling. A refugee couple in their eighties, who also lived in one room in our house, gave me a bowling set for my birthday. Its pins were tiny and the bowling ball was a steel marble that was shiny.

After we played with our new toys for a few weeks, or a few months, they always mysteriously disappeared, and I suspect that Ma traded them for food and clothing. We celebrated our birthdays only when we received a present and this was rare. So rare that when I went outside one morning a neighbor, *Fraeulein* von Mark, asked me:

"Whose birthday is it today?"

"I don't know."

"Congratulations for your birthday," she responded.

I went back into the house and wanted to get a present.

Aunt Adele said, "Invite your friends after school, and I will make Jell-O."

Jell-O was unknown here, but we received some from America. Since Aunt Adele did not read English, she boiled the mix and let it sit. We had no refrigerator and waited with our friends around the table, willing it to solidify. When it did not, we drank this sweet birthday present instead.

When Siggi and I were really bored, we carved a room into the ground through red, brown and yellow layers of sand to the water table and below. We used a rope and bucket to bail the water that kept seeping in. We sculpted benches and shelves and covered our bunker with leaves and branches. This was a colorful part of Simonswolde, and for me only the red beech tree in our front yard and the oak trees after the first frost in the fall were more vivid.

During our month-long summer vacations, Siggi and I often walked to the other end of Simonswolde to go swimming naked with other children in the man-made lake, *Sandwasser*. Ma did not allow me to go into the water, but I did so anyway because I enjoyed it so much that I forgot her orders. She did not tell me that water in my ear caused great damage and sometimes punished me for swimming until the day I figured out how she always knew that I had done so. Messy, wet hair. From then on, I waited until it dried before going home, and this provided my head tribe the perfect milieu to thrive in.

We also caught fish in the *Sandwasser* with night crawlers knotted to the ends of reeds. While lying on the bank of this pond, we dipped the worms and watched them squirm. When we saw a fish bite or felt a tug, we jerked it out of the water, surprising it as much as us. Sometimes we made high-tech fishing gear from a bent needle tied to the end of a string. Once I thought I hooked moss with it, so I pulled hard, but landed an eel that Aunt Adele fried in a pan. It was delicious.

Siggi and I spent a lot of time perching in our beech tree. It was the only such tree in Simonswolde and probably also the highest. This was our secure world far above the fights and miseries below us. We climbed as high as we dared to sway gently in the breeze, to listen to the whisper of the leaves, to watch the people on the street, to study the moss and grooves in the bark, and the ants busily moving up and down the branches.

One day I climbed to the top of the apple tree on our side of the house. As I reached for an apple I lost my balance, and on my way down I strafed a barbed wire fence at great speed. A barb hooked my home-sewn shorts on my left side and ripped them open from top to bottom as if cut with scissors. Miraculously, the fence did not touch me, the earth gently caught me, and I was unhurt. *Who was always protecting me?*

On the south side of our house was another apple tree whose long, slender trunk sloped at a steep angle. During the war a bullet from the sky had ripped a scar through its side at an opposite angle. This tree was easy to climb, but we did not because we rarely went to that side of the house in order to keep out of sight of Mrs. Heddens who lived there. But its apples were bidding us to eat them. We ducked under her windows and cast a hook fashioned from heavy wire into the tree. I jerked on the string that we'd fastened to it and made apples rain down. Then we rolled them with sticks towards the house until we could reach them without being seen.

The reason we kept away from Mrs. Heddens was because we did not have her permission to live in her house. But there was no other place to be had in Simonswolde. We never spoke with her but for the terse greetings when we accidentally met in the hallway, and I could never understand why nobody ever visited this lonely lady.

At various times different refugees lived in this house. They resided there until they found other places to live. One of them was an old woman with giant teeth and a coarse voice. She lived above us in one room, and we could hear her praying rosaries for hours and for days. When she died, a male refugee moved in but he kept quiet. He owned only the clothes on his back and a greasy comb. He had no job or next of kin and was a smoker of homemade cigarettes of dried cherry leaves that he skillfully rolled in strips of newspaper.

◆   ◆   ◆

One summer day, Waltraut, a neighbor girl, a refugee from the East, who was a year or two older than I, led me down a dirt road to a grain field outside the village and into the rye. Deep into the rye. The air was warm, the setting romantic. She lifted her skirt, lowered her panty, and asked me to bare myself also. I studied her, and I felt the same luring fascination I had had once before when I had bent over to watch my cousin Maike squat in a pasture. Now I wondered what activity required nakedness in a grain field as Waltraut held on to my spigot and said:

"Stick it in here."

"Why?" I asked inquisitively.

"Big people do it all the time," she replied knowingly.

I tried but it didn't work. It made sense to me anatomically. But why could we not join? And I did not know how or for what purpose. Without further explanation she ceased her endeavor and I spent little time puzzling about this as we went back to the village. A little voice informed me, however, not to tell Ma who claimed that children grew in kindergartens, children gardens.

I was not yet ready for this sly catcher in the rye.

◆   ◆   ◆

One of the most popular native entertainments for men that we boys also really enjoyed was *Klootschiessen*. It could be called road bowling. There were *Kloot* clubs that held contests and drank beer to celebrate afterwards. A *Kloot* was a round oak ball approximately ten centimeters across and without finger holes. Boys also competed against each other on an informal basis for none of our spare time was organized. All of our games were spontaneous whenever, or whatever, a group of children decided to play at the moment.

Two teams of one or more players each tossed their *Kloot* down the road from the same initial mark by the roadside. To build momentum, the thrower made a quick dash down the road while swinging his team's *Kloot,* then hurling it with a final thrust from this mark. Wherever his ball came to rest, a mark was scratched into the dirt. From that point, the next team member threw its ball again, continuing in the same direction. After a few kilometers they turned around and played back toward the starting line. The ball of the team that reached it first, after each took an equal number of throws, won the game.

Since there were no curbs or gutters along either side of the road, and the ball bounced roughly on the brick pavement, it often ended in the ditch and sank. Wet feet again. Then we tried to stay away from home until they dried in order to relinquish our reward from Ma.

But at times she would summon us with her shrill high C too soon: "Amiiiii! Siggiiiiii!"

When the wind was right, I could be scared home from two kilometers away, especially if I had my hearing ear tuned homeward. Once I was not sure if I heard her call and not wanting to be whipped for not coming home, I responded to the crow of a distant rooster. If I were a killer, I could have killed that rooster.

Ma often called us home, and when we got there our presence was not required except as objects for her intense psycho-catharsis. When she whipped her tool across our behinds, Siggi's and mine, it caused swellings there and created ghosts in our souls, but this exercise relieved her frustrations. I received this treatment considerably more often than Siggi because I was a half-deaf dreamer. I paid little attention to the great wisdom kind people tried to instill in us with their whippings. Blithely I went swimming, treeing, digging and muddying, interspersed by screaming during Ma's catharsis until I could no longer draw air.

◆   ◆   ◆

To fit into my second- and third-hand pants, stockings and shoes, I customized my legs as I grew. Over the years I wrenched and twisted them to accommodate these items; some were too big, some too small, and all full of holes. And if they came without, I put them there. My feet pounded each other, rubbing holes through my boots, socks, and sometimes through my hide. Then I had to dampen my socks to get them off in the evenings because they were blood-caked to my ankles.

Not all of our clothes were hand-me-downs. Aunt Adele and Ma knitted some with locally spun wool: *Bostrocks,* scratchy prototypes for barbed wire undershirts. We wore them to help us fend off the tuberculosis that Mrs. Heddens spread around our house. They also knitted scratchy full-length stockings that were so heavy that they had to be held up with garters, like those on the girls swinging their legs dancing the cancan in glorious cities.

I asked Aunt Adele to teach me to knit. I knotted instead of knitted and created a scarf as stiff as a board. She unraveled it again, to re-use the yarn, to darn the holes in our socks.

To force my legs to grow straighter, Ma wanted to have special insoles made for me. She wrote to Pa in Bavaria to send us plaster of Paris bandages, but he was unable to procure them. Later Ma acquired some herself, and I remember when a nurse in Aurich wrapped wet and cold matrix on my feet to form molds for my insoles. These were to help me walk like the hero that I was forced to develop into but did not want to be.

Pa was, however, able to find other items that we desperately needed. He wrote with a typewriter whose characters were filled with dirt:

"Today I sent you a little package with three bottles of *Esberton* and three bottles of *Ephedrin*. I cannot get any gypsum bandages here, and need a prescription for grape sugar. For the dear boys I have included a small picture book…

"I will bring seeds, if I can find them. Since I am not tied here professionally and you have become a little friendlier and more decent, I will leave here on March 24th. I will arrive in Oldersum with good train connections the next day at 20 o'clock. For our birthday I will bring a bottle of liqueur, which we will drink in the name of the children. I will bring sugar and wheat flour for the torte, so that we at least can celebrate our twin birthday.

"I will bring the bike without tires because they are worn out and can't be used anymore. Maybe you can have some shipped from America. I have to keep my bike here to use for my job, inasmuch as I cannot buy a small car yet.

"I have to use my fountain pen daily for <u>professional</u> purposes since I have to sign a lot of plans, and that is our bread."

Lots of plans, lots of bread! Why are we so hungry? Why are we so cold?

In many of his letters Pa complained to Ma that he could barely read her writing. Her pencil was too hard; her penmanship a scribble. She wanted him to send her a pen, but Pa needed his and would not, could not, buy her one. Ma asked me to also write letters to Pa in Bavaria, but this was very difficult for me at that time. I had to repeat my first grade because there was a shortage of teachers, had no classes for months, and then only two hours a day for the remainder of the year. Ma described my predicament to Pa in a letter as follows:

"All children born after April 1, 1939 have to repeat the first grade and I am sorry that we tormented Ami so much during the winter, that everything was in vain. He does not want to return to the first grade again."

*You **know** that you torment me?*

◆   ◆   ◆

I had a difficult time in school also because I was paying little attention to my teachers; their droning often put me into a trance. They considered me slow-witted and dull. Just because my speech was a slow monotone, people seemed to assume that my brain was the antithesis of Albert Einstein's. As a child, Albert must have appeared to be slow-witted also until the age of six when he had surprised his parents with the first words he had ever spoken, saying that the soup was too hot. I had talked, and screamed, a lot by that age, in relative terms. *Had he not said a lot more by not speaking? Did someone torment some brains into him also?*

Pa wrote to Ma that he discovered that there were not enough teachers in our school, and that after Mr. Lindeman retired these were all women. I remember how Ma had cried when he moved away from Simonswolde, but I was happy to get him out of my hair. Pa also wrote that because Siggi and I were attending school, Mr. Lindeman returned again to continue teaching us and implied that there was some sort of chummy relationship between him and Ma. I also had an intimate relationship with him because he spanked me, and better yet, he boosted my fragile ego by calling me "Moon Face."

Other titles that he honored me with were, *"LL, Lange Leitung, mit Knoten,"* (long pipe, with snags), referring to my slow responses. He also assigned me the hero's designation of *Suelzenkopf.* This suave name translates as follows: head full of headcheese, jellied pork loaf. He informed the world that my head was filled with ground up pigs' ears, snouts and tails. Headcheese. *Suelzenkopf* stuck to me for most of the six years that we lived in Simonswolde, and I was rarely called anything else by my schoolmates because they had forgotten my given name.

Siggi and I were not yet baptized, and like name-calling, our baptism would be yet another one of the spirit-lifting experiences that would be totally out of our control.

Our classroom walls and ceiling were white and bare. The children quietly sat at desks, in precise rows, facing their master. The pupil who sat next to me was Jan Luitje. He had fifteen brothers and sisters, aged minus-something to fourteen, because his father did not understand why his wife always became afflicted with big stomachs. He had never suffered from that disease himself, but Mrs. Luitje must have suspected the source of her ailments because she accused her husband: *"Du kannst nix as kinner makken,"* you can only make children. Fortunately her scent appealed only to him.

Jan's youngest siblings ran around their yard with dirty rags covering their tops because they were so poor that they could not afford dirty rags for their bottoms. They had no bedrooms and slept in straw-covered, closet-like holes in the wall. If I had to sleep there, I would bounce off the walls and three-foot ceiling all night and beat myself unconscious. One of my ghosts would make me do this.

Since no one in his family ever bathed, Jan scented our classroom with the smell of generations. This smell carried me far away to Adam. Jan dressed like Adam when God created him from mud. He was made of mud. I always wondered when his shredded clothes would be carried off, bit by bit, by the organisms living in his mud. His presence interfered with my concentration on the teacher, and I didn't know if Jan concentrated as much as I, since he had reached his highest level in school. He had been in this grade two years before I arrived there, and that's where he remained until he was fourteen or fifteen, never to graduate. Dropping out of school before this age was never allowed and would result in immediate and severe corporal punishment. *Was it illegal to punish adults in such fashion? Or was this just* adult *entertainment?*

We were not allowed to whisper, to move from our seats, and no one seemed to realize that I could not hear at all with my right ear. My enticing outer ear did not seem to give the pedagogues a clue about this. They probably only noticed its design and sometimes its rot, but not its uselessness. Once I failed to hear, to understand, Lindeman's homework assignment. His vocal cords vibrated too weakly for me to receive it clearly. I wondered and thought a few moments, as I did often, about what I had heard, to interpret what he had said, but failed to decode it and was too shy to ask him to repeat our assignment. It could draw another unkind remark from him.

Back home, I meekly mumbled to Ma that I did not know what I had to do for my German homework. Her mother instinct drove her, on her bicycle, to Lindeman's house to ask him what he had assigned. Upon returning, she informed me that I was to compose sentences using adjectives such as "dumb," "fat" and "lazy." With uncharacteristic lightning speed I understood the message Lindeman had sent me.

"Headcheese is dumb." "Moon Face is fat." "Ami is lazy."

Although I was skinny, I had a full moon face, but I did not think that it glowed in the night. And I truly believed that I was dumb because Ma, Adele and my teachers often told me so. Adults treated me as such, gave me special names and frequent spankings for not paying attention and for not knowing the answers. Insults, scolding and spanking were the only *special ed* that I ever received in our Aryan society.

Siggi and I always worked diligently, not because it was fun, but because of the whip. We even had to rake the footpaths on our side of the house to embellish the dirt with parallel lines for Sundays. Parallel lines looked nice on the pathways because no one else had them.

To escape from the effects of my *special ed,* I read everything I could find. I disappeared in books. The first one was *Robinson Crusoe.* I daydreamed in class, soared with birds, swayed in palm trees and drifted in lagoons. When I paid close attention to the teacher I could hear and understand what he said, but I was unable to concentrate for very long and often drifted away to my palm trees by my blue lagoon.

Silently a wild animal sneaked up from behind and tore my ear. I suppressed a cry. But this did not seem to be the solution to loosen the knots in my gristle. So Lindeman decided one day that more drastic measures were needed.

According to protocol: "Suelzenkopf, come here," he shouted.

I fell out of a palm tree.

Nooooeeeee! Don't punish me with paid administrative leave!

Tail between legs, I followed him to the front of the class.

"Lean over this desk."

Trembling, I complied. Forgot my name. Gristle demagnetized. The pupil sitting at this desk obligingly moved aside to give us more room. He had manners. Lindeman gripped his stick; I gripped the desktop with both paws, pressed my face to the cold oak and tightened muscles to flee from my body. *Dirty wood. Smell of ages.*

"When" whip, I further tightened my sphincter to keep stuff from blowing out,

"will" whip,

"you" whip,

"pay" whip,

"attention?" whip.

When Lindeman thought that he had cured my post-traumatic stress syndrome caused by fire bombings and other human affairs, he ordered me back to my desk and said something that I had felt to be the case for a long time:

"Suelzenkopf, there's no hope for you."

These were the wisest, and falsest, words ever spoken in Simonswolde. They caused the saddest feelings anyone ever had in this little village.

After school, Ma and I met Mr. Lindeman on the street.

"I tried to beat some brains into your son," he proudly informed her.

"Gut, immer tuechtig drauf los," good, stay always firmly on him, she encouraged him further. In America she would be a good football coach. I will remember her words much, much longer than the pain from Lindeman's whipping. *Will we always have to be punching bags? Become unwilling heroes?*

At home Ma locked me in the coal closet. To be spanked by a teacher was a punishable offense, to be rewarded with long sulking in the blackest night in the universe. Ma and Lindeman were so intelligent that they did not know that they were unwittingly creating another ghost in my soul. Neither did I, but it would come to haunt me later. Along with all the others.

> *"Children afraid of the night*
> *Who have never been happy or good."*

As much as Lindeman was enamored with me, he was even more so with Siggi, but in the opposite way. He spoiled him. Siggi was quick to respond to his questions, and Lindeman noted on his first report card that "Siggi made a very good start." He liked him so much that he even offered to adopt him. An old man wanted to adopt a little boy. Besides his quick wit, Siggi was charming and had long golden locks, while I wore an obstreperous brush like our Uncle Fritz, and with an additional persistent tuft like the hair on the back of a frightened dog.

◆   ◆   ◆

Pa and Ma knew that written words could be efficient weapons. They could destroy targets at great distances, like missiles, with *collateral damage* to their little children. Pa's letters made Ma grouchy, and when she wrote him she also became grouchy. Siggi and I always worried about our hides when someone became grouchy. Consider the impact of salvos delivered by mail, hundreds of kilometers away, for a few pennies, with deadly accuracy. Mama to Papa, after both experienced the joys of two world wars, hyperinflation, depressions, Nazis and starvation, with great affection wrote in various letters as follows:

"...I sat with the boys for hours outside without protection on the railroad tracks to wait for a train. We could have been there overnight. You could have been at least a little concerned, or made an effort to help us with the luggage into a cattle wagon. But my Dandy chased after his passions!!!

"...Since 1945 you came here to scoop off the cream from us, but you never said that we should live with you or anything like that. All your letters are lies in order to create a basis for a divorce. But the reality is quite different!!! Let me illuminate your black soul before a judge, you poor soul.

"Have you already consummated your marriage, or is your dear bride still lying in bed? It is nearly like a thrombosis after a birth...

"...What is happening there and with your Ent.? (sic)"

(Ent. probably referred to *Entnazifizierung,* de-Nazification. People felt so guilty, fearful or devastated that they would not even mention the word "Nazi" after the war. During this time period, in order to be able to get employment, every person had to present witnesses and prove that he or she had not been a member of the Nazi Party.)

"A general amnesty is expected. There is a 3600 marks yearly income limit. The money which I received, or the monies you received extra for rent, were social additions and were not considered income.

You probably don't earn more than 3600 marks anyway. Dr. Hagen could certify it for you and it would be finished with this hullabaloo."

(Hagen was to certify that Pa had not been a member of the Nazi party.)

"…And I have written about wooden pegs for resoling our shoes. I cannot have Ami's shoes resoled because they are totally worn through. These pegs come from Bavaria and cannot cross the zone borders…"

She referred to the different zones of occupation of Germany: Soviet, French, English, and American. Laws controlled the movement of goods and people and permission was required to travel between them. The Allies also inspected the contents of packages and letters, and this could have been the reason for Ma's abbreviation of *"Ent."*

Ma also wrote him about other concerns, but Pa did little to help or console her:

"Since Adele had her operation she has been much worse. She says that it is better with her thyroid, but she is now quick-tempered, in an evil mood like never before. She grinds on our nerves from morning to night. She will certainly end in a mental institution when she does not have her mother anymore who allows her everything, and will end in suicide. The day before yesterday, she said to a woman that it would have been better if she had been allowed to die rather than let her suffer. Little Siggi wants to console me and has already said: 'Mama, Aunt Adele will soon be dead.' Ami says, 'No wait, I will soon be a strong man and then I will spank her thoroughly.'"

"Because of the food we have to stay here. It is of no use to be hungry every four hours. It is like a sickness. Ami and little Siggi have red cheeks and are misbehaving. I have a lot of grief with them, they should get more whipping."

Want to create sadists, masochists or terrorists?

"Siggi looks more and more like Mathilde and is just like you. Ami is a dear one to me, but he is easily despaired and cannot stand his ground."

Should I have cried or burned down cities?

"Can you get plaster of Paris bandages there to make gypsum castings of Ami's feet? I could send you a prescription for it. Would you like to have insoles? Who knows how long one will be able to get aluminum?"

(The insoles made specifically for me were of leather and aluminum.)

"Also when I have to go to Aurich, I always like to take Ami with me. When Siggi comes along, then it is Ami who takes him by the hand. He is the good and dear home spirit, is tired in the evening, readily despaired and despondent. On the whole he is sensitive and easily lets his head hang down. Courage is not his forte. It is a difficult development until he learns normal self-defense. He does not learn particularly easily and always goes for practical work."

◆   ◆   ◆

Because of our incessant whippings, we always walked on eggs, being careful not to break them. By now Siggi and I had learned not to even think about lying, stealing or vandalizing. We had learned to always wash our hands before eating and to do our schoolwork to the best of our abilities. We were not allowed to interrupt adults when they conversed with each other, and when they did so we had to ask them:

"May I please have the word?"

Other than doing a few stupid things, we were almost angels. In sum, these acts consisted of throwing a *Kloot* through the window, scorching the cabinet and coming home late for precise meal times. And of course always getting wet and dirty from the puddles and ditches.

Ma referred in her letter to Adele's thyroid operation, and that she consumed grape sugar and pearl rice by the spoonful, every few hours, in order to become healthy. Often Adele warned us, Siggi and me, to be still, while holding her hand to her heart, exclaiming: "Quiet! My heart is beating!" Oddly, she did not time its beats, and when she felt that her heart was beating incorrectly, she adjusted it by beating Siggi and me. We learned the meaning of life; we were on this earth to keep people alive. Once her heart raced so much, or skipped so much, that she threw a hard kilo loaf of Frisian bread at Pa's head. *Do people kill houseguests? With bread?*

She missed and knocked the hanging, sliding door to our living room off its track. Pa was already off track from too much alcohol, too much war and too many women, and this speeding bread might have helped to knock him back on track!

◆   ◆   ◆

Unbeknownst to Siggi and me, Pa filed for divorce. The sparring partners kept this fact hidden from us until much later, when this would become all too obvious because we would move in with him. In the meantime they continued to lay the groundwork for their divorce by writing lots of letters with excuses and accusations, including what Ma wrote to her attorney in Aurich:

"(A family from Simonswolde said that my husband with his friend Dr. Hagen drank 300 bottles of schnapps according to his own words. He told me during his last visit here that he pays up to 200 marks for a bottle of schnapps!) He wants to take in a *Fraeulein* Koessler and establish a triangular relationship with us. Besides *Fraeulein* Koessler, he has a dozen more such, and similar relationships, simultaneously and sequentially, all with sexual traffic. He can never live with these always-new acquaintances. I have written proofs that make this evident..."

To defend himself against Ma's accusations, Pa wrote to this same (Ma's) lawyer: (Someone cut off the letterhead (?), to remove evidence?)

"...I myself have not traveled to get abortion medicine, nor have I undertaken anything with another person. The premature birth by the railroad embankment is an erroneous, misunderstood interpretation and came about by a girl through her fright. If one will threaten me with an alleged punishable offense, so will I remember the sheep wool auction in Simonswolde..."

Blackmail versus blackmail?

In Pa's letters to his own lawyers, he listed some of the reasons why a divorce should be granted:

"...The accused one proposes to marry an American, emigrate with our children, then return after ten to fifteen years to marry me again. In several dozen letters she has called me a swindler, imposter, deserter, coward, a lazy person, abortionist, a tramp, dirty from top to bottom...

"The accused one is always very pessimistic and critically engaged. She always sees the future as black and is possessed by a psychological delusion, even though I accumulated through my own earnings a complete household of about 15,000 DM and a car for 5,500 DM, all without debt during our married years 1934–1940, and at times employed a maid. We lived in good circumstances...

"For the dear children I will as a father, as far as possible, support them financially, economically and morally whenever I can, have them trained according to rank, and obtain for them a happy youth..."

Did our father really mean this?

"My wife and I have personally discussed in 1940, that if I had to leave the family for reasons of war, that I would be permitted to traffic with another woman. My wife advised me that I should be careful so that I would not catch an infection...

"I never attempted to play my wife into the hands of an American, although I was thankful to get some things from the occupation forces that one could not buy here, nor to sell my wife into prostitution to the Americans...She took a third American, a 'bull' of a human of about two hundred plus kilograms, a brewmaster, into her heart even more."

Was it only into her heart, Papa?

"But the accused one likes messes. For example, in Herten she kept the kitchen so dirty that it was impossible to move even one step because of all the boxes and cans. The accused one even licked off the eating utensils and did not wash them for weeks, so that old food was stuck on them for days…

"…What kind of impression does the court have, when my wife reads the newspaper and eats apples during sex, with the cynical reason this was the only time she had to do so…"

Even though Pa puffed that he would do a lot for Siggi and me, he never made, nor ever would make, a formal claim for our custody or even for visitation rights.

Ma and Pa's missiles did not miss their targets and were employed numerous times, in slight variations, over a period of years. Ma wrote to Pa that she would not return to Southern Germany until he quit drinking and guaranteed us enough food. She reminded him of some of the worries that they had had toward the end of the war, when each had tried to pawn off the other one to other potential spouses. Ma wrote:

"I would like to refresh your memory: The Russians did not have to stop in Hof, Bavaria. They could have come to Diesenbach. We were also subjugated by the 'chloroform' of the Nazis and thought our children would be abducted. You often said that if we lose the war, we could count on the fact that we would be carried off and the children would be taken away from us. To prepare for our worst fears, we secretly kept close to Walli and Wastel, so that in case of emergency, they would have pity on our children and take them with them and care for them. Still today, the boys would answer to people that they want to go with Walli and Wastel.

"At the end of the war we had great horrors. When the Americans arrived instead of the Russians, you gave me the advice to search for an American, to at least achieve that the children can escape the undeserved misery…"

She also credited Pa's side of the family for my slow-motion wit, and strangely, claimed part of the credit for our robust health, Siggi's and mine:

"…Send our boys into the *Gymnasium* (a high school with a purely academic curriculum). It won't work with Ami anyway without tutoring; he is a mixture of father and Fritz. He is slow, as is his entire appearance…"

"…You know that both we parents are at fault for Ami's and Siggi's illnesses. We have always said that we could not raise children in that apartment, and now we cannot repeat the same mistake again."

For years, every now and then, the names "Wastel" and "Walli" have come to my mind. They also had lived with the Pirzers and had a baby. I asked Ma to confirm my memories, and she wrote that they indeed had lived there and had been forced laborers for the German army. With the army's retreat they came through Diesenbach where they remained to have a baby.

Wastel must have liked me because he gave me a wooden airplane that I took into a bomb shelter during a raid. I was sad when I left it there, and we could not find it later. Another time he gave me a pellet gun, and we went to a meadow where American equipment was being assembled. We sat down on an embankment, and he told me to sit on my rifle in order to hide it, because he was afraid that the American soldiers would take it away from me. But when I brought it home, Ma threw it into a privy because she worried that the Americans would arrest us for possessing an instrument of war.

Ma also wrote me that during this time she always rose at five in the morning to heat milk for baby Ivan on her electric hot plate, to save Walli from having to build a fire. Eventually I would disassemble this gadget to find out where the heat was coming from, thereby destroying it. She also wrote that on the day the war officially ended, she had spied through a knothole of a privy and had observed Wastel walking through a door with a pistol in hand, and that she had worried that he was going to shoot someone. This could have been the time that I remember seeing him going into a barn with a gun and closing the door behind him. I had felt that his expression had conveyed, "don't tell anyone," but fortunately he shot no one.

◆   ◆   ◆

Pa also credited Ma for the many illnesses that Siggi and I had had. To show that he was a concerned father and she a careless mother he wrote her:

"I am worried about Ami's TB symptoms which were discovered through the test patch on his chest. (All children in school were tested for TB.) Please let me know about the health of the child. Early on I saw this coming and warned for many years that in your house, where Mama still is so afflicted with it and has much expectoration, the danger of infection is much greater. Now we have a sick child and I will take the dear boys with me during the winter, and both of them will be educated by me in a higher school…

"Now I am stuck in the middle of a gigantic project and don't have a minute of time. I have spread myself thin, inasmuch as I have to depend on strangers. With all my energy I will now build a *Grundstueck,* property for a nest egg, so that the children in later years will have some possessions. I ask you to leave them with me during the winter, leave them with me for always, so I can as a father abundantly take care of them. You can get them from time to time, or visit them here.

"…Father wanted to bequeath me three forests. Mathilde and Hermann (his sister and her husband) protested against this, that I do not need anything, and are against my getting anything at all…

"My shirts and suits are now all together kaput. As a start, I have begun to acquire new shirts and have bought six of them for 126 marks from Fritz. A new suit of Swiss material cost me 380 marks. Within the year I will need a minimum of 1000 marks for further suits, socks, etc.…"

◆   ◆   ◆

One fall afternoon we heard a desperate squealing and grunting coming from a farm up the road. Siggi and I ran to the commotion at this Frisian country scene. Next to the obligatory manure pile in front of a thatched-roofed farmhouse were two men wrestling a pig. The pig was squealing, the men were grunting.

To calm down the pig, someone hammered a spike into its head.

"Ami, look. They're washing a pig," Siggi observed.

"We'd better be careful," I responded.

We cautiously approached to watch this slaughter. Someone slit its throat, drained its blood into a big bowl and then wrestled it into a hot tub. It was made with steel-banded wood staves and was identical to the one we bathed in weekly in our kitchen. While the men scraped off its dirt and bristles, the farmwife stirred the pig's blood with a bare hand while adding ingredients.

"Why are you stirring the blood?" I inquired shyly.

"I am making *Blutwurst*," she replied.

I had eaten *Blutwurst*, blood sausage, before. It was black, contained chunks of lard, tasted delicious and had no government-mandated warning on its intestine skin.

A man proceeded to cut open the pig's belly, removed its innards, some of which he threw onto the manure pile. Little Siggi and I stood side by side, holding hands, watching with earnest faces.

"You will be next!" the farmer exclaimed while looking directly at us. Instinctively we stepped back because we were not sure if he meant it.

He tossed something at us.

"Here's the bladder," he said. "Blow it up and you can play with it."

We fought over our new toy and excitedly took it home, where I rinsed it, inflated it until I felt that my lungs would burst, and then tied it shut. It tasted bitter. I didn't think that pig's pee would taste bitter, I thought it would be salty. Maybe it was the little trichinas that I'd heard about, but I didn't see any. We were anxious to cure our translucent pig bladder so we could play soccer with it.

Aunt Adele asked where we had found it. She commanded us to go back to retrieve the pig's lungs and anything that looked edible. Siggi and I balked because we ignorantly assumed that anything from manure would not be edible but agreed to fetch it, always being aware of the ever-present whip. Enthusiastically we returned to the scene of slaughter. Slowly we approached the manure pile while looking around for witnesses. When we felt unobserved we climbed it.

Pigs root for truffles. Vultures rip cadavers.

Ooooooh, this is soft.

The viscera glistened on the soggy manure altar, our public trough, our *pork barrel*. We grabbed some entrails, quickly wrapped them in newspapers and dropped them into the shopping net that we had brought with us. *Was this the same one I dripped from at Doebele's?*

We hurried home. I felt guilty for stealing and for not having washed my hands. Oma, instead of pasting reminders in our communal waterless privy, simply told us to always wash our hands before handling foodstuff, and we always obeyed. Now Siggi and I grabbed the food while ignoring the advice that was so often pounded into us. Maybe we could wash the food instead before eating it. After we placed our mouth-watering quarry on the kitchen table, we went back out to play.

◆   ◆   ◆

"Eat this," ordered Ma.

Siggi and I stirred around our potpourri, each waiting for the other one to take the first bite. I could not bring myself to try one, thinking about where these innards had been. *What's worse? Hunger pain, eating pain, whipping pain?*

As we wavered, Ma helped in our decision when she reached for her waist ornament.

"I will eat it," I mumbled courageously.

Under the threat of punishment, and with proper and formal table manners, Siggi and I slowly consumed most of this nutritious, if not delicious, meal of lungs. Chunks of rubbery air tubes provided good exercise for our jaws, more so than the gum that we received from America. It also nourished us and strengthened our characters so we could deal more effectively with future gourmet meals.

The moral then is, when times are tough, stay close to a manure pile.

After we finished, we washed the dishes, a chore we greatly disliked, Siggi and I. Since I was older, I had to fetch water from the pump in the barn. Adele heated it on the white enamel wood stove in the kitchen, and after doing dishes we discarded it into the gutter of the cow stalls, from where it ran into a cesspool outside.

Within hours the results of our *haute cuisine* hit us. Pain in the gut, which had spared us the pain in the butt, which would not have prevented our pain in the gut, since we would have had to eat this stuff anyway, properly, after the pain in our butts. After rolling around the floor for an hour or two, parts of the pig escaped again. We released it with competitive up-chucking, Siggi and I. Then Ma fed our chuckings to her chickens, and they seemed to like them.

We were often aware that we had guts because we induced intense feelings there by eating anything resembling food, wasting nothing. Often we did not know what strange morsels Aunt Adele disguised in soups and sauces, and I would not be surprised if there had been mice and maggots! But other people had not much to eat either because they came from Aurich, went from door to door, to beg or trade items for whatever food they could get, although there was not even enough for the farmers. One of these beggar-traders wanted to barter his iron frying pan and to prove its high quality, he bounced it onto the brick pavement in our barn, and it did not break. Someone else offered us cast-aluminum dinner forks that appeared to have been homemade.

One of the real delicacies that we truly enjoyed was black, whole grain rye bread. The kind that people throw at each other. It tasted so sweet that it did not even require a spread. A local baker baked it every morning, and it was so dense that it was usually sold, unsliced, in half loaves, a kilo at a time, and to this day I still yearn for this bread. It makes my mouth water. One time Ma recovered half a loaf from a secret place. I knew that it was such bread only because I recognized its shape, a block of gray, furry fungus that Ma sliced, moistened and garnished with sugar. Then forced us to eat it.

The pain in the gut.

The pain in the butt.

Since we survived the pig's lungs, we discovered a new food source. Ma asked the town's butcher to tell her when and where he went to slaughter so that Siggi and I could retrieve the choicest tidbits. She wrote me that I often woke up at four o'clock in the mornings that fall and winter. We rose and she'd cut the unspoiled parts from apples and pears from undisclosed sources to feed them to me. I chewed them slowly, to savor the flavor, and by six o'clock I was playing outside when our neighbor Kattlose would yell:

"Janna, get up! Katje's kid is already out on the street."

One morning, I woke as the rising sun was painting the bedroom bright orange, and I worried that I would be late for school. Although everyone was still asleep, I quietly dressed, tiptoed downstairs, picked up my satchel and hurried to school. Outside the air was still and all was quiet, but one rooster was up. On the way I passed a farmer who was proudly enlarging the manure pile in his front yard. I wondered why there was so little activity in our village, and when I tried to open the door to the school, it was locked. I heard noises coming from the inside that sounded as if someone were polishing the floor, so I returned home where everyone was still asleep. The alarm clock startled me. I was so obedient and duty-bound that I only now realized why no one had been stirring.

We were hungry, and Pa in Bavaria did not eat much either. To help feed his ill father, he wrote to farmer Zulauf, asking him if he could trade him some food and received the following reply:

"Very honored Mr. Neuman!

"I am in possession of your esteemed writing of 16 Jan., 1947 and have to report with great regret, that in spite of my best intention, it is not possible in this respect to help him, because I, in spite of my pursuit of agriculture, receive food vouchers myself and have only as much to live on as I can get with them. And this is too little to live on, and too much to die on. We don't know anymore what bacon is since the occupation here, because there are no pigs anymore and we receive **monthly one hundred grams of fat per person**. Everything else is taken away from us.

"I am very sorry for not being able to help your father, but under the local circumstances it is absolutely not possible because we don't even have enough potatoes to eat ourselves."

As the new Deutschmark was introduced, the old Reichsmark became worthless. The currency was being converted in incremental stages at a ratio of ten to one. Each month the government issued seventy-five marks of *Kopfgeld*, head money, to each adult and probably less for children. There was little money in circulation, but this did not matter much at this time because there was little merchandise in the village store. Since many people had lost most or all of their possessions and had no earnings, barter was a way of life. I heard Ma talk about the black market with other people but did not know what that meant. She wrote me later that one egg represented approximately one Deutschmark, which was worth about twenty-five cents at that time. At today's valuations this sum would amount to several dollars.

Since we were so poor that we had to grub on manure, we were fortunate to have two aunts in America who sent us packages. These always smelled delectable, like marshmallows, spearmint, cocoa and candy. They smelled like America. I could smell America's newness, its far away places, even before we opened them. In one of these packages was a used coat that fit me quite well, therefore it became mine. It was of wool, with brightly colored square patterns unlike the dark clothes everyone wore. This package also contained a whistle that I put into the pocket of my new coat which I proudly wore to school. The whistle also became mine because I was bigger than Siggi.

During class break I retrieved this coat from the hook in the hall to go outside. There my coat seemed to be newer than I remembered. I checked the contents of its pockets and found the whistle, but it was shinier. Puzzled, I returned to the hall and found an identical coat hanging there. It also contained only one whistle, but I still thought that I had picked the wrong coat. I knew that other families had relatives in America and concluded that coincidentally someone else must have also received these items. Not being sure which coat was mine, I exchanged it and kept the older one.

Many of our packages also contained cigarettes, tea or coffee because these were scarce and expensive in post-war Germany, did not spoil and were easily shipped. East Frisians craved tea as much as the English and Dutch, and some less fortunate addicts even drank ersatz coffee of roasted cereal grains. We bartered these American items mostly for food, wool yarn or used clothing. Since Ma and Aunt Adele thought that the farmers would have pity on us, they asked Siggi and me to solicit them for milk. We offered them tea or money, and they usually traded us a liter or two of milk for one tea bag, rarely wanting money.

Ma traded a pack of cigarettes for one black chicken. I misunderstood her name Gretchen, called her Gettchen, and was very protective of her. When the neighbor's rooster mounted her, pecked at her comb, and somewhere else, I courageously chased him off with a stick. Ma also had bartered for one dozen brown eggs that were fertilized. Gettchen patiently hatched them and created twelve baby chicks, all hens and no roosters. Remembering the good old days, Ma wrote me years later:

"…It was a miracle that these eggs all hatched females, and we lived a long time from our Chickens of Luck because we had little other income for Pa never sent us anything. We used our excess eggs for bartering and these chickens provided the greatest source of income."

One very cold winter morning, Aunt Adele expanded our livestock collection when she opened the front door and found a snow-white bunny sitting on our porch. She grabbed him by his frozen ears and brought him into the kitchen. Siggi and I were excited to have a furry friend, but Ma wanted to pull his pelt over his head, so we could eat him. When we bawled in unison, we prolonged his life, and our chickens had to share their feed with him. We kept our pet until the following fall when we ate him. That's when we realized why Ma had encouraged us to rake hay from the roadway that fell from the farmers' hay wagons, to feed to, and to fatten our rabbit. Our pet would probably have lived longer if we'd kept him skinny.

Our poverty would have been less severe if Pa had not gotten his paws on Ma's inheritance. After her two brothers perished in Russia, and her father stretched his neck, she inherited some of their Holstein cows. She sold them and macho Pa took this money to build a house for us in Bavaria. Or so he wrote us. He was in deep denial that we were freezing and starving. This was evident from the total lack of concern that he showed for us in the numerous letters which he wrote to us in Frisia, and because he generally ignored Ma's request for help and sent us little.

We were so starved for toys, food and clothing that Siggi and I tore into the packages from America like hungry hyenas. Shortly before one Christmas, Oma was resting on her couch and watched us rip one open. Among the usual items we found a red balloon. Oma ordered us to put it back into the package so she could present it to us for Christmas. We had never seen a real balloon, like the ones in the coloring books that we received from America. We were anxious to fly our new toy, like we did our kites that we built from the wrapping paper of our packages.

We bragged to our friends about our balloon, and they arrived on Christmas day to witness its launching. We blew it up and tied a long string to it. Instead of rising, the balloon tumbled to the ground. As with our kites, we ran with it to give it lift, and I tried to force it up by sheer will power because our honor was at stake. To lighten its load I cut off its string and let go. A gust of wind blew it over the house and across the fields, and even though we ran after it we never found it again.

◆   ◆   ◆

Siggi and I spent all of our spare time outdoors whenever the weather allowed. We played hide and seek with our friends and wandered about, always curious, always looking for something to find or to do. Occasionally we found something from the war, such as a potato masher hand grenade. We tossed it about and had no idea that it might be dangerous because it was only a wooden handle, like a cut-off baseball bat stuck in a can.

In a ditch we found a military-type canister that contained a rotten egg in a lot of salt. Nearby we found a steel helmet and ribbons of bullets that we also carried home. We spread the shells out on the cover of the cesspool and hammered the bullets off to empty the powder. Ma came out and was horrified. I didn't know why she was horrified because I wasn't horrified, and I was always the first to be terrified. She lifted a cover-board from the cesspool and dumped our powder into it, creating explosive fertilizer. Then she took away our remaining ammo and had a neighbor pound a flat spot on the helmet to make her a bowl.

There were two cesspools behind our house, a covered one for excrements, another open one to receive wastewater from washing and bathing. The latter one was the sanitary one because the stinky black goo was all on the bottom. Whenever the covered pool was full, a farmer scooped out the scum and masses of maggots with a long-handled bucket into a wooden cask. Then his oxen pulled it to his field where he spread about this grubby soup to plow it under. This made big cabbages, beets, oats, rye and delicious potatoes pop out of the ground.

That's when I learned that scum goes to the top.

Striped beetles tried to beat the farmers to their potato harvest. Therefore the farmers recruited us to harvest these beetles before they could do too much damage. Scores of people combed the fields to pick them by hand. While I helped with the beetle harvest, I accidentally spilled a pot of coffee that was sitting on the ground. I was afraid that someone might have noticed and knowing that coffee was like money, I felt guilty and ran home, not telling anyone about my spilling of money. Twenty minutes later the coffee addicts arrived, and Ma reimbursed them for the coffee and scolded me in lieu of spanking me.

◆   ◆   ◆

In the early years after the war, the best way to get to Aurich was on bicycle or with a horse and wagon. Occasionally a farmer took us villagers on his buckboard wagon that had enormous tires salvaged from a crashed airplane and was drawn by a huge workhorse. When I was seven or eight, Ma loaded me on this wagon and told me that she'd meet me in the big city. With my legs dangling over its side, I enjoyed bouncing along the brick road through several villages before arriving in Aurich.

At the end of our trip, Ma was not there. I was lost because she had not instructed me where to go or what to do. I walked around aimlessly until my guardian angel guided me to a woman who also had come from Simonswolde. I informed her that I could not find my mother. She walked me to the police station where I anxiously waited. When Ma arrived in Aurich and did not find me, she had the brilliant insight to bike to the police station. From there she carried me on her bike to a second-hand store where I was to remain for several days, while she returned to Simonswolde that evening.

I was very timid and uncomfortable around strangers. I did not trust them because they had proved that they could be evil, and it did not take long for my suspicions to be confirmed. I was loitering outside the store when an older boy walked by and without provocation, without a word, he pounded his fist into my solar plexus. Since I was tough, his fist did not enter my guts where it might have gotten stuck. However, I doubled over and staggered back into the store, where Mrs. Second-Hand asked me what happened, but I could not talk and tumbled to the floor.

I was glad to return to Simonswolde where I had friends. But the school bully, Rewert Kuhlman, now long departed, attacked me. Bullying was his hobby, and I was always his favorite target, because I was always a chicken. As usual, I ran away as fast as I could to escape him. Our father, the potent hot rod, had not taught us, Siggi and me, to have courage, or how to defend ourselves against bullies, and more importantly, how to **be** bullies.

The bloody face of a schoolmate flashed through my mind. I had breathlessly watched when Rewert had pounded it with a stick until it was no longer identifiable.

My temper rose.

My guardian angel warned me to defend myself!

Without thinking, I stopped running, bent over, picked up sand, turned around and threw it into Rewert's face. I commenced pounding it with both fists as rapidly as I could until blood and tears were flowing. I gained further courage from the cheering of friends. Rewert stood paralyzed like a post, until I was afraid of what I might do to him and therefore ceased to apply justice. He ran home. I basked in the glow of my victory. Although I felt relieved and proud, this was not I, because I was always timid and never wanted to hurt anyone, and I still do not like to harm spiders or flies.

◆   ◆   ◆

We were not only under attack by horrible humanoids but also by other creatures. We hosted hostile lice, fleas, microbes and who knows what. A neighbor always cut my hair regularly with hand clippers, and unbeknownst to me, Ma once instructed him to skin my head in order to render my louse colony homeless. The barber began to trim normally, made small talk, then without warning went across the top of my head and sheared away all of my brush and my louse village as well.

I knew that I would be teased again in school because no kid here had ever even seen a hedgehog bristle style before on people, and I was now bald. Even though it was not permissible to wear headgear in class, Ma asked me to do so anyway, to wear my red leather riding cap from America. Fully protected, ashamed of wearing the cap, and also because it was so out of the ordinary with its quality, newness and bright color, I walked into the classroom followed by Ma who waved to the teacher and whispered something to him. This embarrassed me further because no parent had ever come into our classrooms or even into our school before. But neither Ma, the teacher, nor the cap could protect me because later a sneaky pupil pulled it off in order to thrill everyone but me with *Schadenfreude.*

I wanted to enjoy *Schadenfreude,* because Ma had taught us that *Schadenfreude* was the greatest of joys, the enjoyment of other people's miseries. But I rarely could get any *Schadenfreude* because I always felt guilty or sad instead and therefore could not wallow in one of the greatest delights that mankind could experience. On my way home from school I provided even more *Schadenfreude* for my cousins, Maike and Gerd, when, without warning, they pulled my upper-crust cap off again, no bright colors allowed in Simonswolde, filled it with sticky mud and put it back on my shiny head. Cold, wet mud in a red cap on my head made me feel inferior, but I could make inferior people feel happy and superior.

We enjoyed many other results of our romantic, old-time hygiene. Another example was that since there were no public toilets, we often relieved ourselves wherever we could hide outdoors. On one occasion I felt a strong and sudden urge, so I jumped into some bushes. A tickling sensation informed me that my product was going to be unique. I turned around to see what I had created: Dozens of pale, long, live worms wriggling on the ground in the groovy spaghetti party. *Were they eating me? Or only my food?*

Scared to death, I hurried home and asked Ma if worms could eat people.

"What kind of worms?"

"I am full of wiggly worms."

"*Ja,* but we will get rid of them," she assured me but never went out to the bushes to admire them or to feed them to our chickens. Days later, she fed me a bitter powder to exterminate the parasites inside me, but this did no harm to the ringworm fungus that was on my skin.

Then there was the time when I had to display my boyhood because I felt a burning sensation, and the end of my spout looked like a pink raspberry. Ma inspected it, was appalled by it, and hurried to fetch the village nurse before it would grow riper. The nurse came back with Ma in great anticipation and asked me to show it to her also. Upon their insistence, I shyly stood across the living room and delicately retrieved my raspberry from my scratchy underwear. The nurse's jaw dropped in admiration. She told me to wash myself and that was her singular attempt to cure me. *Should I also wash my hands **before** going potty?*

Ma continued to write Pa in Diesenbach about our food and health problems. So to protect himself from our great pain, he blasted off into outer space denial and replied as though he never read her letters because he did not answer her concerns. For example he wrote:

"Now we definitely have the building permit for our little house in Diesenbach. Nothing was changed in my plans and the work will continue starting next Monday so that the rough construction will be finished by Christmas. Then we will finally have a civilized residence and also will be able to follow intellectual and cultural pursuits…

"…We can move into our house in March. Hopefully I can build a twin house with the same methods.

"…Should you send me cigarettes or anything, I promise to quit smoking in 1947. I need my health for the future, which can, as I believe today, in spite of the fate of war, become very great for us and I want to enjoy it with my three dear ones in many years of health…

"…I need the cigarettes for purposes of trade for butter, wine, etc.…"

While Ma, Aunt Adele, Oma, Siggi and I cultured worms, lice and bacterial strains in the North, Pa built a house for himself, and the future wife he was dreaming about, in the South. Not only that, he even informed Ma that he wanted to build an identical second one that he could rent to others.

◆   ◆   ◆

The winter of 1947/48 was one of the coldest in a century and paralyzed much of Europe. Trains froze to the tracks, and there was little fuel available. In addition, so much snow accumulated that we did not have to attend school. Siggi and I burrowed a tunnel into the snow and crawled over the top without collapsing it. General Lucius Clay, commander of the occupying American troops, called Germany's predicament "truly appalling."

Fortunately during the previous summer, Ma, Siggi and I had cut peat out of the bog and had stacked up the blocks to dry before carting them home. We burned this peat, along with a little coal that we had scavenged, in our living room stove. On the coldest days we all huddled around it. When someone entered the room and left the door to the hallway open moments too long, Ma would shout in anger, "Coal thief, coal thief."

To save fuel, Adele also cooked there, instead of on the kitchen stove. At night the temperature in our living room, where Oma lived on the couch, dropped below freezing. Ma wrote to Pa that "the chamber pots under the beds froze nightly for almost three months." Even though this was a frozen-pisspot winter, Pa, as always, dismissed this as complaining and had no words of comfort for us.

Oma spent the end of her life on the couch over her frozen chamber pot and under a down blanket. For almost twenty years she had suffered bronchial catarrh and entertained people by coughing and spitting into a mug. According to scientific computations, at a rate of two an hour, for fourteen hours a day, she had produced at least two hundred thousand green blobs in her lifetime, many, many liters of it. Like Mrs. Heddens, she only grew ever shorter and skinnier, but never seemed to get quite empty. She always kept a damp cloth by her sofa so she could wipe her face after spitting. But one morning her washcloth was frozen, as was the pee in her pot.

And so was Oma. She ran out of phlegm and died. Days later someone loaded her wrinkled, ghostly white shell onto a farmer's cart and hauled it to her nearby birthplace for burial. Her set of teeth, which she always kept beside her on the couch, went with her. Pure white Oma rumbled down the brick road, inside a black box, to her grave and was followed by a small procession of dark figures, their heads drooping with sorrow.

◆　　◆　　◆

Ice covered the canals criss-crossing all of Frisia. We children skated about with instruments from medieval times strapped to our feet with leather and string. Our skates were made of wood with steel blades that projected far out in front, curling up at their tips. Although these skates were designed for long distance skating, we played ice hockey with them, and when we hooked our blades, we suffered painful crashes.

One winter Ma acquired a new sled from a stranger who came to our village and paid for it with two handsful of beans that she had harvested from her garden. Excitedly my best friend Kriene deBoer and I took this sled out on a frozen canal. Its ice cracked ominously, and Kriene quickly returned to shore. Since I knew more than he, I quoted him what Ma had taught me earlier:

"If you are afraid, you will never get anywhere in this world."

She never told me that sometimes it was important to be afraid, and that life was full of surprises. I wanted to get somewhere, so I continued along the canal by myself. Crash. Splash. Down I went. I struggled to shore while grasping the towrope of my heavy sled. Kriene helped pull me out and pulled me home. By the time we arrived there, I was lightheaded, and my clothes were beginning to get crunchy as I staggered into our house. I tried to call for Ma who was upstairs and did not see me:

"If I I c confess s ssomething, will yyyou not sp p pank me?" I chattered with dizziness.

"Of course not," she worriedly replied.

"I b b broke through the e e ii ce."

She hurriedly took off my clothes, dried me with a soft towel, put me to bed and did not give me my usual reward for getting wet. She was glad I had not drowned or frozen like Oma.

◆   ◆   ◆

For as long as I could remember, everyone in our crowded house always wore grim expressions. Grief was always present; the constant sorrow on Ma's face saddened me greatly and was reflected on my own. But I never knew why this was so and would ask her, "Ma, why are you so sad?"

"Little Bird, I will tell you when you're older," was her usual reply. She never mentioned her marital problems. The following letter shows the source of some of her torments. While we were freezing and starving, Pa encouraged us from Diesenbach:

"I have through indefatigable writing efforts finally combined our valuables in Herten and Wollbach. In the middle of May, when the cherries are ripe, it would be well if you would travel to Wollbach, to unpack all the things and store them in a big closet and to dry them out. I am thinking that you and the boys then drive with me to Diesenbach and live in peace with the boys for several weeks. Then we'll drive to the Black Forest for fourteen days of vacation and put things in order in Wollbach.

"If you should shy away from this trip and are without happiness and have great reluctance, Miss Lore will travel with me in order to clean and iron.

"…Miss Lore can get room and board for fourteen days in Oberweiler with one of my friends. We could claim that she studies medicine in Freiburg and that her parents are good acquaintances in Regensburg, so that this story has hand and foot. She is exactly like you, dresses simply, is frugal, a homebody and does not want ridiculous pleasures…

"…Please write to attorney Grosswilde to get the children baptized and join the church, which I will do myself also."

We needed a lawyer to get baptized?

"Now Sweetheart, I have another thing. I need a car for the supervision of a big construction site in Regensburg. I can now buy in the free market, a 'Hanomag Sturm' Limousine, with convertible top, for 10,000 marks. Mr. Bleimund says I could sell this car anytime for 20 to 25,000 marks and should buy it under all circumstances. When I think about it, this is right, inasmuch as soon there will be the devaluation of money and instead of 10,000 marks, we will have only 1,000 marks. I myself can immediately make fluid 6000 marks, but I need an additional 5-6000 marks to be able to pay for the car.

"Through construction supervision and planning I still can earn approximately 12,000 marks this year. I would like to choke back my monthly income somewhat; otherwise the taxes will be too high. This is my suggestion and what shall I do now, what do you believe, is this the right thing to do?" I cannot take over the construction supervision with the train and I...

"So in all things, you can be at peace and be happy about my visit in four weeks. Inform me about the auto situation right away, if I should buy it and send me by return mail 5,000 marks."

He wasted a lot of ink to convince Mama that he was in dire need also and undoubtedly had written this letter with the help of some wine. Whenever he did write a sympathetic comment to us, it was to paint artificial empathy in order to make himself look good before a divorce court. Even though Ma always appealed for his help, he usually wrote but two or three sentences about Siggi and me. She asked him to send us wooden pegs so we could get our shoes re-soled. I remember these short, square toothpicks that were pointed at one end and were used instead of iron nails because such were not available.

In spite of our plight Pa wanted to buy a car. There were many things wrong with this. One, one, and one, our bellies were too often empty, or too often filled with compost and wiggly worms. Two, the German law required him to support us. Three, he had the moral obligation to do so. Four, he did not need a car to practice his profession. Previously he had written to Ma who had requested him to send us a bike:

"...A bicycle I have to keep with me in any case, so that I always can control the construction site in Regensburg in the summer."

Five, if he insisted on a car, it did not have to be a luxury convertible. Six, any automobile would draw the envy of people because few of them could afford one. Seven, he wanted to spend all of Ma's inheritance. This was confusing because he also had claimed that he needed this money to build us a home.

When May arrived, Ma did not travel to southern Germany as Pa had requested. The things that she was to take care of were items stored in places where they had lived before and during the war. She was also to help can Grandpa's vegetables and dry his big crop of cherries. Instead, Grandpa packed a lot of fresh cherries into a big wooden box that he sent to us in Simonswolde. When it arrived there, juice was oozing out, and it was mashed, rotten and moldy. We fed this fermenting mash to our chickens and for many days they happily staggered around. *Could someone have made liters of* Kirschwasser *from this?*

At about this time Pa's boss, Dr. Hagen, wrote a letter certifying that Pa was indispensable to the companies for which he worked. This was in response to Ma's request for Pa to move to Simonswolde, which was ludicrous since there was no work for architects in this area. But he could help in our garden, which he never did, not even during the rare times when he visited us. Poor Ma always hand-spaded and tended the garden all by herself.

The letter from Pa's boss included the following:

From: "Dr. Hagen, Trustee of the Leichtbau GmbH and Messerschmidt GmbH"

"Herewith we confirm that Mr. Herbert Neuman, Architect, for the purpose of a proposal to the Bavarian Interior Ministry, Regional Governor of Regensburg, at this time is involved with the following work for the firms of Leichtbau Regensburg GmbH and Messerschmidt GmbH…

"His sudden departure from his assigned responsibilities would cause substantial disturbances in the liquidation of Messerschmidt as well as in the contract work of Leichtbau…

"…We would like it if Mr. Neuman could stay in this locale until the completion of the jobs, and we kindly request the responsible authorities to refrain from a deportation."

Could he not be forced to send us some of his earnings?

While Pa was visiting us later, Dr. Hagen sent a telegram requesting his immediate return. He was in danger of losing his residence because refugee families were making a claim on it. Therefore Pa quickly returned to Bavaria and wrote us from there:

"My Dearest One and Children!

"I arrived here last Saturday evening, inasmuch as I was able to sit for almost the entire trip. Many thanks for your loving kindness and hospitality. A cute traveling companion from Wesermuende/Lehe, a medical student with seven semesters, entertained me and was welcome company for me on this long voyage. She said that *Basedowsche Krankheit* was an illness which can be successfully cured. As the enclosed card indicates, Father will get an operation. I wrote to him right away and included this letter herewith, as well as the receipt of delivery. I was not controlled, and had good luck getting the things through to Bavaria.

"Last Monday evening a refugee arrived here with a family of six people and furniture. He violently wanted to obtain my room as their residence. Through Dr. Hagen's active interference it was possible to prevent this man from his brazen endeavor. After a few days, Dr. Hagen was able to finish this matter with the help of the officials, the police and the Pirzers. A great excitement prevailed here.

"So my treasure, everything is falling into place again. Now I have shortly informed you of everything of importance."

Pa addressed Ma with various titles, depending on his mood or his frustrations with her when she would not do something that he had requested, such as budging from her resolve to stay put in Simonswolde. His eloquent salutations ranged from "My Dearest Treasure" to "Dear Fury of Criticism," and from "Dear Katje" to "Obligatory Critical Theorist."

◆   ◆   ◆

Four years after World War II, Ma traveled back to Southern Germany but did not tell Siggi and me that she was going to court. She also did not tell us that our lawyers could absolve father of his responsibilities and rob us while pretending to help us, because she did not yet know this herself. Now that she had not hooked an American, she did not want to lose her husband and wanted to appear personally before the judge to prevent Pa from achieving his greatest dream, i.e., to get rid of us. So Ma left us in the care of our loving Aunt Adele Murmerele.

During her stay in the South, Ma planned to live in a poorhouse, but when she arrived there, she was told that it was closed for remodeling. When I would become wiser in the games of divorce, I would realize that this might have been a Pa-instigated lie. Desperate and strong-willed Ma went to the city hall and demanded to sleep in jail. When she was refused, her fury rose and with machine gun staccato she blasted the mayor:

"I am the wife of the architect who supervised the construction of the Lutheran church in this city. He has two sons. He refuses to support his family. He has never done anything for his children. Now he wants to divorce us.

"I was thrown out of my home at the age of fourteen. I worked for land barons in Eastern Europe and had to get up at four in the morning to scrub floors and mop kitchens. For room and board only. I will not leave here until you allow me to sleep in jail."

She continued her onslaught, while shaking her finger until the mayor relented, not because he felt sorry for her, but because she was embarrassing him. At night she shared a jail cell with a female prisoner, while the warden also kept rabbits imprisoned outside their window. Ma wrote me that their activities kept her awake at night. *Or was it her worries?*

Every morning the warden would yell: "Women, get up. Turn in your blankets."

During the daytime, Ma sat in the waiting room of the railroad station, to study documents and write letters, and whenever someone came in she hid her face behind a newspaper. She won this court process and the judgment was short:

"The complaint is rejected. There is nothing that can be proved to be a cause for a divorce. The plaintiff must bear all court costs."

Hurrah! Hurrah!

Poof!

Or not hurrah? A wad of our sustenance went to those who were sup-
posed to protect us?

Some time after Ma returned triumphantly to Simonswolde, she
received another summons for another lawsuit, and I suspect that we
had to eat a greater assortment of garbage in order to pay for her train
fare. She wrote me many years later that Pa was so determined to rid
himself of his family that he employed the most influential lawyer he
could find, Professor Dr. Fuhrler, a close friend of German Chancellor
Adenauer. This professor was one of Pa's divorce lawyers for ten years
and was also, or became later, vice-president as well as president of the
European Parliament in Strasbourg, France. A big guy. Ma also heard
on the national radio that Adenauer vacationed with Fuhrler in Cadde-
nabia, Italy, and this confirmed that she would have a difficult fight.

While Pa hired turbo lawyers, Ma could not afford one at all. She
went to a bureaucracy and applied for assistance under the poverty
rights law. Under its program she was assigned a lawyer who was paid
for by the state, that is, mostly by the working stiffs.

She made the thousand-kilometer trip back to Rheinfelden, again
by train, because she was as determined to stay married as her husband
was to get rid of us. A new law had been passed that included insanity
as one of the few reasons for divorce, and Chief Judge Kaulbach said
that Pa offered half a dozen witnesses to show that Ma was mentally ill.
But when the time came for them to appear in court to testify against
her, they all gave reasons for not being able to do so. Only building
superintendent Hilkert, Pa's good friend, rode with him to Freiburg
where he announced:

"It appears to me, I mean, this woman is not normal."

The judge wanted to confirm this accusation and ordered her head
to be examined. The following Monday, Ma met her appointment at
the health bureau in Saeckingen at eight o'clock in the morning.
Twenty minutes before noon she was called from the waiting room,

and years later Ma described this interview in a letter to me in America as follows:

"How you men mistreat abandoned women!" she told the examiner.

"With you the examination will take longer. The others were all examined for tuberculosis and other diseases," he responded.

"What is your name?"

"Where do you live?"

"How did you get here?"

"What is your marital status?"

"Married," Ma answered in a mocking voice.

The inspector concluded the examination: "You are very intelligent. What did you study at the university?"

She answered: "Nothing, but unfortunately I have been forced to study **man**kind."

This was the basic outline of how to determine if someone is normal or not, and everyone should know this. I never learned if the examiner also practiced phrenology to obtain the diagnosis from his scientific observations, but after a life like hers, with a dented head like hers, anyone would be at least slightly loco, and Pa must have known this when he married her.

◆   ◆   ◆

In one of her letters to Pa, Ma included a list of the bills that she had had to pay while they were still together in Southern Germany, before and into the war:

"1.Rent 2.Gas 3.Power 4.Water 5.Garbage 6.Phone bill 7.Ringer fees 8.Coal 9.Laundry 10.Floor waxing 11.Party 12.Women's Work 13.Men's athletics club 14.Women's athletics club 15.Colonial Club 16.Fools guild 17.Tennis sports club 18.Fisherman's Association. 19.Shooting club 20.Men's choir 21.Youth hostel 22.Peoples' Welfare 23.Stamp collectors 24.? Donation 25.NS Federation for Technology 26.SA Victims 27.Chamber of *Reich* Culture 28.Fire insurance 29.Car insurance 30.Accident insurance 31. Life insurance 32.*Der Allemanne* 33.*Lesezirkel* 34.Radio fee government radio 35.*Funkstunde* radio program 36.*Das Reich* magazine 37.Cinema Middle-class-help 38.Citizens tax 39.Income tax 40.Sales tax 41.Reconnoiter tax 42.Chimney sweep 43.Stove pipe cleaning 44.Church taxes 45.Church community taxes 46.Church state taxes 47.Church land tax 48.Land taxes 49.Garage rent 50.Car wash 51.Air Raid Protection Federation 52.Red Cross 53.Gas (2000 km/month) 54.*Triptick* 55.*Frankenetat,* monthly 56. DDA Club."

Ma had found this old list again, added the following note, and sent it to Pa:

"Always paying and then to hear the accusation, 'you squat on the money.' To how many clubs do you belong again in Rheinfelden?"

She also sent him an official statement that was forwarded to her from Simonswolde while she was in Rheinfelden for the court process. It was a doctor's request typed on a half-sheet of cheap paper, indicating the great scarcity that still existed in Germany even six years after the war.

"Official Medical Prescription.

"…Mrs. Ulberta de Vries, born on August 30, 1905, lives in Ostersander. Exhibited for the presentation to the Housing Agency of the County of Aurich.

"Mrs. V. lives at this time with three daughters, one son-in-law and two nephews (since April 3, 1951), in living quarters insufficient for eight people.

"Besides, she has sick lungs.

"A separation of the sick one from the children and nephews is imminently necessary because of health concerns. This is easily carried out when Mrs. de Vries changes her domicile to Simonswolde, where she could lead a combined household with her mother.

"I request to assign Mrs. de Vries a room in Simonswolde in connection with Mrs. Heddens."

Signed: "Official Doctor, Dr. Martin Schmidt, Medicinal Counselor"

Mrs. Heddens, our landlady with early-day body piercing on her cheek, was the mother of Mrs. de Vries. On the back of this notification, Ma scribbled the following note:

"The boys cannot remain here any more, their beds will go to the attic. The doctor and nurse wrote that they cannot help us any more. I myself cannot find shelter. My bed has already been in the hallway for a long time, since 1949. I was told that I can only legally live where my husband resides."

We were about to be thrown out of the sardine can house where we had stayed during the six postwar years. Ma knew that her private war would intensify, and she would have to remain at the battlefront. Therefore she sent for Siggi and me to join her in Rheinfelden. We traveled back to Southern Germany by ourselves, again by train, but this time comfortably in passenger cars and mostly on schedule. I remembered World War II as we passed through many still-damaged cities. This country was still digging itself out of its rubble, and there were many of the tall cranes that became a common sight throughout Western Germany. These were always the first to appear on the construction sites, even for the erection of single-family homes, to hover over the rising buildings until after the roofs were complete.

Fortunately we had survived WWII and its aftermath mostly intact and Europe was at peace. We were now nine and eleven years old and could not know that we were traveling directly to ground zero of another war, and for Siggi and me an unending war, because we thought at that time that with a father...

Life can only get better!

3

IT GETS BETTER

○ ○
Unity, justice and freedom for the German fatherland! Fraternally, with heart and hand, let us strive for this! Unity, justice and freedom are the pledges of happiness. In their radiance flourish German fatherland!

—*German National Anthem*

Our nation makes great promises. Does this include everyone?

◆   ◆   ◆

With great fanfare we arrived in Rheinfelden. Our train, powered by a steam locomotive, screeched into the station. Tons of steel shook the earth and sent smoke and thunder into the sky. Clouds of steam hissed through the giant wheels onto the concourse, shrouding the travelers waiting there.

Our ancestors knew that we had returned, Siggi and I.

The twin cities of Rheinfelden, one in Switzerland, one in Germany, were a great contrast to Simonswolde. Whereas the North German countryside was flat, these cities straddled the Rhine River which meandered along the hills at the southern end of the Black Forest. Not far to the west was Germany's historic enemy, *La Grande Nation*.

Ma, but not Pa, met us at the station. Her hair was noticeably grayer and her skin was pale yellow. Again she had spent days in bed with jaundice which was caused this time by Pa and his frolicking lawyers. She was high-strung excited, not happy-excited, to see us. Since the station was close to the Swiss border, she led us to the Rhine River to give us a glimpse of the old Rheinfelden. She shrilly asked a customs official if we could walk out onto the bridge for a closer look at Switzerland. The river was deep and swift with silent, deep whirlpools sucking down flotsam. Quaint old rowhouses snuggled each other on the opposite riverbank, and someone was fishing from an open window.

We walked to the middle of the bridge, the boundary between the two countries, where Ma pointed back to the German side:

"See that rock outcropping over there? With the steel beams hanging from it?"

We spotted it: *"Ja."*

"That's where your father's fishing hut was before the war."

Siggi and I went ballistic.

"We can go fishing there."

"And with our father."

Ma was silent.

After our detour, the three of us walked to our new home. Along the way Ma pointed out the buildings that Pa had designed, as well as the manicured parks and tree-lined streets. Even now Siggi and I did not know that Pa had built a house, our home, and that we would be moving in with him. *Family matters must be hidden from children? Could it be detrimental to their psyches?*

Siggi and I did not think of Pa as a member of our family. Although he probably had not invited us this time, Ma had moved in with him when she became ill. He had invited us numerous times in the past to join him in the south, even though he had lived in only one room in the hotel *Saengerhalle,* Hall for Singers, into which he had moved from Bavaria. I did not know why he had moved, if he had built our house there, or if he had sold it. The *Saengerhalle* was the best accommodation that he had been allowed here because of the great housing shortage. If we had lived with him, he would have been placed on a list to get an apartment, which was probably why he might have asked us to come back to him before.

Now that he had built a house and we were coming, he did not want us, because it would be more difficult to get a divorce. Ma would be close by to raise hell. You just couldn't throw a mother and her children out onto the street and let them freeze and starve. It would be difficult to evict his burdensome wife and lovable by-products from their new home because Ma stuck to Pa like cockleburs that he continuously attempted to pluck off.

We by-products were still too young to understand that children normally had two parents. The closest contact that we had had with another family was with our cousins, Gerd and Maike, in Simonswolde. They did not have a father either because Ma's brother had been buried in Russia, after which our mothers fought each other over his inheritance.

Siggi and I did not know of divorce because it was rarely a solution under German laws, but we would soon learn that it carried an intense social stigma. Ma had never told us much about our father, except that he was irresponsible and did not care for us, having abandoned us after his climaxes. She did not tell us about such because she did not want us to know that either.

When we arrived at our new home, Siggi and I were astounded. We went ballistic, again, for the second time in one hour. We could not believe it. This could make us "hyper," even though "hyper" hadn't been invented yet and neither had attention deficit disorder. However, if we'd suffer from them, it would be cured with spanking. Now we were overwhelmed to find a new three-story mansion that no one had ever told us about. Three families lived here. A small enameled sign pointed to Pa's office in the daylight basement: "Herbert Neuman, *Freier Architekt und Diplom Ingenieur.*" This was status.

And there was not a manure pile in sight.

Our new home was located at the outskirts of the city, two blocks away from a street that had been built by the ancient Romans. It was still used, had far fewer potholes than the streets in my present hometown, and this was the stability and permanence which Siggi and I so craved.

The size and luxury of our new home astounded us. Its design conformed to the regional uniformity of cubic shapes that were reminders of chateaux without turrets. It was built with reinforced blocks of concrete and fired clay that were finished with stucco and plaster. Like most mansions, it was also covered with a steep hip roof of red tiles that endured for two centuries. These roof tiles were not even referred to as "Deluxe" or "Superior." They were simply thought of as tiles, and there was no lesser quality available. Wrought-iron grilles with diamond patterns adorned the windows on each side of the front door, and most of the other windows were flanked with wooden shutters that could be closed to keep out light and prying eyes.

And raging fathers.

When we opened the oak entrance door to our house and entered the foyer, where an oaken staircase curved upward, I swelled with new emotions of pride, permanence and security. In Simonswolde we had lived in a crowded house where we'd shared one stinky hole with other families, and this one was its antithesis.

I ran up the stairs.

"No, no, come here. We live downstairs. Other people live upstairs," Ma said emphatically.

I turned around as Pa opened the lead-glass doors to the vestibule of our new home. He was smirking and did not say, "Welcome home." He did not hug us and we did not hug him. Instead, Siggi and I dashed around him and looked into the first room to the left.

"Ma, look," I exclaimed, "a bathroom. With water."

It was the first bathroom with plumbed fixtures that I had ever seen. It was so clean and inviting that Siggi and I could finally toilet train ourselves. I knelt beside the white bathtub to twirl the shiny handles. A dull thud drew my attention to the mysterious glow that came from a snow-white porcelain box on the wall behind me, and through a hole I could see dozens of long, blue flames aligned in precise rows. I rose on my toes, drew a deep breath, and puffed into this fiery regiment. A cleft opened and closed with a thump. While turning faucets on and off, I realized that the fire in the box, an instantaneous gas heater, responded to the flow of water.

Excitedly we rushed from room to room. In the kitchen Siggi turned a knob on the stove and it emitted a hiss, filling the air with a strange odor.

"Turn off the gas," Pa scolded him.

In the *Herrenzimmer,* gentlemen's room, Siggi and I admired the bas-relief curlicues on the plaster ceiling, the recessed lights and chandelier. This room also had iron radiators under the double-paned windows like all the others in this house.

"What are these things for?" we queried our parents.

"They are heaters."

"How do they work?"

"Hot water circulates through them."

"But where does it come from?"

"There's a boiler in the basement that heats the water," explained Pa.

We raced back through the vestibule and down to the basement where we found the boiler that heated the entire house. Downstairs in Pa's office, draftsman Sepp showed us the drawings of the buildings they were designing. Pa's practice had become very successful because he was very talented and the reconstruction of Germany was in high gear. Every building, including all houses, had to be designed and supervised by architects. It was the law.

Pa was also successful because he was gregarious, easygoing, and was always ready to joke. With other people but not with us. He was making up for lost meals by stuffing himself in restaurants and thus had grown plump like many of his countrymen. He was jolly with a balding forehead and drank wine or beer only with his meals and in between also. We discovered that he would never drink anything but alcoholic beverages, yet I never considered him to be an alcoholic.

Now that we were united with our father, who looked rich like a banker, Siggi and I felt that our poverty had ended, and we enjoyed the first few months living in our new home. This was the best time of our lives, and it could not get much better. Or much worse. For the first time in my life I felt a twinge of confidence in myself, secure in having a father, a new home, a real toilet, while Pa owned an automobile at a time when few people could afford one. Even so, Ma, like all house-wives, walked to the neighborhood stores for our daily needs, carrying her purchases in her shopping net because she did not drive and most of the stores were within walking distance anyway.

While out shopping, the housewives visited with each other, and this helped build a stable society. Ma gossiped about her irresponsible husband and the mistreatment of women, while others told that they did not have husbands or had only partial ones. Some were dead and gone, others partially gone having lost limbs on battlefields, while still others sat at a *Stammtisch* in cafés every night. A *Stammtisch* is a table in a restaurant which is reserved for the same group of men who meet there almost nightly to visit. These were also partial husbands. Here they drank beer and wine and ruminated about the politics of man-kind, and it had been one such group that had hatched the *Putsch,* a secret plot, in Munich that had triggered one of the world's greatest man-made disasters.

Pa was too embarrassed to be seen with Ma, and they never went anywhere together. *Or did they hate each other so much?* He also was too embarrassed to be seen with Siggi and me in our tattered clothes from Simonswolde. Children often teased us, especially here in Rheinfelden, where people were not so poor and were always properly dressed. Pa bought Siggi and me each a new suit with Knickerbocker pants, the first new clothes that Siggi and I ever wore, except for the leather pants that he had sent us in Simonswolde. We had worn them daily for seven summers until our pee rotted out the crotches, and we grew too big for them.

◆   ◆   ◆

After moving in with Pa, we slowly began to realize that our parents did not get along with each other. Siggi and I barely knew our father and did not expect to have one. In the past we had written him only a few times and had received only impersonal notes in return along with an occasional toy. Now that we were all together in one house, there was still not much contact with him. Our parents argued frequently but mostly in private. Worse yet, Ma, Siggi and I were confined to one bedroom, to sleep together in one double bed, while Pa had a room by himself. Siggi and I did not yet know that this was weird. We had always been weird, but did not know that we were weird. We did not yet realize that mothers and fathers slept together and that growing boys had their own bedrooms.

We never entered Pa's bedroom. But one day when everyone was gone, and I must have felt unusually courageous, I sneaked in to snoop around and searched his dresser which smelled of sour sweat, exactly like Pa. Much later scientists would discover that this virile scent attracted women, as did money, like flies to honey. I found Pa's address book and was puzzled by more than seventy names listed therein and realized that they were all women. There was a photograph of an *aunt* to whom Pa had introduced us, Aunt Faessle. She owned a hat store, was cross-eyed, and we did not like her. Ma told us that she was stealing our father. In this picture our *aunt* was squatting down and her pale buttocks were beaming in a dark forest, but I couldn't find *New* or *Improved* stamped on them. So far there had been only very few people that I really didn't like. And I did not yet know that I would someday develop a real soft spot in my heart for lawyers. *When will they classify such soft spots as a sue-able disease?*

I searched Pa's toiletry case and found a rolled up balloon. Because there was no sex education in our schools, and our parents didn't teach us anything useful, I had not yet learned about the birds and the balloons. I could only guess what it was and wondered which *aunt* would get to ride on it. Pa had a great choice of women with whom he could ride, because they greatly outnumbered men, since so many of them had been killed during the war, while others were still stuck in gulags. Still others were hiding in other countries because they had been Nazis and did not dare to return to their furious Fatherland.

Pa dated many *aunts* and brought some of them home, apparently because he wanted us to be a big family. When he took Siggi and me, but never our mother, to restaurants, he always ogled the waitresses, all of whom seemed to know him quite well. He never failed to tip the young ones generously and pinch their buttocks lovingly to check if they were ready. If he were a man, he'd definitely be a buttocks-loving man.

We never did anything together, our big family. Our parents still did not tell their children that they were divorcing, that there would never be a real family, even officially. Siggi and I detected no difference in their relationship with each other. We felt that parents were supposed to fight and nothing changed between them now that we were all together. Opposites were supposed to attract each other; they were opposites but attracted each other only to quickly repel each other in nasty ways.

Ma never went anywhere with us, never learned to drive because Pa would not let her, and she moved about in a very small area, as far as her bike could take her. She either walked or biked to the few places that she visited because she had no money and could not buy much. Pa ate most of his meals in restaurants by himself or with one of our temporary aunts, Siggi's and mine. We did not eat regular meals because Ma did not prepare regular meals and instead, whenever we became hungry, we simply exclaimed to Ma, *Ich Bin Hungrig*. I am hungry. For several more years we would say several times a day, *Ich Bin Hun-*

grig. When we would say so, Ma retrieved a loaf of bread and cut us some slices, and after she thoughtfully covered them with lard and sugar, or margarine, we devoured them.

Someday my dynasty coat-of-arms will depict a chicken brooding on gilded eggs, nestled on a juicy manure pile, because those had helped to keep us alive. My shield will be adorned with a curly ribbon announcing in curly script, *Ich Bin Hungrig,* like the shield of the English queen announces *Ich dien.* I didn't know whom the queen served, but I knew that we were always hungry.

The only other food that Ma fed us included mostly apples and oranges but never bananas. These were too expensive and rotted too fast before Ma could get them. I drooled whenever I saw them on side-walk displays, imagining their taste to be from the world of Tarzan. He liked them and I liked him. Occasionally Ma bought lettuce, cucumbers or tomatoes for us from which I prepared salads for myself. Like a rabbit, I devoured bowls full of lettuce that I drenched in milk and sugar that ran down my chin. I would become civilized tomorrow.

◆   ◆   ◆

Siggi and I still weren't really aware that Ma was extremely lazy and so different from other people. She was outgoing and often embarrassed us with her loud pontifications in public. She still whipped us but only infrequently anymore. She liked to impose her philosophies on other people, deaf ears, closed minds, tender butts, or not. She talked almost incessantly, and her words blew people away like the wind blows paper and plastic garbage. Her way was the only way, and strangely, she never seemed to listen to other people's advice. But if it were in print, it was the gospel. She cut out newspaper and magazine articles by the hundreds and saved them. She was a fountain of knowledge, much in the form of statistics, little of which was of any use to us. The wire cord dangling from her waist was still a handy tool to make sure we did everything her way, and it could still help with her cathar-sis.

Even now that we had a new kitchen Ma never cooked. It was still too much work and still destroyed vitamins. In Simonswolde, Aunt Adele had prepared most of our food, while Siggi and I usually did the dishes. Much of this food had to be cooked, to kill or to disguise the things in it; so there had been no choice of not cooking, and Ma also never cleaned house because dirt always came back.

Since we had no washing machine, doing the laundry was a back-breaking job. The clothes had to be boiled in a big kettle, then this heavy load had to be stirred, scrubbed on a washboard, rinsed at least twice, wrung out by hand, then hauled outside to be hung on a clothesline. After they dried, they had to be brought back in again to be ironed, folded and stored. Consequently we rarely did the laundry, but in Simonswolde Ma had dyed the light-colored clothes from America with dark colors to disguise dirt. Along with these clothes, our relatives also had sent us the dyes that came in boxes similar to Jell-O. After Ma, Siggi and I moved to Rheinfelden, our relatives quit sending us pack-ages, possibly because they thought that Pa was taking care of us.

Because so much of the work in her youth had been heavy and time consuming, Ma learned to be practical. It became one of her basic principles. She never did any work unless our situation became more unpleasant for her than having to do something to rectify it. "Besides," she explained, "the more I work, the more I have to eat and we cannot afford to buy anything because your father never gives us any money."

Pa's philosophy about work was similar to Ma's; do as little as possi-ble. I cannot blame them for their laziness, considering they had lived through two world wars and the aftereffects. Pa loved his profession and excelled in it, but he did absolutely no work around the house or on his car. Besides, German homes are not in a constant state of disre-pair, and it is even difficult to destroy them intentionally. That's why there are few *home improvement centers*.

Ma and Pa shared no common interests and had grown up worlds apart. She saved every piece of paper, every rubber band, while he did not save anything and spent his earnings faster than he received them. He wore only suits; she did not care what she wore as long as she could adorn herself with her whip. He always lived for the moment, for the pleasure. When he attended technical college, our grandfather, who at one time was the richest man in his village, deposited six thousand Reichsmarks at a bank for Pa's architectural study. A few weeks later, Pa had literally spent it all on wine, women and song, even though this was to pay for much of his education. *Did he have a good excuse for doing so, because during the hyperinflation he had learned that people who had spent their money the fastest had received the most in return?*

After the German hyperinflation, grandpa had shown his savings booklet to Pa and had said to him:

"We had over 100,000 marks in the bank. We would never have had to work again if it had not been wiped out completely."

In January of 1921 the wage of a worker was about two and one-half marks per hour. Ten months later this rose to fifty marks. By April 1923 it rose to 1,200 marks. By October of that same year, it exploded to 25,000,000 marks. Twenty-five million marks per hour. Rarely had so many people become multi-millionaires, as well as paupers, and simultaneously, in such a short time. And how did they keep track of the ever faster changing conversion rate? For example, Karl Schmaelzle of Boennigheim had contracted to build a three-story house for a fixed sum. It took, and still does now, about eighteen months to build an average home in Germany. When he finished building it, this sum could then only buy one carpenter's pencil. A three-story masonry house with a full basement for one pencil. Deals like that could get people excited and make them seek revenge on somebody, and not necessarily on the guilty parties.

The currency value declined rapidly, mainly because of the intolerable war reparations imposed on Germany after World War I. When Ma was fourteen years old, Oma kindly had packed her suitcase, had given her some money, and then had thrown her out of their home. In one of her letters to me, Ma recalled that her mother had told her:

"All of your belongings are in this suitcase. Also 1,000,000 marks. If your suitcase gets too heavy, give the money to someone to carry it for you."

For ten years thereafter, she worked as a maid in Pomerania and Tyrol for room and board only. She learned to save because she earned nothing to save, while Pa who had his college paid for and earned a lot after the war, learned to save nothing. Nothing at all. Deals like that could make mothers seek revenge on somebody and not necessarily on the guilty parties.

◆   ◆   ◆

A few times Pa drove with Siggi and me to Wollbach where he had been born and raised. There we visited his brother, Uncle Fritz, who owned and lived in a grocery store that was bought by our grandfather when he was a young man. The date carved into the lintel over its entrance read 1732. Inside this stone and stucco building we absorbed the history with its ancient smells, dark rooms and low ceilings. Its walls were massive and had small windows that shed little light into the darkness of ages, but I felt comfortable here because of its comforting aura of a long tradition.

Uncle Fritz showed us a book that he had written in order to maintain his sanity while he was a prisoner of war in France. The French had caught him after they had drilled a bullet through his chest, which then stuck in the hand holding the reins of the horse that he was riding. His memoir described the history about our grandfather's store and Fritz himself. He wrote that as a young man he came home from a party late one night, and before he went to bed he desired yet another glass of wine. Therefore he went down to the huge wine cellar where he pulled the plug out of the bunghole of a large barrel to fill his glass. But the internal pressure blew the plug across the cellar and wine poured forth in a big arc. He did not want to waste his beloved wine, so he quickly stuck his thumb into the bunghole to plug its flow. He kept it there for the rest of the night until he heard someone arrive in the morning, when he called for help to retrieve the bung, so he could be free of the barrel. I believe his story because his book also referred numerous times to how good this or that wine had been. It also mentioned that people who came to grandpa's house usually stayed to visit over a glass of wine.

Next to Uncle Fritz's store, which was located near the highest point in the village, was an old stuccoed stone church. Its bell tower housed three bells, the largest of which weighed nearly a ton, and for years our grandfather rang them several times a day. To do this he sat on a board tied to the end of a rope, the other end of which was attached to a mechanism that swung the bells high in the belfry. He built a rhythm while pulling on a second rope that was connected to the opposite side of this mechanism. His body served as a counterweight. He traveled up and down to ring them and continued this for up to fifteen minutes, depending on the hour and the day of the week. He had rung these church bells for many years and ringing them was an old tradition throughout this land.

In spite of this long heritage, the Nazis had removed many of the country's bells without permission. They melted and forged them into cannons and other tools of destruction. Killing and conquering had been more important than calling God, or His flocks to Him. But after the war, new bells were cast and reinstalled in these churches. Siggi and I watched two of them being hoisted up to the belfry of the Lutheran church in Rheinfelden. *Was casting new bells more important than housing for the homeless?*

During this post-war period, Western Germany, with a severe housing shortage, built a lot of churches and fortunately it did not crank out mobile huts to accommodate the homeless. Instead of quickly pasting together immobile huts, German families crowded into existing housing. They bunched up, often in compressed boardinghouse style, in the remaining shelters left intact after the bombing raids until quality dwellings could be built. In the meantime, people were forced to get along with each other during their mandatory in-house diversity training.

On the outside of the Wollbach church, near its entrance, were two carved stone plaques built into its wall. Each depicted a coat-of-arms, blackened by time, the same time that could heal wounds. One shield belonged to our family and depicted a spoked wheel with teeth, split in half by a staff held in a fist. The description beneath it referred to one of our ancestors who in 1732 was blessed with eighteen children. Several of these were then blessed when they soon died.

After I read the history of Wollbach, I knew that the dead were more blessed than the living at that time. There were plagues and pestilence, wars and starvation. Catholics killed Protestants and Protestants killed Catholics. No one dared to be an atheist. Vikings, Frenchmen, Austrians and Germans all butchered and burned swaths through the Black Forest and up and down the Rhine River, engaging in wars that lasted for lifetimes. They created witches and burned them on stakes, and there seemed to have been little relief from this sort of entertainment and brotherly love.

◆   ◆   ◆

One time we visited Grandpa's orchards just outside of Wollbach with its assortment of fruit trees.

"This will one day be yours," Grandpa told Siggi and me.

"This orchard has been in our family for generations. We supplied products to the Count von Roetteln," he continued.

This count had a castle, now in ruins, a few kilometers away.

Not to be outdone in generosity, Pa told us:

"If you are good boys, you will someday inherit my house."

We shrugged off his statement and said nothing, but as always, we reported to Ma what he had said and what he had done. She always wanted to know what he was doing, and Siggi and I were her spies. Now we did not believe him because we were taught: *"Wer einmal luegt dem glaubt man nicht, wenn er auch die Wahrheit spricht,"* he who lies once, cannot be believed again, even though he may speak the truth. So there. So long ago he had destroyed the credibility that he was born with because Ma had always told us that he lied a lot. Therefore we did not dwell on Pa's wonderful news and did not get excited. *Did Pa even believe himself?*

When Grandpa died later that year, Pa alone attended his funeral, leaving us behind, and when our relatives asked him why his sons had not come, he replied:

"Their mother would not give them out."

Ma told us that this was also a lie because he had not asked us if we wanted to go or said when he was going. The few times that I had been with Grandpa, I had been happy in his presence. He radiated an ageless stability and smelled like fresh home-baked bread and hard cider. Now I wanted to jump into his grave, but I could never get what I desired. No one ever asked us what we wanted or needed, and he was one of the few people who seemed to take an interest in us, although he did not help. He did not help us because we were on opposite sides in our war. We were on mother's side; she had indoctrinated Siggi and me for many years to be on her side, and we knew little about what was happening on the battlefields of our Progenitors' War.

There was one other relative who seemed to take a little interest in us, Aunt Helene, but she was far away, in America. She had even invited us to move there after the divorce became final, and Siggi and I did not realize that anyone was after the spoils of our war because Ma did not tell us about some of the letters that Helene had written to her. *Family activities must be kept from children. Could be detrimental to their psyches.*

A few years ago Siggi found one of Helene's letters that she had written to Ma in the early fifties and sent me a copy. Apparently she had known that we soon would be a divorced family, and the three of us might be on our own:

"Dear Katje and boys,

"We wish you, dear sister, all the best and good health and God be with you. I especially have the wish at heart that you bring up your children as only a mother can do, even though your hands are often tied. So do the best for the children so that they later will not worry that 'mother did not pray with us…'

"…The German girl, Renate, is also here as a student in the same class as Arlene (our cousin) and gets everything free, including pocket money and much freedom. She comes to us to play piano and goes to church with Arlene.

"We have a house for you to live in at the other end of our farm. You should live there and earn your living by picking berries with the boys, etc. We have many possibilities this summer because our daughters want to continue their studies. The boys can help us make hay. You will say that is a good idea. I think every few days, what will happen with Ami and Siggi…

"…Also young people from Switzerland are here in our neighborhood. They like it better here, even though they have to work, but they are free of many…"

Swiss like it better than their mountains and castles?

◆   ◆   ◆

Pa brought home yet another fornicating *aunt* or so we were told, named Elfi, who moved in with us. Siggi and I did not know if our parents were now divorced, or would soon be divorced, or if Pa had already married our aunt. Privately we called her "Teufi," a derivative of *Teufel*. Little devil. Ma did not have to tell us, "look what the old tomcat dragged in" as we noticed his drag-in immediately and were very uncomfortable with her. She had come from Austria and seemed to desire to destroy us, to exile us from our home. Like *Fraeulein*

Faessle before her, Elfi was also a hatmaker, even though there were not many hatmakers left in this world. Elfi's eyes were not crossed, but we did not dare to cross her path because her eyes emitted poisonous darts that made me suspicious.

Pa liked to make hatmakers. He went mad for hatters. Elfi pressured him to throw us out of our home, but Ma refused to leave even though she would soon be divorced, or was already divorced. No one told Siggi and me about the status of our beloved family, and we could not leave, would not leave, but as Ma would later write me, the judge had shouted:

"Out, all of you!"

Pa's frustration grew unbearable at his inability to remove us, to enforce the court's judgment, and because he was caught between two women. To get out of his bind, to encourage us to leave, Pa pounded Ma with his fists, and when she dropped to the floor he kicked her. That's how her father had apparently cuddled her when she was a baby, our poor mother. I just had come in with my beebee gun and watched Pa vigorously practicing soccer on Ma. Even though he had a heart condition, he had to enforce the judge's order. He was breathing hard now, and I was worried about his heart; I was worried about my mother. My papa was oblivious of me, even though I wished that he would enforce the judge's order on me instead, because I was used to enforcement. Ma had often practiced it on me.

Siggi and I never had any thoughts of aggression even though we had been at the receiving end of immense violence most of our lives. From family and foes alike. We might have benefited from a little tele-violence, reenacting its fantasy, its reality, to send messages to guilty parties, parties who did not peer into our eyes to reach our savaged souls. Now I stood there frozen in tears, withdrawing deeper into my shell. Nobody ever visited my soul in its lonely dungeon.

Ma yelled for the police. I ran out, jumped on my old bike and ped-aled to the police station as fast as I could. Pa yelled to come back but I ignored him. I could hear him only on one side. "I did not hear you, Pa," I could always say.

A pot-bellied, ruddy-faced policeman, a leftover from the superior Aryan armies, followed me back on a taxpayer's bike to the beating scene. He was important, I was a mass of scrambled goose eggs. He was on his way to rescue a damsel, a white knight in a proper blue uniform, but I had to go slowly so he'd be able to keep up. I was young; he was old. I had a wonderful life ahead of me, and I could tell by his rotund physique and pasty, capillary face that his had been less than wonderful. Very-cold-in-the-blizzard-dash-to-privy-like wonderful. I would never allow my life to be thus.

Pa answered our front door and kindly asked the policeman to come in for a beer while ignoring me, because I was only his son and had no fancy uniform. The beating of one's wife could best be dealt with by drinking dark, delicious Teutonic beer with the law.

◆   ◆   ◆

Whenever she met him, Ma complained about our irresponsible father to the very same minister whom she had extorted Siggi and me away from many years before. She explained that he did not provide for us, and that he and his new wife were mistreating us. But as always her complaints fell on deaf ears. Our mother's pain always fell on deaf ears. Siggi and I rarely talked about our pain because nobody asked us. Nobody heard us. The minister's wife even admonished Ma that she should find a job. She herself was supported by our father through his church taxes, therefore she was qualified to advise our mother to find employment.

Ma claimed that she only had learned to raise chickens. Whenever she filled out forms for this and that, she listed her profession either as a housewife, or as *Huehnerzuechtering*, raiser of chickens. Nothing could be done now with fowl. No fowl jobs were to be had in Rheinfelden, and furthermore, Ma thought of herself as an architect's wife.

Housewives did not get paid with money, and chickens were much lower on the pecking order than housewives or architects. But the biggest reason that Ma did not get a job was that she had no hope and therefore no ambition. Her past had had fowl, her future looked foul, and this caused her great pain.

No religious or any other organization offered us any assistance, nor did anyone seem to care about our private disaster. Yet Germans were required to pay church taxes, which could amount to more than seven percent of their regular income tax. I only learned this a few years ago when I visited our cousins in Germany and they said to me: "Let's visit the tax office." This confused me until they explained about the church taxes, and that they really wanted to show me the beautiful old church in their village.

◆   ◆   ◆

When Pa married Teufi, as had been discovered by others, he obviously didn't know that it might be better to stay with the devil that he knew, than to run to the devil that he didn't know. But he'd find out, and soon, and too late. Much too late. Was the minister reluctant to provide us with a second mother because Siggi and I were growing up as heathens? Here was his chance to add two more sheep to his flock because we had never been baptized with water. Pa apparently had made a deal with the minister that if he'd marry him to Teufi, he could baptize Siggi and me. So at the ages of twelve and fourteen, we were besprinkled at the altar of the church that Pa had designed and supervised during its construction. This warm remembrance should have soothed our souls, Siggi's and mine.

After we received the reverend's water, we would be required to pay church taxes as soon as we earned enough money. This was not separation of church and state. This church, and this state, helped in the separation of mother from father, and father from children, and children from life. We did not know that we would not be around to pay those taxes because we would be separated from this state. Soon Siggi and I would be tricked into leaving this state.

Pa invited some of our relatives to be our godparents, although Siggi and I did not know some of them, and Ma was not invited to our baptism. Defiantly she and her fat Swiss friend, Mrs. Grob, came to the church anyway and sat in the front pew off to one side, while everyone else kept to the other side, like Brahmins and Untouchables. Like men and their inferior wives.

The Very Right Reverend Mennicke, wearing a black robe, came in to perform his function. He surveyed the assembly and asked Ma to leave his church. There was a pair of snow-white, starched rectangles of cloth under his chin. What for, I did not know, but when he spoke they moved with his lips as if to emphasize his words. A man of the cloth asked the mother to leave the baptism of her own children. *If I understood this could I be holy? Was this proof that I was a sinner?*

Instead of leaving, Ma and Mrs. Grob climbed up high to the pipe organ loft in the back of the church and, like God, watched our baptism from above. They were far away and kept quiet when they should have made loud heart-rending noises with the powerful organ.

Ours was a poignant scene. Siggi and I giggled as the minister solemnly sprinkled water on our heads. For us his ritual was silly. For us life was serious and we had no traditions. Besides, hadn't we already been baptized by fire during our first war? Surely the bombardiers had prayed when they released their blessings. Now we were baptized with water. Water is easier but fire is everlasting. Pa buttered up the minister to marry him to a sinner. And a robber. She robbed us of our father; later she'd rob our *Grundstueck,* Siggi's and mine.

After our water ceremony we had a celebration. We had never had a ceremony after our baptisms by fire, even though these had been very hot events, where people were scorched, and freed from hell. Or sent to hell. We remained in hell. Now everyone walked to a nearby café where Pa was hosting a dinner. Ma and Mrs. Grob followed us at a distance. Untouchables always remain out of reach. Siggi and I wanted us all to be together, but we were not Brahmins. We were children.

The Brahmins physically barred Ma from coming to our celebration so we would not be touched by the Untouchable. Ours was a magnanimous dinner with mountains of food and gallons of wine. The mountains and the wine were not for us; we longed for our mother. We longed for a father and all the others that make a family. We longed for all that had been denied to us.

◆   ◆   ◆

Reverend Mennicke married Pa to our second mother, but Siggi and I did not know when or where. We didn't know when one of our many *aunts* became one of our mothers. Ma wrote me many years later that she had walked on a blustery day, blistering her feet, carrying a bouquet of flowers, several kilometers from Rheinfelden to Wollbach for their wedding, and I suspect that she went there to raise a scene.

Teufi's move into our house had been easy. She had little more than the clothes on her back. She had wormed her way into our house, on her back. Now Siggi and I had two mothers. Our new mother wanted to throw us out. Our old mother still used us as objects for catharsis. Neither mother cooked any meals for us or did our laundry. Our old mother spoke long monologues about how men had mistreated her, while Pa did not seem to mistreat our aunt-turned-second-mother. *Did she not catch up on the news during intimate moments?*

Up to this time, since our mothers did not cook for us, Siggi and I were barely aware that people ate regular hot meals because we rarely did. We were young, dirty, and had little social contact with our peers, especially since there were absolutely no extracurricular activities in our schools. Schools were strictly for learning serious subjects and discipline and nothing else. Absolutely nothing else.

Ma brooded at all hours about the court battles with her ex-husband. We didn't know what occupied our new mother. We rarely saw her. She played the upper class architect's wife, with lipstick and haute coiffeur. Our first mother fought for justice and stubbornly continued to fight for child support and alimony in the continuing legalized screw jobs. Our new mother found a pot of gold, and therefore fought against justice in order to steal our child support, alimony and future inheritance during this endless mockery of universal moral standards and laws.

I don't want any more mothers. I don't want any more fathers. Good thing I have a brother. We play together and fight each other. Our fights are forgotten within minutes.

◆   ◆   ◆

Unbeknownst to Siggi and me, Ma had disobeyed the judge's order to move out of our own home, and we therefore were in contempt of court. With Pa threatening to beat us, the three of us became prisoners in our bedroom. Our father and our aunt-turned-second-mother became our guards and occupied the rest of our home. The judge did not send us to jail because we were already in prison, and Ma, Siggi and I ventured out into the bath and kitchen only when we were home alone.

Our prison contained one double bed, a wardrobe, a wall-hung sink and our meager belongings that were strewn all about. We had no privacy. We spoke in whispers and referred to Pa as *Buskohl,* Cabbage, in Low German, a language that he did not understand because he had never lived in the lowlands where it is spoken. We were afraid of our guards and tried to avoid them at all cost. Whenever they were home, the three of us did not dare to leave through doors, so we had to climb through our window like burglars in the night. And after about a year, the white paint on the windowsill became gray and polished, except at the sharp edges where the wood was bared.

The three of us continued to sleep together in one bed whose sheets turned as black as our souls. Ma did not, could not, wash our laundry, and we rarely had the opportunity to bathe or shower. We seldom washed our clothes, except in our sink, there never being enough time, because we were always under siege by our father and our second mother. Only when we were reasonably sure that they would leave the house for a longer period of time did we dare to use the kitchen and bath. But we did not linger, since we never knew when they would return, because unlike in our first war, there were no sirens to warn us of enemy attacks.

Often, whenever Teufi and Pa went somewhere together for more than a few hours, we could not draw hot water, not even from our prison sink, because the instantaneous heater would not ignite. We assumed that Teufi shut off the gas somewhere so that we would freeze if we wanted to bathe. This was easy to figure because that's what devils do, they tempt you with warm showers, then deny you the same. But I located the main gas valve in the basement and turned it on. After we took quick baths under duress, always being alert for the return of our next of kin, we shut off the gas again so the devil would not know that we had used it.

Since there were no bath facilities in the schools, Siggi and I could not shower there either.

Even though our house was luxurious, it had no refrigerator. At this time there were very few of them in Germany, and most food was stored in ventilated pantries. Teufi never bought any fruit and stocked few groceries, so there was little for us to eat. She kept mostly staples, like noodles that required cooking, probably because she knew that we could not eat them. Siggi and I bypassed her noodles, but sucked out the mayonnaise that came in toothpaste-like tubes and blew them back up, so she would not notice. Even though the thoughtful judge ordered Teufi to cook for Siggi and me, she did not; she was to cook for us even though we were now living in our home illegally. *Why did he order our aunt-turned-second-mother to cook for us if we were not supposed to live with her?*

The potty-bed combination in our prison was the center of our universe, the basis of our modus operandi. The bed: We slept in it, rubbed dirt in it, dined on it, read on it, wrote on it, were sick in it, cried in it, and kept our potty under it. The potty: Our white enameled chamber pot was antique and these now have great value because I've seen them in antique stores. If only it came with a tight cover. We did big business in this potty only when it became urgent, and Teufi and Pa denied us access to our bathroom. Only when the two beautiful people left our house did we dare empty it. After we'd fill it to the brim and our pressure became unbearable, Siggi's and mine, we let fly into the sink, the same sink where we also washed our hands, faces and apples. In the meantime, our room reeked more impressively than the privies in the Simonswolde cow barns, but over time we barely noticed.

We carried our potty penchant to extremes because it was our only choice. This was so because we could not hide outside from the prying eyes of the high population density around us, and because of the destruction of our reputation through vicious parental truths and gossips. Our shame and social values would not allow us to ask our neighbors to unlock their homes for us whenever we had to answer calls of nature. Nor would they have permitted it.

Had I not been as dumb as Lindeman claimed, or had I not been in a permanent state of intimidation by Ma's subtle waist décor, I would have known where to put our piss 'n it. I would have hidden little reminders around the *Herrenzimmer* and their bedroom so that Pa and Teufi could enjoy them also. Keenly they would have recognized the connection between their extraordinary aroma and our extraordinary pain. They could then have enjoyed the intensity of our pain. Dung beetles don't know that dung beetles dwell in dung. *Did the judge even know that we beetles are imprisoned in a big potty?*

◆   ◆   ◆

One day when I was home alone, I sneaked into the *Herrenzimmer* that was outfitted with heavy dark wood furniture. Someday we might inherit this elegant opulence and someday we might have class, Siggi and I. One of the pieces was a tall cabinet that also contained Pa's important treasures, such as liqueur, cigars, and a set of *Das Brockhaus* encyclopedia. I opened its glass doors to find a metal box hidden in the back corner and tried to open it, but it was locked. I searched for its key, and when I found none, I tried the key to the cabinet instead.

Surprise! I opened the box and found bundles of Deutsche marks banded together with official bank ribbons. I had never seen so much money before. If I got caught stealing our own money, I would get spanked; therefore I did not even think about stealing it. Quickly I locked this box again, returned the key but did not remove anything because Pa could come in at any moment and I would be punished.

When Ma returned home, I told her about my discovery, more as a confession because I thought that I had misbehaved, than to inform her of the money. She wanted to look at this treasure herself. When it appeared that our guards had left for a longer period of time, she asked Siggi and me to be sentinels to warn of their return. I guarded the front yard, and Siggi stationed himself in the back of our house. It was not long before Pa arrived in his car, alone. I was too frightened to move. If I ran into the house, he might get suspicious and come after me. I froze in place, frightened, while he stopped and glared at me. He restarted his car and squealed away. I will never forget his face, contorted by anger, frustration and shame. *Was he mad at me? Or ashamed?*

I ran into the house and told Ma that Pa had just been here. Biting her lips, she quickly closed the box and returned it to the cabinet. Then we rushed back to our prison and locked ourselves in, scared, but relieved that Ma had avoided a certain and furious beating.

I never took anything from that box and never opened it again. That's how weird I am. I didn't know if Ma ever removed anything from it, but I believe that she at least retrieved information that she used in her court processes.

◆   ◆   ◆

Since I always had a difficult time in school, I did not want to attend a *Gymnasium*. Even its Latin name intimidated me, and I did not even know the definition of this word. After I finished the fourth grade in grade school, however, without discussing it with me, Ma signed me up to take the entrance examination, and I thought it a miracle when I passed it to gain admission into the regional *Gymnasium,* the academic high school in Loerrach. But my scores were so low that I was immediately placed on probation. Most pupils did not branch off to a *Gymnasium* but remained in grade school to finish eight grades of primary school and continued in a trade school to become apprentices to learn a vocation. A *Gymnasium* required nine years of intensive study before one could graduate. If a pupil failed one major course, without earning a very good grade in another one, he was required to repeat all other classes as well, even the ones he had done well in. And if he failed yet another one, he flunked out and had to return to the elementary school or to a vocational school.

During this era, only about five percent of the population graduated from a *Gymnasium.* Because of its high academic requirements, the majority of pupils did not attend it. They were still too young to decide what they wanted to be, so their parents made the choices for them. Enduring the final examinations for graduation caused some pupils to have nightmares, even decades later. Contrast this with the last senior class in the town near my present domicile which produced sixteen valedictorians out of a total enrollment of three hundred eighty-five students. For their commencement speech they took turns reading a story. Also, one student received A grades in high school courses and flunked later in a community college even though he had studied harder.

There was no *Gymnasium,* or any other kind of high school, in Rheinfelden, even though it had at least twelve to fifteen thousand people, and the nearest such schools were in Loerrach and Saeckingen. I commuted to Loerrach by train, about forty to fifty minutes away depending on the connections, and I seemed to be the only pupil from Rheinfelden who attended this school; all others went to Saeckingen. There was no one I could visit with during my commuting, and I always kept to myself. I had to change trains in Basel and felt lost among the crowds inside the underground hallways and the huge glass-roofed concourse of this station.

Even though I tried to study diligently, I did not do well because of the physical and psychological convulsions caused by our quiet Progenitors' War, loaded on top of my torments from the earlier noisy and fiery war. My pig's gristle retained barely enough knowledge to pass some of my courses because I was always in dream mode to shield my soul. To protect my sanity, I kept my mind closed to everything except the necessities for survival that included not getting assaulted.

After my first semester I flunked out and had to return to grade school, but the following year I enrolled at the *Gymnasium* in Saeckingen, where I passed the entrance test also. Siggi was now old enough and was also accepted there. We commuted to school together, and during our thirty-some-minute trips we often caught up on our homework or played cards with our classmates. During the first semester in Saeckingen I was essentially repeating the courses I had taken in Loerrach. I was in my fifth year of schooling, the first year in high school, called *Sexta* in a *Gymnasium.*

The pupils, called students only after they enrolled at a university, had no choice of courses. All were required to follow the prescribed curriculum that was almost purely academic in nature. Our main subjects were German, French, mathematics and sciences, while English and Latin were added in later years. These main courses were taught several times a week, while other classes such as music, art, history, geography and physical education were offered once or twice a week. Since we could not choose subjects that we might have enjoyed, and there were no extracurricular activities, we found little relief from our problems at home.

There was also little distraction inside the school buildings, and unlike in today's classrooms, all the walls were white and devoid of posters or displays of any kind. The starkness of the spaces forced the attention of the pupils on the teacher, and the artworks of the pupils were displayed only on the walls of the art room.

Once a week we also studied religion. The pupils were separated into two classes, Catholics and Protestants. I liked these classes, mostly because they provided relief from the intense study, and we did not have to take the tests that I so abhorred.

Our schools also instilled us with a great amount of discipline. We had to write everything with pen and ink; we never used pencils or erasers. This forced us to think carefully about what to put down on paper, and when we made an error our only choice was to cross it out. Neatness was also graded. All lining had to be done with a straightedge; freehand ruling was not allowed. If a pupil ignored this rule, the teacher would be likely to embarrass him with an unkind remark:

"Ami, *Dummkopf.*" Dumbhead.

Sulk.

"Can you not follow rules?"

We never used preprinted forms for homework or tests. Multiple choice, true or false questions and such were completely unknown to us. Most of our examinations were much more challenging. For example, our teacher dictated sentences in German, and we had to write the translations in ink in the foreign language that was being taught. The pressure was enormous because we had to respond to the speed of the dictation, and we could not return to re-read questions or think about our answers later. Ten to twelve spelling or grammatical errors on a language test resulted in failure. For other kinds of tests, the teacher usually wrote the problems or questions on the blackboards and later erased them again.

Even though several hundred pupils attended this school, it had no valedictorians, school board, logo, school colors, mascot, advisors, counselors, nurses, librarians, cafeterias, vending machines, copy machines, newspapers, reader boards, bands, sports teams or coaches and clubs. There was not a single club. Or gang. *Resource officers,* with or without guns, did not exist because each teacher had the ability to mete out immediate and severe punishment, along with its associated shame, which no student wanted to suffer. There was no scapegoating either. *A willow switch, a pull on the ear, more effective than guns?*

There was only one non-academic employee in our school, a janitor to keep the building clean. We had no study hall, teacher's aides or tutors. If we needed assistance with our schoolwork we had to hire our own tutors after school. And if we still could not meet the academic standards, we simply flunked out because there were no *alternative schools*, or "GED" (General Education Development) programs.

There were no loudspeakers, radios, telephones, movie projectors or sound equipment to distract us. We had no invited speakers or demonstrations, seminars or parent-teacher organizations. There were no courses in self-esteem, sex or social agendas. Instead of learning to mix drinks, we learned French. Instead of bouncing around in tutus, we beat our brains out with algebra. We were not taught how to dress with condoms. We were deprived and unprotected in this cruel world, but we were taught all the basics, including sciences, mathematics and foreign languages. We learned a lot and at a much smaller cost than it does today. Because we had to study so hard some of our textbooks often fell apart and became severely dog-eared and dirty.

There were no school buses even though the pupils came from far and wide. They commuted by trains, buses and bikes, or on foot, and had to pay for their own transportation, textbooks, and all other school supplies.

Our school taught facts, logic and no hocus-pocus of any kind. We had no distracting entertainment such as dances or assemblies in our boot camp. In other words, we were totally deprived but learned absolute discipline and obedience. We actually learned too much of such, Siggi and I. Even before we had entered school, we were the paragons of discipline and urgently needed some hocus-pocus. Unfortunately our school did not provide us with such relief from the torments that were caused exclusively by people. If our parents, lawyers, teachers or other pupils mistreated us, there was no one to help us. We were expected to be silent when we wanted to scream and simply had to frown and bear whatever miseries were heaped on us.

There was little opportunity for socializing in our school. Breaks between classes lasted five minutes, with fifteen minutes for a mid-morning sandwich and some fresh air. School was usually finished by noon after which the pupils returned home, where most of the families ate their meals punctually at the same time every day. This was possible because the wives stayed home and cooked, while the fathers often worked nearby and also came home to eat.

There were no organized or coached contacts between the students after school either. All intercourse between them was between individuals pursuing fun, creative and physical activities. There was no alcohol drinking, no shopping mall loitering or TV, because there were no shopping malls or televisions. Instead the children read, visited, talked, roamed in the forests and pursued individual hobbies. Most of them were close to their parents, especially their mothers who were home most every day, and were allowed to be children; and to be children, girls did not paint their faces to attract boys. They did not even shave their armpits or legs, but I would discover that they still could be enticingly sexy.

There was not only no hocus-pocus in our schools, there were few, if any straight A pupils and no honor societies. We did not get publicly recognized for outstanding performance, and there were no accounts in the news media of achievements by teachers or pupils; nor were there reports of them committing crimes. Our motivation was not the carrot but the stick. We were not bribed to do well; we were instantly punished and embarrassed if we didn't. Few pupils could achieve perfection in all subjects, and it was an exceptional person who could excel in a wide range of academic courses, especially since we could not choose them.

The pupils of a class remained in the same room for most courses for the entire school year; only the teachers changed rooms from hour to hour. Once we were assigned our seats, that's where we stayed for the duration. When I was seated toward the back of the room, my daydreaming intensified because I could hear the teachers less clearly. But since I was very shy I liked to sit there, because I was able to hide so as not to be called upon for answers. I was always nervous about having to answer the teachers' questions and usually tried to hide behind the pupil in front of me.

One day the algebra teacher startled me: "Ami!"

I jumped to attention.

"What did I just ask you?"

I did not know but I mumbled: "Man has to learn to control himself."

My compassionate classmates snickered. The teacher had made this statement much earlier, even though it was unrelated to the subject. Now he had asked me to answer an algebra question. Surprisingly, this kind teacher ignored the class response, agreed with me, and asked no more of me.

The teachers in our *Gymnasium* were a motley collection. Some were friendly and helpful, others grouchy and mean. Mister Danner was boorish and frustrated by his lack of vision because he had one glass eye, as well as false teeth. When he talked he spit, showering the pupils as he walked among their rows. We called him Muni, colloquial for "bull," because of his broad forehead, stout neck and lack of refinement. One day Muni was standing before the pupil at a front desk, lecturing, spitting and intensely boring his eye into selected individuals.

The pupil on the side of his glass eye, Siggi, slowly lifted his arm and held up a finger next to it. It was his index finger as the *bird* had not been imported yet. A titter went through the room and Muni wondered why. Not knowing, he flew into a rage, and with his powerful ham he beat the head of the pupil sitting directly in front of him. This head recoiled from the desktop and this surprised even Muni. He told the pupil who suddenly suffered a headache, *"Das war die Muliplikation der Ohrfeige,* that was the multiplication of the box on the ear."

An example of the legendary German efficiency and justice?

Professor Asal, much more polished and cultured than Professor Muni, did not beat us but left his mark through memorable discourse. Regal, with a mane of white hair, dressed in an almost-white suit, he advised not that I was dumb, but that I would become a *Guellefahrer,* someone who spreads human effluence over the fields. This prediction would come true in a way because I would someday be in *nutrient management* spreading similar stuff over the pastures in America.

◆   ◆   ◆

Speaking of stuff, at this time my ear became so productive, that when I was in dream mode, green goo coursed down my neck. Since Ma had no money, Papa Buskohl kindly suggested that she take me to his friend, Dr. Lupfer, so it would not cost anything. Since Dr. Lupfer could not help me, Ma took me to Dr. Metzger who also could not stop my infection. Finally she traveled with me to the ear clinic in Freiburg where I was diagnosed as having proud flesh.

Surgeons sliced out my wild meat, not through the big old scar behind my ear, but through my ear canal. But when they removed my bandage sometime later there was rot in it. The doctors did not guarantee their work, so I just kept oozing until such time that Ma could save enough out of our meager subsistence to pay for another surgery, at some future date, in another hospital.

We never had insurance.

When I'm empty like Mrs. Heddens, fill my hide with concrete and place it in front of the divorce court. On a pedestal festooned with my coat-of-arms, "Ich Bin Hungrig."

◆   ◆   ◆

As the months passed our guards increased their harassment to expel us from our castle. Pa became increasingly abusive, and in a rage he bent the door handle to our prison. While he was pounding the door, we moved our bed to block it and secured our window shutters as well.

Suddenly I suffered from powerful peeing pressure.

When Pa could not get in, he went outside to beat and shake our shutters while screaming insensibly. Fortunately we had no tools around the house that he could use to force his entry. I held on to my nozzle and aimed for the sink and just in time. I had to control my aim and flow; it was difficult under pressure, and so I splashed all over the place. What a relief to splash all over the place to release my pressure! I should have aimed through the slats of the shutters, but I didn't think of it.

Pa must have realized that he could not get into our cell because his shouting faded into the distance. I peeked through the shutters and could see him stomping down the street waving a pistol. I was more relaxed now; he was still uptight.

Some time before, I had surprised him when I walked into the *Herrenzimmer* while he was buying a pistol from a salesman. His face had turned beet-red with embarrassment. He obviously did not want us to know this. Never let your enemy know your strength. Afterwards he took Siggi and me out to a field and festively shot colorful flares into the sky, to show us that his pistol was harmless. He did not tell us that it could also launch teargas. *Will he try to flush us out of our potty?*

It was illegal to own guns that shot real bullets. I had heard that Hitler had taken them away to protect the people from themselves. The Nazis wanted to protect them instead, and had this not been the case, I might have collected another hole in my head. Our own father persecuted Ma, Siggi and me in our own home. Our own people tyrannized us in our own country; people were always persecuted in wars. We were ever alert and suspicious of our father and Teufi and their whereabouts and stayed away from them but always observed their activities. Siggi and I were spies and developed distrustful personalities. We moved about like guerillas in enemy territory, always out of sight, always gathering information. We kept looking for facts that could help Ma on the judicial battlefields. What projects was he developing? What cafés did he visit and with whom? How many miles did he drive? How many cigars did he smoke?

At this time we did not yet realize that the court was a farce, that the biggest guys with the biggest lies and the most money always seemed to win. Just like today and also in other countries. Ma never told us anything about the court decisions and the activities of the jurists, puppeteers and bombardiers. Siggi and I only knew that we always lost because we never had enough to eat and no proper place to pee. *Had we attempted to kill somebody, would the judge have sentenced us to a warm place to pee and three hot meals a day?*

Our father knew that we were in a war because I found another piece of equipment in his arsenal. When I sneaked a look into his car, our car, I noticed a black rod sticking out of the door pocket. It was a hard rubber truncheon with a leather wrist loop. He must have bought it recently because it was still shiny and had no hair or blood stuck to it. *What ghosts is he afraid of? What other weapons does he hide?*

◆   ◆   ◆

We lived under siege in our cozy one-room prison for about one year after the judge, the almighty, had commanded our exile. Because we were guilty. He did not tell us what we were guilty of, so we must have been innocent. Our father committed the crime but we were guilty. He was guilty and we were punished. When you starve your children, you are innocent, but was this not a crime? Had I thought about this for very long, I would have been very confused as to what was right and what was wrong. Now I know. Murderers could get five to twenty; Ma, Siggi and I could get life.

Life.

Could a judge at least lock a steel condom on our father so he would not make any more babies that would be guilty? Why am I so sarcastic?

It was a rainy day before Christmas when Siggi and I came home from the train. Our enormous pressure to study was off because it was the start of our vacation, a time when people were especially joyous.

"Think we'll get any presents?" Siggi asked me almost cynically on our way home.

"Don't know."

Never said much.

We had always received something for Christmas in the past, even if it were only a few pieces of candy. This was the first year that we did not have a Christmas tree, with tinsel and real wax candles of fire. We even had them in Simonswolde, even though Ma and Aunt Adele were devout atheists and believed in the devil in a human form, although they never swore to call for him.

Now we had Teufi.

When we arrived at our mansion, we found our biggest Christmas present ever: Mountains of clutter in our front yard, all of our worldly possessions from our prison.

In the rain.

Our present from devils.

They had scattered the sum total of our lives out on the precisely manicured lawn.

Like dog piles.

We walked around to inspect our belongings and went to the window entrance to our cell. It was locked. Siggi and I never had keys, and we tried to open other windows and doors, but they were all locked, and nobody seemed to be home. Always keep your doors locked or your children might find you. Our courageous father had left the scene and could not face us: His sons, his enemies, ten and twelve years old. I stuttered when I told Siggi that our father had thrown us out. Just in case he hadn't noticed. It was better to bawl now, in the rain, than later when people would notice. They'd think that we were weird. We did not want to be weird; we wanted to be proper.

Ma was nowhere to be found.

We sat down in the shimmering clutter and waited because we didn't know where else to go. While we were waiting for another miracle, we might as well be actors in this Christmas scene.

My little brother and I.

We did not speak. Nobody ever listened to us. The lawyers and judges were too high; they could not be reached. *What will happen to us next? Do miracles happen, especially at Christmas?*

While we were getting soaked in the gray evening light, a few people passed by but did not see us. Or pretended not to see us. They knew that we were proper and did not want to embarrass us by stopping to admire our setting. No one offered us help; nor did we expect any. No one had ever done so. No one called the authorities to find missing children. No one yelled for missing parents. It was a holy time to give presents, and we had no beer to offer to a policeman.

Thirty-five years later, I would learn a few details about this episode in a letter from Ma. At the time I received it, years before, I quickly read it and promptly forgot it, as always, and I would never think about it again until now. But I had saved it, as always. Even though the divorce court had ordered our eviction a long time before, Ma had refused to move out. She wrote me that she had yelled at the judge in the courtroom when he had issued our eviction:

"We need a shelter for two abandoned boys. There is central heating in the double garage and a water faucet. Now the products of Ford are stored there."

This is what she wrote me, that she had said, our poor mother. Now that I am no longer dumb, I would have told the judge something else.

I would have shown him something as well; I would have forced him into our hell.

"No, no," said the Saeckingen judge, "you cannot live in this house."

Ma wrote me that two bailiffs executed the judge's order. In less than two hours they had dumped everything from our cell in hell onto the lawn, piss pot and all, and locked us out. The products from Ford remained home, while we did not have one.

While Siggi and I sat basking in faux euphoria on our veranda, Ma arrived with a borrowed quaint little handcart. With a Christmas-spiritless face she confirmed that we had been evicted and told us that she found another place to live. See, miracles do happen; it could only get better. We piled our mattress onto the cart along with a few other things. Ma pulled our load through empty streets, and Siggi and I followed. All was quiet, except for the squeaking and the rumble of the cart's steel-treaded wheels grinding along the shimmering wet pavement. My feet were cold and I could feel them squish. *Will Ma spank me?*

"Where are we going?" we asked her.

She did not answer and hid her face from us. This could be a signal of our future. About twenty minutes later she turned into a driveway and stopped at the entrance to an old three-story apartment.

"Here we are," sniffled Ma.

She wiped the rain from her face. Nobody sniffles on the Eve of Christmas.

"You mean we live here?"

"*Ja.*"

We lugged our wet mattress into the building.

"Which floor?"

"Top," she said.

We grunted up the stairs, one step at a time. Our world was heavy. On the second floor a tenant peeked through the curtain of his apartment door, and I pretended not to notice. My soul curled up like my

Simonswolde friend, the gentle hedgehog, and like his, its bristles pointed outward. *See nothing, feel nothing. Soon we'll eat some garbage in our very own kitchen.*

When we arrived at the top floor Ma asked us to rest, but Siggi and I were anxious to see our new home and turned to open the door to that apartment.

"No, no," Ma said, "this is not it. One more floor, to the penthouse." As with our last home with Pa at Hardtstrasse 45, we could not find our new home, Siggi and I.

With renewed vigor we heaved our mattress to the top of the stairs where Siggi ceremoniously opened the door to our penthouse.

My digestive system convulsed.

Surely Siggi's did too.

Penthouse?

Attic.

Bats.

At the far end of this attic Ma opened a door to our aerie high above the city. It had a floor, a ceiling, a dormer and a door. That was it. Fortunately we could stand up in half of it, because the ceiling sloped almost down to the floor. There we dropped all of our furniture, our mattress, and it covered nearly one fourth of our eagle's nest.

"I have to pee," I exclaimed and began to dance.

Whenever I was nervous, or frightened, the float valve in my bladder tripped and urination became urgent. There must be a name for this condition, but I had not heard it. *Could it be RMBBS, reverse miracle bladder bursting syndrome?*

"I will ask the people downstairs if you may use their toilet," graciously offered Ma.

"Nooooo," I moaned, while I continued to dance.

"Everybody in the world has a toilet! It's Christmas Eve and we don't even have a place to sit," I continued my discourse, although my thoughts were much fouler.

I would have cussed but might get whipped. Instead I began to bawl.

Siggi thought this to be a good idea and joined me. Ma followed our chorus. Our glee club must have confused the tenants below because now there was agony in the carols of Christmas.

Silent Night, Tearful Night…

Dancing and bawling, I relieved myself in the neighbor's one-holer on the stair landing two flights below, but I could not wash.

After we brought up the few remaining things from our "moving van," we holed up in our attic for the night. The owner of the building was out of town, and Ma had not asked for permission to live here. We were squatters now without electricity, water, sewer or heat. And we were without a father and without hope because a judge had decided that we still had no right to live on this earth.

How did Ma find this penthouse? Did she have connections with powerful people?

Ma had planned ahead. In the spirit of Christmas she had brought a candle and some matches. She lit it but we could not afford a tree. The three of us curled up on the floor, while our mattress was drying, slowly, forever, in our cold room. While we remained bundled up in our clothes, we tried to ignore our exhilarating imbroglio the only way that we knew how. We searched for some old magazines, stared at the paper, pretended to read and did not talk. We dwelled in separate voids in this holy and silent night. I locked my soul in a deep dungeon but didn't know where Siggi's and Ma's were stored. There was nothing we could do, short of throwing a Molotov cocktail through Pa's window to help Teufi light his fire. Or we could do this at the judge's house to get his attention, but no one told us this, and we didn't think of it.

This evening, amidst millions of real candles of joy burning on Christmas trees throughout the land, our lonely candle cast flickering shadows on the narrow confines of our new prison. *Will its dark specter remain with us until we pass out of this existence?*

A day or two after our holiday celebration, the bailiffs came back and loaded our remaining possessions into a truck with the order to move us to the city of Schwoerstadt. But Ma refused to leave Rheinfelden because she wanted to stay close to her ex-husband. Why this was so, we didn't know, Siggi and I. There was still a housing shortage, and only a few of Ma's precious possessions fit into our new cell. Therefore she directed the executioners of justice to distribute our belongings among about fifteen different acquaintances in the city.

I was certain that the other remnant of our family was faring much better: Pa and Teufi were celebrating their liberation with fine wine under the baroque ceiling of the *Herrenzimmer*. They crawled under their goose down blanket and fluffed it up and down frequently, until they pumped out the start of a baby who developed into Oliver. It was at least his fourth known product. Ma had miscarried one, with circumstantial evidence of more from other mothers. Oliver was Teufi's first, she claimed.

During the months following our eviction, Ma ordered Siggi and me to retrieve some of our stuff with the quaint little handcart from the places where she had stored it and haul it up to our attic. Years later, she wrote me that some bedding and a suitcase full of stuff turned up missing, and that she would worry forever as to what might have been in it. We piled most of our belongings outside of our room and did this obediently, always following orders from adults because they intimidated us. Carting this stuff through town was humiliating, but she still had her control device pinned to her skirt, where it was mostly a permanent fixture. It did not have to be used much anymore because it activated us into action by its mere presence. The thought of not obeying or rebelling never occurred to Siggi or me, even yet.

Our minds were primed for slavery.

◆   ◆   ◆

Ma was out digging in garbage, or packing people's ears with garbage. Everyone always thought that what she had to say was garbage. Siggi and I were alone and were lounging on our mattress in our new hell when there was an unexpected knock on our door. We were afraid because we thought that no one knew that we were here. *Are we going to be evicted again? Who could have found us already?*

I opened the door and a white-haired stranger, dressed in a suit, handed me a cake and wished us Merry Christmas. That's all he said and we thanked him. He did not live in our building, and we never learned who he was. Ma did not know him either. Siggi and I discussed whether it was safe to eat this cake. We were hungry but couldn't be sure that the devil had not sent it. *Could it be that someone actually felt sympathetic about the* Massenschlachtung, *wholesale slaughter, of souls?*

When the owner of the apartment returned from her vacation, Ma informed her that we had moved into her attic and had had an electric meter and outlet installed. We had improved her dusty attic. Thoughtfully Mrs. Braun had them removed again and demanded that we move out immediately. We could not even be stored in the attic of a stranger. You always want to stay away from riffraff. But Ma refused to leave. It was easier for the three of us to hide in an attic than in the streets. And in the streets people would know that we were riffraff, the dregs of society, the offal of an architect, a professional man.

After we shivered through our heartwarming Christmas vacation, earning our doctorate degrees in heroism, Siggi and I returned to the *Gymnasium* to pursue more trivial studies that were supposed to be useful for successful living and survival. Since we were modest children, we did not tell anyone about our advanced degrees. We tried to keep our accomplishments to ourselves and became totally withdrawn. Snobbish.

"Now everyone knows about our divorce," I said to Siggi.

We had heard people talk about "the divorcee," namely Ma. We sensed the stigma. None of our classmates had divorced parents, or they kept it secret, for in this society everything followed rigidly established mores and divorce was strictly taboo. Siggi and I were ashamed about our dilemma even though we were only innocent victims in idiots' battles, years before big bucks could be sucked out of victimization games. A book on the teacher's desk in our classroom listed the names of the students, along with the names and professions of their fathers. Our father was an *Architekt*. It was important that everyone knew the professions of the fathers. A more appropriate entry for us would have been "Abandoned by Father," or "Never Had One."

Germans were so formal that people who had known Pa for decades still addressed him as *Herr Architekt*. This was to show respect for his person and his position as a highly educated man. There were not many higher up the social ladder than architects because they designed almost our entire environment, including all of our homes. Lawyers, maybe a little higher, created our hell. They were addressed as *Esquire* and *Your Honor. Was it an honor to send people to hell?*

◆   ◆   ◆

Our predicament became all consuming.

Will people notice that I am not normal? My dirt? My stink? I'll stay away from them. Never smile again.

We had not had a shower since long before Christmas and did not even have water to wash our hands after calls of nature. The three of us slept in our clothes, which we did not change during our vacation, because the temperature in our cell barely rose above freezing. We had been taught that it was fiery hot in hell, but we also learned it could be very dark and very cold as well. One could shake there and shiver.

On the morning we returned to school it was particularly cold. Around seven o'clock Ma lit a candle and shook us awake, so we grumpily crawled out from under our blanket. I sat up, thump, whacking my head against the sloping ceiling. With cold noses puffing mist, we did not take long to get ready as we tied our shoes with freezing fingers and combed our greasy hair. Ma went through her usual feeding routine by cutting a few slices from a loaf with her gloved hands to serve our standard meal, bread with lard and sugar, and pieces of rescued apples.

"I need a drink," I said coldly. "This bread is dry."

Ma reached for the bottle of water that had begun to freeze and handed it to me. I drew a few sips and gave it to my little brother. After we quietly finished our continental breakfast, Siggi and I brushed our teeth because Ma always insisted on this. We gripped our brushes and sawed without toothpaste. Since she always bought the hardest brushes, I eventually would saw grooves at my gum line. I did this even though my teeth are very hard. This is probably so because I absorbed a lot of fluoride that some factories spewed into the air and into the ground, along with other chemicals. They provided this community service free of charge, except maybe for occasional cancers far in the future.

Thirty minutes after waking, Siggi and I descended the waxed and polished wood stairs. Two flights down we stopped at the neighbor's toilet hole that did not have a cover. A hint of dawn barely lit the unheated three-story high privy, and I wished that it had at least a light bulb. I struggled to unbutton my fly. My thingy shrank into my newly growing manhood hair, as I probed and tugged it with icy fingers, to get it out from my wooly underwear, to get the proper aim on the hole. I thought I had it and let go. Pee splattered off the bench, temporarily warmed my fingers and soaked my pants. The paint on the bench was worn off in front just like that of the windowsill of our former prison.

When I finished soaking, I struggled to button up my fly. I dried my hands and the bench as best as I could with newspaper and went back out to let Siggi take his turn to get pissed off for the day, in case he wasn't already. After he enhanced his attitude, we continued down the stairs, ready to face the challenges of a new semester.

Outside it was barely getting light.

"Are my ears clean?" I asked the usual question whenever we went out in the mornings, knowing well that they were dirty because I could feel my dirt. I could feel it in my ears, I could feel it in my eyes and I could feel it in my soul.

"No," he said.

I pulled a handkerchief from my pocket. Stretched it over my little finger, wetted it with spit and stuck it into my left ear. Reamed out the wax and dead skin. Moved my finger to a cleaner spot and repeated this procedure several times until no more came out. Then I scooped out the usual cheese dip from my right ear with a bare finger to get out most of its crud. Wiped it off somewhere and finished the cleaning with my handkerchief. I always worried how far away people could smell my ear and therefore tried to keep some distance.

Whoosh, whoosh,... *Why is my ear whooshing? Can my goo be seen? Can I **feel** the waves of distant shores? My heartbeat?*

"Come here. Do you smell anything?" I asked Siggi, as I had many times before.

"No, I can never smell anything. Why do you keep asking me?"

I never believed him.

"But smell this."

Siggi repulsed.

He also spit-cleaned his ears with a handkerchief decorated with crusty stuff. Everything in our lives was always gusty, crusty, dusty, fusty, musty, or rusty, and rarely lusty or trusty. And worst of all, Siggi and I could not get close to someone busty. Ma didn't count. We inspected each other to make certain that we looked clean. It was important to look clean since we were upper crusty, our father was an architect, and we went to school with the elite.

"You have crud in your eyes," Siggi told me. How uncouth he was, to tell me that I had crud in my eyes. He had crud in his eyes too, in both eyes. After we wiped them with our crud cloths, life didn't look so cruddy anymore. I enjoyed my refreshing spit shower; it woke me up in the mornings. But I resented the smell of spit. I resented it when Ma's nesting instinct got out of control, and she cleaned her brood with her spittle. She spit on the seam of her skirt and wiped us clean. We were growing tall now and did not want her to do it, especially in public. But she always insisted on cleaning her brood; she never listened to us; she insisted on smearing our dirt around, on making it transparent. *How does she know which way the dirt travels? From skirt to face, or face to skirt?*

When Siggi and I arrived at the train station, spittle clean, people were already crowding through the gate. No one ever stood in line and there was a mad push to get a seat. As I sat down, I noticed that my fly was open. I had had a frustrating time trying to button it up with wet and icy fingers, but these pants were worn out before I received them, probably because of this very defect. Ma did not sew; sewing was work and interfered with her brooding. Cleverly I kept my satchel over my lap until I could find a safety pin in school to secure my gateway.

◆   ◆   ◆

Winter continued to be bitterly cold, and our attic was not insulated. When the streets became icy, Siggi and I strapped on the medieval skates that we had brought from North Germany and skated around the city; this exercise warmed us until we ran out of steam. Then we returned to our attic to shiver on our communal mattress, our entertainment center, where we spent much of that winter.

To counterbalance our freezing in the winter, this attic boiled us during the summer because it also had a Mansard roof just like Doebele's tuberculosis ward. Therefore we spent little time there during the hot afternoons but roamed outdoors as much as possible. I always expected to be shrouded in a cloud of flies, buzzing to get into my head. But even with my luscious bait, these would not help me, to lay eggs there, to hatch maggots, and maggots again into flies. Strangely, few showed much interest in me.

Nowadays we have antibiotics, nuclear bombs and spaceships, electron microscopes and cloned sheep. We have machines that transform virtual reality into reality and reality into virtual life. An elderly man I know recently had an ear infection and to cure it, his doctor placed a maggot in his ear. While it grew roly-poly it healed his infection. Had I known this, I could have raised organic maggots, to cure myself, as well as sell them to doctors to cure all the infections in this world.

Even though the flies did not show much interest in me, people sometimes did. I sat in class, in extreme dream mode, and forgot to empty my ear. Goo ran down my neck. I was startled by the snickers and whispers from the admiring pupils behind me. I could not understand them and did not have to. I always tried to ream out my ear unobtrusively with my little finger and wipe it off on my clothes since a handkerchief drew attention. I never gave up hope that the goo would not stink and instinctively sniffed it, but the diagnosis was always the same: *Still stinks, still rotten. When will I get empty and die?*

My home class teacher must have detected that something was rotten about me, and that I was very shy. His name was Mr. Haecker. He was always jovial, never punished anyone, and I really liked him. He asked me to be the class speaker. Every grade had one pupil who held this position. It only required collecting money for excursions or donations for the cemeteries of the war dead. It involved no paperwork and all payments were made in cash. I was happy to do this because this teacher had shown faith in my ability and my honesty even though I was rather dumb and somewhat dirty.

◆   ◆   ◆

We were squatters in the attic for one year and continued to survive at a subsistence level. We commuted to the *Gymnasium* to get educated for what reason I did not know. Since there was no study hall, the pupils were assigned enough homework to keep them busy for several hours after school. After Ma made sure that we had finished it satisfactorily, we could go out and escape. But our main diversion was reading and more reading, especially when it was raining. The only other hobbies that we could pursue and would not cost us anything were to vandalize, burn, steal, rape and murder. But these activities were not in vogue, were not advertised anywhere, and we did not think of it.

We borrowed books from the libraries, a dozen at a time for each of us. An American bookmobile passed through Rheinfelden every two weeks, and we read most of the books in its youth section and many of the adult books as well. Many were about America, such as *Gone With The Wind, The Egg And I, My Friend Flicka* and *The Naked And The Dead*. We also read *Cheaper by the Dozen* and about Manitou and Tecumseh, and traded comic books, such as *Hopalong Cassidy* and *Donald Duck* with other pupils. Almost every day we lounged on our comfy mattress to develop our minds as Americans.

During winter evenings we lit a candle, and the three of us huddled around it. Our severe eyestrain was the cost of relieving our severe soul strain, to let our minds wander to faraway places. We swung from vines in the jungles of Africa, fought gangsters in America, and sailed around the world with Magellan. We learned a lot, except how to improve our own plight.

We found no self-help books in the libraries. Few had been written, mainly because up to this time in Germany the masses did not pursue higher education, thereby not producing scores of social scientists who must research, publish or perish. We would have greatly benefited from publications such as: *Waterless Personal Hygiene, How To Duck Lawyer Attacks, Shelters For Soul Bombing* and *Surviving Parental and Judicial Terrorism*.

Besides a lot of reading, Siggi and I spent much of the earnings from our magazine routes on movies to relieve our ever-present gloom. Over the years we saw dozens of them, most of them American, many of them about cowboys and Indians, which for us helped create an American Dream.

◆   ◆   ◆

As time went by, we grew extremely apathetic from lack of incentive or hope, and there were no prospects of finding jobs. We knew of no other children who worked for money, and no one ever suggested to Siggi and me that we should do so, because we were pursuing an academic course in the *Gymnasium* and not a vocational one. We were not qualified for German vocations because they did then, and still do now, require several years of apprenticeship. Part-time menial jobs, other than paper and magazine routes, were non-existent. There were no gas jockeys or hamburger slingers because there were very few gas pumps and no fast food joints. Ma was an architect's ex-wife, and at this time it was generally unacceptable for women to work outside the home. Even so, she did some work away from home when she gathered special treats for us: grapefruit, oranges and other fruit that she retrieved after dark from the garbage pile of the nearby wholesaler named Buehrer.

Aunt Adele's intense etiquette training was of no use. We still had no table to sit at, no plates or silverware to hold properly. Fork in left hand, knife in right hand, sit straight and raise your spoon to your mouth. Don't play with your food. Aunt Adele had trained us over the years in Simonswolde in these refinements as it gave her a purpose in life; a bona fide screaming relief to rid herself of the demon when the premenstrual syndrome attacked her. Her training sessions had also helped distract us from the delicacies that she had served us.

Siggi and I remained social klutzes until our girlfriends would fine-tune us in later years. Or we would fine-tune ourselves for them after we could afford a toilet and girlfriends. In the meantime we continued using the toilet of Mrs. Lenz downstairs, instead of standing on the edge of our roof and peeing down on the city. We were modest children and did not want somebody to build bronze statues of us, nude, in the middle of Rheinfelden, like the one of *Mannekinpis* in the middle of Brussels.

◆   ◆   ◆

We could not afford to move into any kind of low rent housing, and I didn't even know if such was available yet. Pa provided a few marks now and then but always much less than the court had ordered. Ma and Pa continued sparring professionally, which officially started in 1949, but I suspect, unofficially many years earlier. Pa would waste more money on lawyers, in attempts to evade his obligations under the law, than he would ever pay for the support of his sons, Siggi and me.

Again, this is what our dear father did: He gave more money to lawyers than could be squeezed out of him for his family to live on. *Was there anybody in this world so intelligent and yet so stupid? Was he firing on only one piston? Or was it because of his one firing piston?*

After the judge's army exiled us from our prison in our own home, I saw our father but once, when he stopped his shiny car, while I was strolling down the sidewalk. He rolled down his window, spent ninety-two seconds of quality time with me and gave me one Deutsche mark to get a haircut. He thereby absolved his fatherly duties for the year. He drove away, undoubtedly swelling with pride because his son would now get a haircut. He would look proper for two weeks, as if he had a father who always helped him and took good care of him. *Did Pa even know that we were stored in a very cold, and a very hot, stranger's attic?*

Father looked into my eyes. He had intense will power; he could look into my eyes. Ma had told us that he wore glasses not to see better but to hide behind them. I always looked into the eyes of the strangers that I met on the street. Many did not like this and looked away as if I were not there. Now my father looked into my eyes. *Was he in denial about what he was doing to us?*

During the year that we had been under siege in one bedroom in the Hardtstrasse and the subsequent year in the cozy attic, not a single relative contacted us, helped us, or consoled us. We did not contact them, rarely thought of them and barely knew them, Siggi and I. None of them lived in Rheinfelden, except our father and our second mother. *How well did they know our parents? Had there been discord between them before we were born?*

> **"Who can reach the dead,**
> **Who can speak for the dumb?"**

◆   ◆   ◆

In February the Catholic holidays of Mardi Gras offered a break in our dreary existence. It was *Fasnacht* and school and work stopped for a few days. It started one morning, even though there was barely a sign of it the day before because it was not commercialized. There were no decorations in the stores or in the schools, and there were no annoying, aggravating, mind-numbing, insulting noises to suck bucks out of these affairs.

Adults did not make fools of themselves. They became fools, kings, queens, wild men and shysters. There were groups dressed as barbarians and court jesters, wise men and idiots. But no one knew who they were because they hid behind masks that were carved out of wood or molded from papier-mâché, all painted in bright colors.

There were parades, music, drinking and dancing.

Siggi and I dressed up in makeshift costumes and joined the crowds in the city. Since Ma did not sew, and we could not afford to buy anything, Siggi and I improvised and fashioned our own. We made cowboy hats out of cardboard and hid in crud-crusted scarves like in the movies, to roam the city as gangsters and cowboys. We scared the crowds with our cap guns while we were rambling around robbing, raping, burning and pillaging. An official, religious time for mayhem.

We robbed little old ladies and threw them through store windows. Women became pregnant, whether they chose to or not. We spat into the faces of teachers and lawyers and followed Jonathan's *Modest Proposal* to cut up babies to eat them.

But we didn't think of it.

It was all make-believe. There was little crime even though robbers could move about unrecognized during the time of *Fasnacht*. We never heard sirens or screams for help and rarely saw a policeman. And when it was all over everything went back to normal, and there was never even any litter in the streets.

◆   ◆   ◆

We sat in the shade of a tree on our beloved mattress, alone, far out on the prairie. The air was still and the sun had come out of the clouds. It lightened my mood and I became a cowboy. Our screenless window was open, and a swarm of vultures was buzzing around the epicenter of our quiet savanna. Ma was having a conversation with an invisible judge about a court document that she had received earlier. Deep in thought, she whispered something about the "heartless children's judge Blaersch" and was unaware that I was observing her. Cowboys and Indians always keep still to watch and listen.

I fell off the cliff of sarcasm into the chasm of her brooding. My discourse went something like this and was a spontaneous outpouring akin to gallows humor, the kind that comes when one's situation is completely hopeless. It comes when it was easier to die than to live. I mimicked the judge I'd never seen before, visualizing *His Honor*, Judge Blaersch, in his black robe addressing Mrs. Neuman in the serene courtroom with its fine furniture:

"You are looking very chic today, Mrs. Neuman," I said in a judge-like voice.

Proudly Mrs. Neuman rose, "Thank you, your Honor."

"But what is that thing hanging from your waistband."

"Ach Du Lieber, oh my dear, I forgot to take it off," I screeched with embarrassment, imitating Ma's voice. "I'm sorry *Your Honor.* I'll take it off."

By now Ma's face lightened to a smile, surprised that there was still one gram of humor left in me. Humor powered by desperation.

"Don't take it off here. Take it off at my house tonight. But please remove that silly strap," I continued as *His Honor.* "What is it for anyway?" I added, imitating the dignified judge.

"To protect my boys, *Your Honor.* Don't you protect your children?"

"How do you protect them with that? Do you wire them? And please be civil. The court always treats you with respect," I continued, encouraged by Ma, who was now laughing hysterically, tearfully.

"It protects them from themselves. Prevents them from getting silly ideas. Like seeking revenge on fathers and judges. And then they'd go to jail," I continued as Ma.

"Thank you, Mrs. Neuman, for your great idea. I will ask the plaintiff to wear a whip also; about where you have yours. Like a tie over his fly to wave at the ladies."

I continued my imitations until Ma was gasping with belly-shaking laughter. When she regained her composure, she looked at me in wonderment as if thinking there's an imagination in Ami that he's been hiding. I always thought he was dumb; perhaps there's hope for him.

Clouds hid the sun again darkening my mood. Reality shut off my discourse. Once again we squatters were still squatting on our beloved mattress in our forgotten prison.

◆　　◆　　◆

One hot day, after living in the attic for more than a year, Ma announced that she had found a real apartment two buildings down the street. It also had a Mansard roof of black slate, or dark tile, to boil the people within. Anxious to move, Siggi and I carried our stuff to our new home and discovered that it really was an apartment. We moved down four stories and back up three stories, below its attic. Around noon, we slouched down to rest on our mattress back in our old home that we had grown to love. Siggi and I announced in unison, *"Ich Bin Hungrig,"* our usual battle cry. Ma sat down with some bread, cut off a few slices and smeared on some spread.

While I wolfed down some cottage cheese, I dropped my spoon and reached for my trembling jaw. My entire body began to shake. I fell back. Ma screamed. She grabbed me under my arms, dragged me out of the attic and down the stairs because my limbs were paralyzed, but my body was trembling. I could hear and see Ma screaming, but I could not spit-clean her face or otherwise move or talk. I wanted to assure her that I was all right and felt no pain, as she continued to struggle with me, while screaming hysterically:

"Mrs. Lenz. Mrs. Lenz. Ami is dying!!!"

No such luck.

By now I must have weighed more than she, and I'll never know how she was able to drag me down the stairs.

Someday someone else would drag me down some other stairs in some other country.

Mrs. Lenz came rushing out of her apartment, helped Ma carry my body into a bedroom and onto a bed, whereupon my tremor ceased. Later a doctor came to examine me and gave me some pills but did not tell me his diagnosis. I remained there alone until evening, nestled in heavenly fresh goose down and brilliant white sheets while I studied this tidy room. The afternoon sun streamed through the white, delicately embroidered curtains, and I soaked in this quiet luxury. Had I not been as dumb as Lindeman said I was, I would have faked a more intense illness even after I recovered, liberally drooling slobber, or mimicking some other impressive symptoms, in order to remain in heaven a little longer. But I did not think of it.

That evening I returned home. I curled up on our bedding with Siggi and Ma, whom I questioned about my paroxysm, and she told me that I had suffered heat exhaustion, and I believed her. Only many years later did I realize that this could not have been true, but that it must have been a seizure caused by too much parental affection, combined with heat, exertion, dehydration and malnutrition. I felt no chills, fever, perspiration and the shaking attack passed within minutes. It would never recur, even though I would pursue my post-doctorate studies of heroism for many more years.

◆   ◆   ◆

Slowly the three of us settled into our new apartment at Werderstrasse 3, Rheinfelden, West Germany. This meant that *pre-owned* treasures, great and small, kept mysteriously accumulating in our *sanitary landfill*, increasingly crowding us. This apartment was like most others in our neighborhood in that it had a dark central vestibule with curtained, glazed double entrance doors, from which other doors led to a kitchen and three identical rooms. Practical Ma would use all of them as multi-purpose rooms, with sleeping and living as the secondary purpose in the tiny spaces left over. The architect thoughtfully had provided each door with a lock which had keyholes for peeping Toms to see what Ma was doing in her clutter.

Our kitchen had a sink, a cold water faucet and an electric stove but had no built-in cabinets. This was no drawback because it was becoming an ever more complex multi-purpose cube, with important treasures carefully entangled from floor to ceiling, and from ceiling to floor, just like our other rooms.

So far Siggi and I had slept mostly in hallways, railroad stations, boxcars, beer halls, and bomb shelters, or had shared rooms and a mattress with Ma. At first we were excited that we at last would be able to bounce around in our own rooms. But as we gathered the rest of our belongings from where they had been stored throughout Rheinfelden, it became evident that this could never be. We discovered many things that we had not seen before because Ma had busily acquired a lot of stuff and added it to that which was stored at various places. In retrospect I realize that Ma must have asked these families to add their throwaways to her reserves that Siggi and I had to retrieve to outfit our quarters.

Ma's packrat syndrome continued to intensify. She had to do something to fill her desperate time while amassing irreplaceable heirlooms for Siggi and me. She acquired clothes, furniture, bags, broken or unidentifiable items, or whatever she thought would be useful, once, one hundred twenty years from now, and hoarded them in our small apartment. Maybe she thought that she could barter such items as she had done during the wars, hyperinflation and depressions. Time had bypassed her. People bought new things now and rarely acquired used clothes in increasingly wealthy West Germany. Even so, could Ma have divine foresight?

Our agony, Siggi's and mine, slowly crawled up the walls. Dust accumulated and it became more and more difficult to find anything. Ma's packrat syndrome tangled with her laziness syndrome. Lugging stuff up three stories took some doing because she did it mostly herself while we were in school. Siggi and I noticed only that our world slowly densified, and our space kept shrinking to the point that we could barely move or open doors.

Mother's entangled heirlooms were her heaven.

They were our hell, Siggi's and mine.

Now, though, we had our own toilet, and it was located off the stair landing, half a flight down from our apartment door. Fortunately it was open to the public because it could only be locked from the inside. If this had been possible from the outside, Ma would have entangled it, and we would not have been able to roost in comfort. It had a small window and was an exact replica of Mrs. Lenz's toilet that we used so lovingly before. After two years without a toilet, or one that we had to sneak to under duress, a toilet was a welcome addition to our family. We had become acutely aware that a toilet was a basic implement for man's survival.

When I dropped bombs down the tube, they resonated back up the three-story-high stool pipe. During cold and windy days, a frosty breeze caressed my bottom, creating a shivering, shriveling response in me. At times, the wind played a mournful tune in the twelve-meter high pipe organ with grand finales, when duds tumbled to the bottom to land with a kerplunk. We now had it made. We had our own kitchen and high-tech privy, freshly vented and sound enhanced during the performance.

I mention this private subject only because I thought that it was important.

◆   ◆   ◆

To stay away from our paradoxical space as much as possible, Siggi and I learned to become great outdoorsmen without the coaching that abnormal kids received from their fathers. We learned this avocation by rumbling and rambling around the city. Day in, day out, we walked, biked, climbed, kicked, crawled, and played spontaneous soccer, with caps and coats marking the goal posts. Just like in Simonswolde.

We squirmed around in a transcendental world that we could not fathom.

We joined the *Stadtmusik* orchestra but had no idea what we could play. The instructor-conductor looked at our lips and teeth and told me that I'd play the clarinet and Siggi the trumpet. He would be able to toot his own horn and I would squeal. The orchestra provided us with instruments, and the conductor taught us twice a week along with two other boys, and after a year and a half, I began to practice with the band to perform in concerts and other fun functions. Siggi was still too young to do so because often our music mixed with beer and wine until late into the night.

All of the band members wore light gray uniforms during our public performances, but Ma requested that I be furnished with a regular suit instead. Therefore this orchestra bought me a dark blue wool suit that I could wear for personal use also, and this made me stick out in our band when I wanted to hide. But I greatly enjoyed playing at funerals, weddings and *Fasnacht* parades. When I was sixteen we played at a New Year's ball in Swiss Rheinfelden, where hundreds of revelers in costumes and masks drank, smoked and danced to our music. The air in the dancehall became so enhanced with cigarette combustion and digestive gases that it burned my eyes and throat and impaired my breathing, so that during a break I pushed through the crowd to go outside.

"Ma! What are you doing here?"

I recognized her even though she wore a mask and had nothing dangling from her hip. She was with someone whom I could not identify, and I did not ask her about her man.

Our music deteriorated from ever more free beer and head-splitting gases, so that by midnight, I was the only one still stable enough to usher in the New Year. Only my lonely clarinet still kept this dance in motion because my cohorts had filled themselves, and later also some of their instruments, with beer and pretended to shave their faces with its foam. But one hour after midnight I drank my first bottle ever. When our melee finally ended my world had become wobbly. So I ambled through dark and empty streets back across the Rhine River to Germany, back to my rat's nest and fell asleep in my lair.

Burp.

◆   ◆   ◆

At this time I entered puberty; I was a late bloomer. This further helped strengthen my character during my hero formation. Unexpectedly I was conquered by a new emotion, more intense than the one that kept me hostage for so long. I fell in love. Deeply. One day I turned the corner of a building and there she was. We almost collided. My eyes locked into her brown eyes.

I felt the sizzle. *What happened to me? I just want to hug and kiss you. Never let go. What's your name?*

We stared and said not a word. We passed each other. Bouncy, golden, curly ponytail. I bumped into something. She smiled. She entered my mind. And stayed there. Over the next year our paths crossed often, on trains and on streets, always evoking the same passion in me. I followed her to a park where she sat and talked with a girl-friend. I sat down nearby and stared so hard that my gaze invaded her liquid eyes and our souls merged.

I was so bashful, and my feelings about her were so intense, that I was afraid that if I talked to her, I'd blabber, because so often I stuttered. I wore threadbare clothes, could not bathe and did not have the courage to show off my hideout.

I dressed my best. My best was a long-sleeved black shirt with a bright yellow tie. Ma had carefully selected them from her favorite store, Quack's Fifth Alleyvue. Pa had his tailor; I had my slick, rancid hair. I didn't like the black and I didn't like the yellow, but it was the best I had. Black was depressing, black was for fascists and yellow was disgusting, and did not belong on a man. I was so ashamed and timid that I never said one word to my girlfriend while, in my mind, we went steady for more than one year.

Then I would leave the country and would never even learn her name.

I was so befuddled during this time of my life that when Ma asked me to buy a newspaper, I asked for the *Nordwest Zeitung.* The clerk told me that he did not have it. I realized that I had made a mistake and asked for the *Nordost Zeitung,* then *Suedost Zeitung,* whereafter he volunteered that he also did not have the *Suedwest Zeitung.* That was the one I wanted, and I did not know if the others even existed. He probably sold this particular newspaper but thought that I was just playing a game.

If I were to design hell, my unending dilemma would be its leitmo-tif.

After I met this girl, I became extremely conscious about my looks. I was going to be a real man, a strong man and a handsome dude. I checked myself closely to see if I had big muscles, to see if I looked clean but discovered that I was a very greasy guy. There were blackheads sprinkled on my nose and when I squeezed them, tiny spaghetti oozed from my pores. I also grew an impressively big carbuncle on the back of my neck and as it became shiny, purple and ripe, its pain stopped the motion of my head. Ma squeezed it; I screamed, so she sought advice from the eighty-year-old neighbor below us, who then operated on me instead. She looped a rolled up handkerchief around my boil and applied peripheral pressure to force out a nice stream of deceased blood cells. This did not hurt nearly as much as Ma's method of operation, and therefore everyone should learn how to do this properly.

◆   ◆   ◆

Ma must have noticed a change in me and decided that it was time to teach me about sex. She was going to teach me about something that could not be talked about. People didn't say the word "sex." There was something taboo about this word and probably also about its deeds. This society was pure. Had it been purified by the torments of its past? Or had this subject simply gone under cover? There were no pornographic magazines or strippers, and was this why our father had brought us new aunts? During this era, the best that we boys could do was to bore our stares through ladies' blouses and hope to burn through to get a glimpse. When I bored, I could feel my eyeballs crowd into the cleavage of their breasts and remain there like baby birds in a nest.

In spite of our lack of privacy, Ma had always kept her body hidden from Siggi and me. Living together in one room in the Hardtstrasse, in the attic and the present no-room, three-room apartment, with three of us rotating around one privy hole, did not give us much privacy. But body-exposure privacy was easy because there was not much reason for us to run around naked. There was no tub or shower, and we washed our few clothes only when we nearly fainted. And when we were cold we also slept in them. The sheets of our beds were gray with grime, body fat, dead skin, bed bugs and live and dead dust mites. I had an advantage over others in that my pillow was sometimes especially adorned. With goo from my ear. I studied my brain that kept oozing out, but I never learned anything from it, or about it, not even why I never ran out of brain.

It was not long after I became immersed in my powerful new emotion, when Ma casually shed her clothes and sponge-bathed in my presence. A suppressed instinct struck her to wipe off body odor, teach her pubescent son preening and educate him about the birds and the girls. If she could not talk about sex, she could maybe drop a hint, to hint that a woman had different parts than a man, and that these got tangled up with each other if one were afflicted by a lack of self-discipline to overcome the most powerful heavenly bodies attraction in the universe.

So Ma wanted to demonstrate that girls were different from boys. But I already knew that. However I learned one of Ma's secrets. She had no belly button to collect fuzz in. In Simonswolde she had had it replaced with a nice fifteen-centimeter horizontal scar, pouched out at the ends. She did this because of the hernia that she had acquired while manually spading and fertilizing our survival garden. A doctor had opened her up and had put her innards back into their proper places. This condition had been very painful, and she already had more pain than she could handle. Siggi and I had never known this. Courageous Ma had not told us that she was in pain, that she had been cut open, and the doctor had rummaged around inside her. She just had left and come back later. That's all we knew. Therefore dear Ma, I thank you for sparing us your agony.

◆   ◆   ◆

Suddenly there was going to be lot of nakedness in Rheinfelden. Concentrated nakedness. The advertisements showed that there'd be naked boys and naked girls. I didn't care about the boys, but I wanted to squeeze naked girls. So far they had been impossible to find and here was my chance. The theater posters advertised *Dangerous Love,* and there were no clothes on the actors. But the important parts, those necessary for the continuation of the species, were just out of sight.

I had to show identification that I was sixteen to get in, and I was barely old enough to join this orgy. Before the curtain rose we waited anxiously in the darkened theater. Most people in the audience were boys. I played cool. I was a connoisseur and didn't want others to see when my eyes would bug and my tongue would hang out, therefore I had to keep myself under control.

The movie started and soon a doctor dressed in a white frock appeared on the screen. He was lecturing seriously about the growing venereal epidemic, and he was here to frighten us. He told us about the cause of the scourges of mankind. He showed us the results of sin, of lack of self-discipline during the heat of passion. He introduced us to stark naked boys and stark naked girls in sterile hospital rooms. They looked cold and sad; they were not hot. They all had sexually transmitted diseases. They had sores all over their pale bodies, faces and groins. My eyes bugged out but not for the reasons that I had anticipated, and this movie dampened my desire somewhat. I would have to be careful when I would be able to get near naked girls.

There was no whining, convulsing and contorting in this society or in its schools if, how, when, where and who was to teach sex. One movie like this would teach everyone to be cautious when entering the minefields of passion. It would scare the hell out of boys and girls and prevent them from becoming too adventuresome.

◆   ◆   ◆

Ma realized that Siggi was also growing up fast and must have figured now was her last chance to provide him with one final lesson, to
make sure that he would not be morally confused and would remain a
hero for life. I cannot remember what he did, but it was inconsequen-
tial, if he misbehaved at all. Ma ordered him to bare his buttocks and
to lean over the foot of the bedstead. He willingly complied, as always,
because if he didn't he could get spanked. She whipped him with the
braided electrical cable that she'd brought from Simonswolde which,
after many years of vigorous use, refused to unravel.

I stood by frozen, suffering the same inner-body, out-of-body experience as when Pa had beaten Ma. I felt each lash as much as Siggi and
wondered if she'd lost her mind. I counted twenty rhythmic swishes
across his young behind. Twenty sharp lashes whipped through our
souls, Siggi's and mine. *Did Ma know that she was also slicing me?*

Swish! Slice! Scream! Swish! Slice!...

Then she threw him out and told him never to come back. He ran
out and I followed. I tried to convince him that she didn't mean to
hurt him, and that she was just frustrated with men, specifically with
Pa and his lawyers. We wandered around until we got hungry, then
returned to the warm bosom of our haunt. Recently I asked Siggi
about this incident: "Do you still remember when Ma **really** whipped
you in the Werderstrasse 3? And then threw you out?"

His faraway gaze signaled great pain; the greatest pain I had ever
witnessed in anyone's eyes, as he responded: "No. I guess I must have
blanked that out too."

◆   ◆   ◆

Whenever it became obvious to Ma that my ear was rotting severely,
becoming an environmental hazard, she sent me by train to Basel,

Switzerland, to a world-famous ear clinic. Doctors took turns gazing into my head with great interest through a funnel, as if there were a peep show inside. When they couldn't see much, they squirted water into my head to flush me out. Clean water in, a bowl of sewage back out. They also wondered if I was unbalanced and asked me to close my eyes to walk a line on the floor, to see how straight I could walk and not fall over. They were amazed that I was quite stable and would be even more amazed if they only knew how unstable my life had always been.

After my treatments, my infection usually cleared up temporarily. But it always returned, and vigorously, mainly because of neglect, poor nutrition and hygiene and lack of proper counseling. Even though I've been forever told not to stick anything into my ears, a few years ago I started cleaning my defective ear out with cotton swabs. When I visited the ear doctor the next time, he looked and blurted: "What did you do?"

"I kept dry by not taking any showers," I teased him. I wanted to see if he could figure it out himself.

He replied: "I hope not."

He also warned me that the bone to my brain was as thin as an egg-shell. This was hopeful, because someday I might still be able to hatch great ideas. He then advised me to pour a fifty-fifty mixture of white vinegar and rubbing alcohol into my ear, especially after showering, to prevent infections. I have visited many doctors many times over the years, and this was the first time that someone informed me of such a cheap and effective preventative treatment. My decades-long rot and embarrassments could have been avoided from the very beginning, and now I can even go swimming. *Should I sue?*

Earlier, this same doctor had suggested that he could remove a bone ridge that caused stuff to accumulate in my ear cavity. This ridge had formed over the years in response to infections. After I asked him for details, he explained that it would be a two-hour operation and that the nerve to my face might get damaged, paralyzing my face. I asked another ear specialist if such an operation would be helpful but received a negative response. He has had several patients with similar conditions and they were getting along quite well. I was glad to have declined my long-time doctor's offer, especially because one day he made an irreversible decision. He died *under the influence* of some sort of popular mind-twisting self-indulgence.

◆   ◆   ◆

After Ma threw Siggi out, I became totally withdrawn. I brooded, did not talk for hours and did not respond to Ma who tried to cheer me. There was nothing in my life that could do so, except being able to love my girlfriend, but I could not get near her. I needed a little crumb of normalcy; throw out this crap and give us some room. But at the same time I felt so sorry for Ma that I did not want to kick her, to tell her that my rot and her junk were now the greatest burdens in my life.

I wanted to hug my girlfriend.

My brooding caused Ma to take me to a specialist in Basel. She did not tell me where we were going, and I assumed that she was taking me to another ear doctor. But as we entered the waiting room, I realized that this was not a medical clinic because it lacked the disinfectant smells and the white-gowned nurses and doctors. A man in a suit showed me ink stains and asked me what I saw in them. I guessed that he wanted to glimpse into my soul to study its bruises. I inspected his blobs and returned my verdict. I saw animals, trees, faces and airplanes but had no idea what meaning could be extracted from what I saw in these blotches. He did not ask me, what is bothering you? Were you abandoned by your father? Do you ever smile? Do you like anything? He did not ask me any questions, did not look in the right place because he did not look through the windows to my soul. Afterwards he talked to Ma in private and told her his verdict. He must have told her that apparently I was not going to kill anybody, at least not for the time being.

◆   ◆   ◆

Our magazine routes were our first and only jobs, Siggi's and mine, when once a week we delivered magazines on our old bikes. What earnings I did not spend on movies, I put into my savings account, which slowly grew to the equivalent of over twenty-five dollars, a huge sum for me. Ma must have noticed this because she informed me that I was going to have another ear operation. She checked me into the Citizens Hospital in Basel where I was carved out again for the third time. This time I was not cut through the old scar at the back of my ear or through the ear canal as before, but through a new cut in front of it.

Neither Siggi, Pa nor anyone else contacted me in the hospital, and I wasn't sure if they even knew that I was routed out again. Siggi was probably happily miserable at home, or residing in a secondhand store, while Pa was probably miserably happy chasing women. But a friendly Dutchman, who was also a patient recovering in my hospital room, gave me a banana. I was astounded that somebody, especially a stranger, would give me something that did not cause me pain.

After about ten days I returned to the mother of all rats' nests, the headquarters of our magazine empire. When I made another deposit into my savings account, I discovered that Ma had withdrawn it all and blown it on hospital bills. I had been saving to get out of hell, and I still remember this well, to travel to Peru, to live in the jungle by Lake Titicaca, away from people, white people, but now it had been wasted to cut rotten meat out of my head.

Pa was so concerned about us that he wanted to do radical surgery himself. On all of us. But I did not know this, or had suppressed it in my conscience, but I found copies of one of his letters entangled in Ma's heirlooms during my last visit with her. My father's letter to an attorney stated:

"Very honored *Counselor* Laule!

"With great disappointment I found out that the support for the children was increased by DM20 (20 German marks) for each child, that is DM40. With this, my monthly responsibilities to the divorcee would be DM200 + DM190 = DM390. Since I…(three lines blackened out on the copy I have)…I have not had a single penny of income this year. It is completely impossible for me to pay this amount to the divorcee…(one line blackened out).

"I see no other possibility anymore, except to cause a total catastrophe, no matter what consequences it will bring. I will grasp the final and heaviest means, to cause an end to this shameful situation. This I will do, if the court does not comprehend my situation as a provider of the divorced family and the founder of a second family. I will not let my honor be so dirtied, inasmuch as I am so indebted, that my creditors are pushing me to fulfill my responsibilities. If it has to be, **I am ready to eliminate the entire family**, before I will take this shame on me. Afterwards the court will be responsible for this, which this decision has brought about."

Yippee!

Why did nobody ever warn Siggi and me? To light up the end of our tunnel. Why did nobody ever come to arrest, compliment or serenade our father?

Our father wanted to kill us in order to save ten dollars a month, less than he spent on his cigars. Big, expensive, imported cigars, singly packaged in gilded aluminum cylinders that probably cost more than their contents. To protect them from a mean environment.

◆   ◆   ◆

Ma became so distraught that she even wanted to do something. She wanted to make soap. Soap? Why, I didn't know. She could have been suddenly blessed with a gift, like the charming of cobras. This was on an ethereal level that we did not understand, Siggi and I. She started to make soap in her usual fashion. Big time. Like big time bed sitting, big time butt whipping, big time house stuffing, big time court battles. And now big time soap making.

From somewhere she got the ingredients for her project, enough for at least several dozen bars of soap. Carefully she measured and mixed them together, opened the oven door and set the mixture on it. And let it sit there. By the next day, this sticky concoction had oozed out or fallen over, thus ending her project. She left her project that way for months while the hardening blob was fusing to the door. However, there was no need to remove it because we never baked anyway.

Because of her torments Ma could not force herself to finish her project. She lost her inspiration. Finally I de-blobbed the oven myself because I had an inspiration to start a new project.

Bomb making.

A friend had discovered a chemical that burned rapidly under certain conditions, and it was sold in granular form at a local pharmacy. My creative impulse went to work. After dissolving the crystals in water, I soaked newspapers in this mixture and dried them. Since I was too impatient to spread them out on the kitchen décor and wait for them to dry, I placed them in the oven and turned on the low heat. When the window of the kitchen steamed up I opened it.

While I was waiting for the drying to complete, there was hissing in the oven and smoke belched from it. The papers smoldered so quickly that the kitchen became very hazy. I closed the window to a narrow opening and frantically smothered the smoldering papers, hoping that the smoke would diminish to invisibility from outside, because I did not want anyone to think that our building was on fire and I would get caught. I scanned the neighborhood to see if anybody was staring up at our apartment, or rolling on the ground laughing, and saw no one. After the smoke cleared, I continued my fuel production more carefully, removing the papers from the oven while they were still moist, draping them over the décor to dry them completely. After they dried, I rolled up this fuel paper tightly inside sheets of untreated paper to make solid-fuel rockets, with strips for fuses that burned with a sizzle.

When I was finished, I stored the leftover fuel paper in the dark and dreary basement laundry of our apartment building, then searched out a vacant lot to launch my rockets. I lit a fuse and ran for safety. As it burned it generated an unbelievable amount of smoke. My paper rocket blasted off with a swish, trailing a random smoke pattern, while bouncing repeatedly off the ground. I noted that future rockets should have tail fins to control their flight paths.

Siggi and I experimented to produce rockets, fire crackers, smoke bombs and hand grenades. Over the next few weeks we spent our spare time developing an assortment of *peacekeeping* materiel that also included pipe bombs. We discovered other chemicals and even mixed our own black powder. One dark red concoction boiled in a slow chemical reaction that also created a lot of bloody red smoke that scared us. Our explosives acquired ever-greater force until we realized the danger of our hobby when we detonated a pipe bomb next to the Catholic church. Shrapnel whistled around us, chipping the stucco off the wall. Oddly, no one ever paid any attention to our activities, even though our games made loud noises and were simulating urban warfare in the middle of Rheinfelden. And no one seemed to care that we might become our own *collateral damage*.

Wisely we decided to discontinue this hobby when we came home from school one day and a fire truck, with flashing lights, was parked in front of our apartment house. Spectators were lined up across the street and were looking up to the top of our building, thrilled by the smoke that engulfed its roof, and I recognized its light-gray color. Since we lived on the top floor, we were worried that we would lose our home again but, fortunately, the firemen could not find the source of the smoke and departed. When the smoke over our roof diminished, how-ever, we could see that it was only coming out of a chimney. Then I realized that someone must have found and burned our secret paper in the laundry boiler. It looked like regular newspaper, except that it had a rougher texture, and it would not require much of it to generate a lot of smoke. If it were not closely confined it did not explode because it would burn too slowly. Siggi and I sneaked down to our arsenal, and sure enough, the boiler was cooking and our paper was gone. Only we knew where the smoke had originated, but for obvious reasons we told no one.

◆　　　◆　　　◆

I accidentally discovered that Ma also pursued a dangerous hobby that could result in *collateral damage* when I opened the "wardrobe" in her "bedroom" to fetch something. Hanging there in the clutter was a limp, long, whitish balloon. *It's so long. Do humans use this? Is it a "time-share" condom?*

I confronted Ma about the fatigued condom in her wardrobe, wondering why our parents couldn't pursue the world's most popular hobby together.

She squealed: "I found it in the city park."

And as Dave Barry would say, "I'm not making this up."

"Was Herr Graf in it?" I asked humanely.

"Nein, nein, why should he be?"

Ma befriended Mr. Graf, a gardener *under the influence,* who had a World War II souvenir shrapnel stuck in his chest that caused him great pain, especially when he smoked. He was a kind man and often brought us fruits and vegetables to help us survive. *Was he in pain because he was so kind? Did Ma barter her body to make him so kind? To help keep us alive?*

◆　　　◆　　　◆

Ma kept on doing what she did best and that was to enlarge her hoard. When she found something that was cheap, she'd buy it. When she found something in garbage, she'd confiscate it, but Siggi and I didn't realize this yet because she tried to keep her mining sources a secret. And the more she could get the better she felt. Once a store sold wool/synthetic, knitted swimsuit-style pants. They were not swimsuits or underpants but were in a classification not yet identified by the fashion world. Their price was greatly reduced, and for good reason: nobody wanted them. Therefore she bought all of them for Siggi and me. They fitted tightly, itched magnificently and colored our privates liberally, literally and metaphorically, but fortunately, in my favorite color. To wear them imparted a singular wisdom that could never be taught in the hallowed halls of universities.

Ma also bought dozens of loops of dried figs beaded on real vines, like the ones on which Tarzan swung through the jungle. Aaahouu…eeeaaaaah. We feasted on figs for weeks. Since I had the biggest stomach, although also the smallest bladder, and go for the mostest, I hogged them. As other fruits came into season, such as cherries or grapes, she bought them by the box full, and we ate pounds of them in one session. She also continued her raids on the wholesaler's reject pile where she collected fruit under cover of darkness and after we were asleep. Fortunately by this time, we had nearly developed immunity to post-vintage-fruit overindulgence.

Since Ma never cooked, Siggi and I were surprised one day when we came home from school to find her locked in the kitchen.

"What are you doing? Do you need to be rescued?" we asked through the door, expecting that she was cooking up something with Mr. Graf or someone else.

"I am cooking," came back her reply.

"You? Cooking? Why are you destroying vitamins? What are you cooking?" we wanted to know.

"A rabbit," Ma's strained voice muffled through the door.

Rabbit? Really rabbit? With Knoedel, Strudel and ice cream?

(I had rarely entered a butcher shop emergency room, and then only to cure my severe drooling caused by strings of pudgy frankfurters that I could see hanging on the white tile wall through the store window. I was Pavlov's dog. At times I would forgo a movie to buy up to six at a time and wolf them down, cold and schmaltzy, drooling on my way out of the shop.)

"Unlock the door," we ordered Ma.

"I can't, I am busy," she replied.

Busy? She had never been physically busy, except in her garden in Simonswolde, but that had been long ago, and during her sporadic spurts of energy when she busily wired us. Now she was always busy sitting, brooding, reading and writing.

As usual, Siggi and I were hungry as wolves and salivating. Rabbit? Juicy, tender, tasty rabbit, instead of the unending rye bread and semi-spoiled fruit that we consumed almost exclusively for years. Early on, Pa had taken Siggi and me a few times to restaurants where we had eaten the only hot food since Simonswolde. Except lately Siggi and I also ate soup in the café of the railroad station after we returned from the *Gymnasium*. It was always the same watery broth, and we didn't have to pay for it. Was this one of Ma's schemes to demonstrate to the judge that she was a fit mother? Or did we have an unknown benefactor?

Cooking odors overcame the musty odors in our dark vestibule and confirmed that Ma was indeed cooking.

"I can't believe it, Ami, Ma's cooking."

"But why? It destroys vitamins."

"This cannot be, there's something wrong."

"But what?"

"Do cooks cook in private to keep their recipes secret?"

"A pot full of dying rabbit vitamins could be murder."

Siggi and I anxiously waited in the dark. I peeked through the keyhole but saw no light. This heightened our suspicion. *Do chefs always cook best in the dark? Why is Ma hiding her activity?*

Finally, without fanfare, she unlocked the door, pushed aside some carefully arranged junk on the table, fished a critter out of the boiling pot and dropped it on a platter. There it lay, pinkish and steamy, lonely, without head or potatoes to keep it company. Its guts and hide had been thoughtfully removed and hidden somewhere. Siggi and I sprinkled some salt on it and tore away at it.

"Not bad," Siggi mumbled with his mouth full, "tastes fresh," forgetting the table manners.

"Why is it so pink, is it female?" Siggi wanted to know.

"But what is this? A claw?" I wanted to know.

Why don't rabbits climb trees when dogs chase them? Like cats. This is a cat.

I spat out a mouthful of cat.

"This is a cat, isn't it?"

It was Ma's secret recipe, a legacy to be cherished. After some prodding she confessed that she had served us a cat.

"Whose cat is this?" we wanted to know.

"I don't know," Ma replied meekly.

"Where did you get it? Just asked the little pussy to come up and jump into your pot?" I asked inquisitively.

"No."

"Then where did it come from. And who butchered it?" we demanded angrily. We could not believe that Ma killed anything, least of all somebody's pet. Besides work always scared her.

"I found it on the road," she said with tears.

"You mean it had the guts squeezed out?"

"*Ja.*"

We said no more. We felt very sorry for Ma; we always felt so sad for Ma. I also felt like I had to reverse eat as we had done so often in the past, but I was empty.

Pa eats mountains of food and I almost devoured a flat cat-rabbit. Parents stink. This junk pile stinks. Lawyers stink. I stink. The whole rotten world stinks.

◆   ◆   ◆

To find and to do something that didn't stink, Siggi and I joined the *Christlicher Verein Junger Maenner,* the YMCA of Germany. It did not own any facilities like in America, such as swimming pools and dormitories, and this group pursued only religious studies and not much else. We met weekly in church with other boys to study the Bible and pray. If we prayed things could only get better.

Our group vacationed four weeks in Caslano in the Italian Alps and even though this would cost only about fifteen dollars per person, Siggi and I could not afford to go. Neither the CVJM, nor the tax-supported church, nor our father offered to pay for our trip, although this vacation would have sent us temporarily to heaven. Ma wrote me years later that she never thought of borrowing our trip money, and that she had never paid one cent of interest in her life. Was this a narrow outlook on life?

I also had a very narrow outlook on life. I observed it as though through a crack in an outhouse, seeing only a tiny sliver of a better life outside, and for months I considered how I could escape from my privy. Ma must have realized that I wanted to check out of our privy because I rarely talked and never smiled anymore. To improve my mood, she arranged for me to spend my vacation with the owner of a last-hope, secondhand store in Basel, and for this I needed a passport. I remember that when the photographer asked me to smile for my picture, I forced a grin from ear to ear. Later I discovered that instead of a smile, I looked as sorrowful as if somebody had stolen my lollipop.

My hosts were poor by Swiss standards and lived in an apartment above their store in the *Totengasse,* Alley of Death. But I felt comfortable there, even though the air was pungent with old cat pee. The husband was in the armed reserve and kept his weapons at home. When I was upstairs alone, I aimed his unloaded, I think, rifle out of the window. The passersby thought nothing of it because Switzerland was armed to the teeth, and even boys belonged to the military. *Why are there no exuberant gun battles when there's a gun in almost every house?*

Even though I did not know anybody, I enjoyed this sojourn. I spent hours strolling around, watching people and absorbing the sights and sounds of one of the world's richest and most cultured cities. I admired lavishly adorned buildings, beautiful treasures in store windows and the bustling traffic of autos and streetcars rolling across arched bridges over the Rhine River.

When I had to return again to the *Gymnasium,* Ma asked me to stay with the Grobs. Mrs. Grob had been an organ loft witness to our water baptism and was the owner of a secondhand store in Swiss Rheinfelden, which was close enough that I could walk across the border to the nearby railroad station in Germany. They had no children and I lived with them for many months. To keep me fully occupied and further enhance my mental health during my stay there, Ma made arrangements for me to work a few hours every week in a nearby bakery mopping floors and putting ice cream bars into wrappers. But I received no pay and didn't think that Ma collected it because I would have needed a government permit to work in this country. My reward was that I liked it there much better than all other places where I would have had to spend my time.

But having to return to Germany for school every day did not do much to ease my consternation. So to make myself feel better, to be macho, I bought one or two packs of cigarettes from a vending machine, and soon I was hooked on smoke bullets. It was not long before I had to quit shooting myself, however, when I ran out of money, and to steal never entered my misguided mind. To reward my honesty, Mrs. Grob informed Ma that some day I would become a murderer. Or rapist. She did not say why she thought so and I did not ask. Did she think this because I was so forlorn and never smiled, or did she read tea leaves? I did not want to know this, lest it would become true. Up to this time I still believed people who told me that I was stupid because they had made comments that I still remembered:

"I don't understand how you got into the *Gymnasium*."

Or: "You will someday spread feces."

No one could get much lower in society than a spreader of feces, except rapists and killers. Now someone said I would become a murderer. *Is this what you tell children in hell?*

Up to this time I had sojourned only with families who were unrelated to us and were secondhand-store owners as well: in Aurich, in Basel and now in Swiss Rheinfelden. Ma had arranged all of my stays, and I met my keepers for the first time when I was deposited with them. Siggi also stayed at the Basel store but at a different time from my visit there. We were the pawns of our parents, who stowed us in such stores for safekeeping, in order to keep us from getting too scorched during our most despairing times.

While we were in hell, our father seemed to be in heaven. He played with his young wife and guzzled the best wine to forget his lost sons. He continued to dwell in an opulent home, drove deluxe cars, dressed in fancy suits and professional pride and continued to do whatever people do in heaven.

Even though Ma did not guard us anymore with her whip, Siggi and I tried our best to always behave well. We never thought about drinking alcohol or sniffing fumes. Only adults drank and sniffing hadn't been invented yet. We never took even one aspirin to deal with our haute cuisine and parental torture. None of our schoolmates were *under the influence* because their parents seemed to love them, took good care of them as best as they could and taught them discipline and respect. We knew of no children who imbibed, even though it was legal for them to drink beer and wine in this country.

Siggi and I were chips off the old blocks and would soon be men, but no one seemed to ask: "Will they follow the examples of those who had taught them so well? Will they be lazy like their mother? Will they become vigorous fornicators like their father? Will they drink in excess and mistreat their wives and torture their children? Will they say 'We *made mistakes* and become *victims?*' Will they buy attack lawyers like their father? Will they someday outdo them because…"

**"Those to whom evil is done
Do evil in return."**

◆   ◆   ◆

We did not visit any of our relatives. When we had in the past, it had always been with Pa, but only for an hour or two at a time, when we first moved in with him, and Siggi and I were still new and shiny. We were now old and tarnished. Our relatives had never invited us and had never stayed with us, except once, when we had hosted one of our numerous cousins, while we had still lived in the Hardtstrasse before the arrival of Teufi. Friederle, Uncle Fritz's son, had come from Wollbach on his big motorcycle to ride with us to the wedding of his sister, Lotte, in Switzerland. The only reason that he had joined us was that he knew he would be very drunk in the end and would have to recover before riding home on his motorbike.

After the wedding ceremony, a bus or two took the guests to a hotel by a lake. A band played for the party, and Siggi and I rowed around the lake. In the evening Pa played the piano, allowed us a puff or two from his cigars, and let us sip his wine. For all the guests he appeared to be a caring father who provided for his children, and for Siggi and me this wedding was the mother of all parties. Having never been to one, never having met so many friendly relatives, never having eaten so much good food, we were in belly-bursting heaven.

When we returned home, Friederle crawled into bed to sleep off the pain in his head. The next morning, while he was still recovering from his overindulgence, I rode his shiny motorbike. I barely could keep it from falling over because it weighed much more than I, and I did not know how to start it. So I coasted downhill and left it there because it was too heavy to push back up. I was caught. When Friederle came alive again I confessed what I had done. He never offered me a ride, nor did he scold me as I had anticipated. Maybe this was because he did not yet feel like making any fast moves that might have disturbed his overindulgence.

♦   ♦   ♦

Ma, Siggi and I continued to struggle along, subsisting on next to nothing, as always. She wrote Siggi many years later that for a while we received about fifty dollars a month from a welfare agency, and that she had to repay all of it from Pa's intermittent court-ordered payments. But during this time an American visited us and lit up our dungeon with brilliant hope. Siggi and I did not know him, nor did we know that he was coming. His name was Maxo Harman Hinderk Schitzma. Very impressive.

He was the brother of Fullo Schitzma and Deepo Schitzma, our uncles in America. They had migrated to the United States in the twenties or before, and later had married two of Ma's sisters, Helene and Houwke. In the early thirties Deepo had come back to East Frisia and visited Oma and her family, and mentioned that he was looking for a wife. Uncle Jodokus had pointed to the pictures on the piano and had asked him to pick one of his four sisters. Deepo had liked the looks of Ma and had wanted to take her back with him, but Ma wrote me that Oma had told him:

"She grows up to her required tasks. Helene is a cleaning fiend and a spendthrift. We want to get rid of her the most."

Helene worked in the Hartz Mountains as a household apprentice, so Oma and Jodokus traveled there to fetch her. On the bus to the ship for America she was struck by influenza, and Deepo was afraid that he would have to leave her behind. But she recovered enough before his visa expired, so they traveled together to his home in the New World. They married and had several children in quick succession. Later they had another daughter and much later, perhaps because of some sort of oversight, or insight, another boy.

Aunt Helene had convinced Uncle Deepo to also fetch her sister Houwke, who subsequently visited them in America, and Fullo had married her on the day her visa expired.

Maxo who was visiting us now was still single.

Houwke and Helene were our aunts who had sent us the packages in Simonswolde after the war that helped keep us alive. Thank you very much, dear relatives, because there had been so little to eat that the new German government had issued rationing vouchers which permitted each citizen **as little as two hundred calories per day**. This would have been even less if the Soviets had not improved our situation by sinking refugee ships in the Baltic.

During Maxo's visit, Siggi and I became infected with excitement and embarrassment. *Amerika* excitement, an American came to visit us. Junk embarrassment. We were very improper in very proper Germany because we could barely move in our rat's nest. There was a constant danger of tripping and getting stuck in Ma's nesting material, and I felt that we would be mired in this soul-trap for all eternity. Our visitor took a lot of interest in us, a red flag waving, but Siggi and I did not see it. Whenever a stranger gets friendly, watch out, but America was special; it had cowboys and Indians, mountains and prairies, wealth and freedom. During the course of his visit Maxo casually asked us: "Would you like to come to America?"

"Jaaaa," Siggi and I almost shouted in unison, without considering the hows and whys. We had learned to like *Amerika* from the many books and movies and could not wait to visit there. But Ma did not answer Maxo's question, and we assumed that she would come with us. She never hinted about such a trip and voiced no objections about it now. She suggested a walk around our neighborhood, and when we came to a city park, Maxo wanted to take our picture. He asked Ma, Siggi and me to stand on the lawn in front of a flowerbed. As he snapped our picture, an acquaintance strolled by:

"You can't walk on that grass. It belongs to the city," this man scolded us with an authoritarian tone.

Always this damned "Don't Do This." Always this damned "Do that." Always, "This Is Verboten."

No one ever said: "You poor, little victims! You try so hard. You can live in garbage like maggots. You are neglected, beaten, tenderized, chewed up, and *processed* in *court* cases, again and again. Yet, you never rebel, lie, cheat, steal or kill. You are heroes."

Along with the constant emotional and physical pummeling from our parents, Siggi and I received a total lack of recognition and support from our next-of-kin and not-next-of-kin. It was getting to us and we were ready to visit *Amerika*.

We were set up, my little brother and I.

After Maxo left, Ma informed us that we were going to *Amerika* alone. She had always kept us on a very short leash, pinned to her waistband, but now she willingly traveled with us to Frankfurt, to the American consulate to apply for our visas. The red flag kept waving, but Siggi and I were too naïve and too innocent to see it. We had outgrown our use for her catharsis and were now strong enough to reciprocate any proffered whipping, and with interest. If Siggi and I would have been able to spend a few weeks in today's enlightened culture, would it have triggered the defense mechanism in us, or were we too set in our squeaky clean ways?

◆   ◆   ◆

At the consulate an official questioned us separately about our political beliefs. We didn't have any, and this helped us qualify to come to America. When he asked me if I were married I giggled. No one married at the age of sixteen. But the official remained serious, and I was hoping that I wouldn't blow it, causing him to not let me go to America. When he then asked me if I had children, I found this really bizarre, but I tried to remain earnest. Children didn't have children, and during this era German mores allowed boys to barely look at girls. These ethics developed long ago to keep them from connecting, to prevent the untimely creation of babies. This was a fail-safe method of birth control that also taught us intense self-control.

We also received thorough medical examinations at the consulate. While we were waiting for many hours, I observed its people. I could tell which ones were Americans, even if they did not speak, because of the comforting aura that surrounded them. They wore bright colors, had light-hearted moods and casual demeanor. Even the marine guard, dressed in a blue and tan uniform and white cap, was casually chewing gum, and I could not remember ever seeing someone so nonchalant and self-confident.

◆   ◆   ◆

Months later we received our visas, and "Uncle" Maxo made arrangements for our passage to the United Sates of America. Even during this interim period, Siggi and I did not discuss our upcoming voyage. We had no idea why we were allowed to travel ten thousand kilometers by ourselves at such a young age. I barely thought about our upcoming adventure because I was still living from minute to minute, even though our future would look bright: Big, fast cars, smiling people, chocolate, marshmallows, rock and roll bands. And of course, cowboys and Indians.

Amerika.

We remained totally uninformed about our trip, and Siggi and I did not even know about the different types of visas, or which kind we were going to get. Important questions that we should have asked ourselves never entered our minds. Such as: Why are we allowed to go to America? Whose idea was this initially? How long will we stay there? Who is paying for our trip? Will we be able to continue our education? How will we get along with almost no English? Will we miss our homeland? Will we get jobs? Will we ever see our friends again? Will we play in a rock and roll band? And most of all, why was Ma not coming with us? Was it because she could not take her precious possessions, or did she know something that we didn't, and wouldn't tell us? Did Ma send us away because she was at the end of her rope? Or thought that we were at the end of ours? Ma's silence about these questions was another warning signal about our future, but we did not recognize this, Siggi and I. No one else posed these questions either, at least did not bring them up with us. Our daily lives ground forward as if our future would not, could not, improve. Such was the state of our universe.

◆   ◆   ◆

We hadn't seen our male forerunner for months even though he only lived about a kilometer from us. On the day we were leaving to board the train for our long voyage into the unknown, he arrived at our apartment as Siggi and I exited from it. We mumbled good-bye to the jolly fat man in the suit and kept on going. He stood there as if dumbfounded, but smirking, and acted as if he had only now learned that his sons were leaving the country.

No hugs, no kisses, no good-byes. I wonder if he were thinking:

"Good riddance. Now I won't have to kill you."

Three stories above, Ma was leaning out of her bomb-making, soap-making, rat's-nest, road-kill and cat-house kitchen window. I looked up when I heard her say, "We will never see them again!" *Is that good? Or is that bad for Siggi and me?*

The lesson then is, if you send your young children alone to the other side of the world, to give them courage and confidence, your last and only suggestion to them should always be that you will never see them again.

◆   ◆   ◆

In about the middle of March, at the ages of fifteen and seventeen, Siggi and I left behind everything: shame, cold and hunger, parental love and affection, homeland, culture, orchestra, friends, relatives and the world's best educational system. And our judicial umbrella, the excitement of our Progenitors' War, the war of our silent torture, which, amazingly, would continue for another seven or eight years. But by visiting America, like Pa, we did not know that it was better to be with the devils that you knew, than to run to the devils that you didn't know.

Siggi and I had never met, nor talked, to one bureaucratic soldier in our war, neither on our side, nor our enemy's side. We had never met, nor talked to, one single lawyer, judge or social engineer, because they had been silent and invisible to us since the start of our war eight years before. Not one of them had ever asked us, how's your life in prison? Do you have enough food and water? Not one of them had questioned, do you want to live with your father or with your mother? Do you prefer to be stuck in a rat's nest, or would you like to live in a mansion?

And worst of all, no one knew that we had been little heroes. Heroes among skeletons. Heroes from a stranger's attic. Not even Siggi and I knew this, because no one told us and we didn't think of it.

◆   ◆   ◆

We traveled again by train back to East Frisia where we met Maxo. He bought us some new clothes, and we spent a few days visiting his, and our, relatives. While he was driving us to the Port of Bremerhaven to be shipped, and he thought that we had reached the point of no return, he casually asked us:

"What are you going to do in America?"

Again Siggi and I did not detect the warning flag. We had no idea what we would do, but hoped for a better life, and Siggi, ever submissive, like I, wanted to accommodate him and simply guessed:

"Work."

Maxo was quiet.

Maybe Siggi remembered the German adage: *"Arbeit macht frei."* But we know better now, we learned it the hard way, it is this: "To think makes you free. To act on your thoughts makes you free." Slaves are told: "Work makes you free."

I did not answer Maxo's question because I never wanted to impress anyone with my quick wit. Had I done so, I would have told him that I did not know what we were going to do in America because I really didn't and had never thought about it. I was sure that in America you were either a cowboy or an Indian, and I wanted to be friends with the Indians and hunt buffaloes with bows and arrows and spears. Many years later, Siggi would send me a newspaper article about himself, which stated that when he came to America he had looked forward to hunting buffaloes. Our dreams had been the same, even though we never discussed them.

In Bremerhaven, amid great fanfare, we boarded the huge ship, the "MS Berlin." A brass band played happy melodies, while colorful streamers and confetti fell from the gray and drizzly sky. *Is this a happy time or a dreary time for Siggi and me?*

On crossing the Atlantic, our ship pitched and rolled through a hurricane and was blown far off course, and because one of the ship's propellers ceased to function, we further lost speed and control. The ship's crew thoughtfully decorated the handrails in the hallways with brown paper bags to help celebrate this event, this lack of control. When passengers suddenly lost their contents, they could quickly unload into one of these bags. But Siggi spent most of this festive period in his bunk in our tiny cabin, far-out seasick. Many of the passengers, as well as our crew, also decorated and "perfumated" our ship, throwing barf against the walls and on floors. I was frightened to death, because I was convinced that we would sink. Even though the whole ship smelled of vomit, I was spared the distraction of seasickness. *The unbalanced balancing system in my ears?*

◆   ◆   ◆

The "MS Berlin" limped into Halifax, Nova Scotia. Two days later, after eleven days at sea, we arrived in New York City where thousands of brightly colored cars cruised through deep canyons. This and the Statue of Liberty made me shiver. It was the first time in my life that I shivered from thrilling pleasure and not from hellish cold or terrifying fright.

On debarking we followed the crowds through customs. We had no idea how to find our way around New York, much less across a continent. We had had only a few years of English in the *Gymnasium,* not enough to be able to travel that far and not get lost. But we were so overwhelmed by what we were experiencing that we were not the least bit worried. Our hope for heaven overcame any concerns. After passing through customs, a friendly lady informed us in German that she was with the Travelers Aid Society and was here to take us to the train station. Even though we wore nametags, we wondered how she was able to find us in such a huge crowd. The three of us rode a taxi to Grand Central Station, where she ordered us bread and butter sandwiches at a snack bar, and the clerk confirmed that's what we really wanted. Bread, lard or margarine had always been one of our main foods, and our guide might have suspected this. Since we still had a long trip ahead of us to the west coast of the state of Washington, she wanted to make us feel at home. After we ate, she gave us our tickets and put us on a train bound for Chicago.

When we arrived in the windy city, another Aid representative informed us that we had to change trains ten hours later. She said that she would leave us and requested that we wait in the railroad station until that time. But after Siggi and I explored the huge station, we disregarded her request and ventured into Chicago. Hungrily we passed a building that displayed a sign: "Hamburgers." We did not know if these were edible or if this were a restaurant. To us a *Hamburger* meant someone from Hamburg, as *"Ich bin ein Berliner"* was someone from Berlin or a jelly-filled doughnut. The smell drifting from that building drew me in, while Siggi waited outside to rescue me in case that should become necessary.

The people inside this restaurant were all extremely well tanned and looked at me with great interest. *Did Ma not brown me enough?* Siggi and I also had fried ourselves in the sun for weeks to tan ourselves as dark as possible. These people were curious, I was nervous. But they also fascinated me. I still remembered the friendly black soldier who had given us oranges when we had been so frightened and so hungry in Diesenbach. I approached the lunch counter and meekly said to the waitress with a thick accent: "I like two *Hamburger*." I did not understand what she said to me, but I guessed that she was asking me questions, so I responded by nodding affirmatively. As I waited I felt quiet stares on my back. After she handed me my order, I gave her several dollars and received some change. I had no idea how much the hamburgers cost, but I trusted her to give me back the correct amount.

Back outside, I shared the hamburgers with Siggi. They were enormous, piled high with condiments and were delicious. A few weeks later Siggi still remembered this when he wrote our friend Juergen a letter describing our adventure:

"...courageously Ami went into a store and came back out twenty minutes later, pale and sweaty. Yes, it took a long time for Ami to explain to the clerk what he wanted to buy."

We both desired another hamburger, but I was too timid to go back into the restaurant, as was Siggi, so we continued our sightseeing and eventually found our way back to the station to board the train to continue our journey.

In this letter Siggi also wrote to Juergen:

"To describe a railroad station like New York or Chicago would take too long and I don't have enough room for it. By the way, Ami is already attending school. I will start maybe in a few days. Ami says there are one hundred twenty subjects that one can choose. For example, to give speeches is a subject. I mean speaking before a crowd…

"…the girls put on make-up, and during class. The teachers don't have much authority here…

"When I was in church I saw people with their hands in their pockets, chewing gum…"

◆　　◆　　◆

As we traveled across the continent, we spent much of our time looking out because we did not want to miss anything. We absorbed the vastness of America as we passed through mountains, plains, deserts and cities. We quickly learned that Americans were different from Germans. The people on our trains smiled a lot, wore colorful clothes, were relaxed and light-hearted, and not harried as the Germans had stereotyped them. We liked Americans, and we could hardly wait to meet our relatives at the evergreen coast.

We had it made, Siggi and I. By coming to America we could quickly crawl from the bottom of the pit where we had dwelled all of our lives. We were heroes heading for greener pastures and our future looked rosy. We were going to be cowboys and as such…

Lives of heroes are always better!

4

AND STILL BETTER

Whom God wants to show real wonders, he sends into the
wide world…

—*Old German Song*

Will we see great marvels? Or will we suffer a clash of cultures and
classes?

◆   ◆   ◆

Siggi and I arrived in Everett, Washington, at four o'clock on a Sunday morning. We had slept only fitfully that night, feeling elation and
trepidation. When we got off the train, some of our relatives were waiting for us on the station platform. There were two aunts, two uncles
and several cousins and at six feet I towered over them.

"Oh, what big boys!" exclaimed Aunt Houwke.

"Strong enough to shovel my manure," undoubtedly thought Uncle
Fullo.

"Ja, groote boys,*"* echoed her sister Aunt Helene, mixing Low German with English. Cousin Frauke raised her arm to greet me.

"Wo geiht Di denn?" she asked confidently, how do you do?

"Gaut," I replied. I did not expect to hear Low German in America and looked her over like a youngster looks at a circus clown because Frauke was much shorter than I.

After introductions and handshakes everyone got into two big, racy cars. *I want to be an American. Oh no! Our aunts and uncles don't look American.*

Siggi climbed into Uncle Deepo's light-blue spaceship-like Mercury, and I was invited into Fullo's older-looking Chevrolet. We did not say good-bye to each other because we assumed that we both would go to the same destination. After about a half-hour drive, Uncle Fullo made a sharp turn off the county road. Our heavy chrome bumper scraped the pavement as the tires began crunching up the steep gravel drive to his house, while Uncle Deepo's family continued down the highway. They honked good-bye and Fullo returned their signal; I saw their taillights disappear around the bottom of the hill. There went Siggi, where to or how far, I did not know. I hoped that we would soon be reunited because we had always been very close, had done everything together, and greatly depended on each other. Our souls were fused by our mutual singular experiences.

On the hillside the house was wrapped in darkness. I wanted to explore it, but my adrenaline was spent, and I soon asked to go to bed.

"I'll show you your room," suggested Houwke. "Follow me. We built it especially for you. It's not quite finished yet."

I felt a twinge of guilt. *Somebody built a room just for me? I have kind relatives!*

Houwke led me outside to a room in the attached woodshed, where I climbed into bed and fell asleep.

◆   ◆   ◆

What is that knocking?
"*Ja?*"

"Rise and shine!" came from the door, so I immediately and obediently crawled out of bed. It was still dark, and I did not understand why I had to get up so early, especially since I had barely slept that night. In the past I was roused in the dark only when sirens had scared us. *Is there a gunfight? A stampeding buffalo herd?*

I dressed, looked out of the mirror hoping to see the moonlit mountains and prairies, but instead saw a tired kid straightening his hair, and went back to the house.

"Good morning," Houwke greeted me with artificial cheer, while handing me a bundle of faded cloth. She herself was in stocking feet and dressed in faded pants and a flannel shirt. I found this really odd because I had never seen a woman wear man's clothes before. They always had worn dresses or skirts with blouses.

"Here, you can wear this for now."

I took her present back to my room and changed into my new clothes: a flannel shirt and torn blue pants with a front flap held up with integral suspenders. They belonged to Fullo because its legs were far too short and almost two of me could fit side by side. I wondered why she asked me to wear these rags, because as poor as I had been, I had only seen such ragged clothes on the Luitje family before. *Cowboys wear this? In the movies they always wear tall boots and big hats.*

And it was Sunday.

This clown tiptoed back into the house in his stocking feet, quiet with embarrassment. At this time Houwke was out on the back porch, putting on some rubber boots and asked me to do the same, while pointing to a used pair nearby. I figured that these belonged to Fullo also because they pinched my feet severely.

"Let me show you our cows," she said gleefully.

"OK."

I wondered why I had to wear rags to look at cows. I thought we needed elegant boots and distinguished hats to ride fast horses. Even though it was dark and raining, Houwke led me down the hill across the highway into a barn where she turned on its lights. I followed her past the stanchions on each side, to the opposite end of the cow barn, where she opened a pair of big doors so the waiting herd of Holsteins could come rushing in. These were black and white on top, plastered with a mixture of mud, and this cannot be described in lesser terms because it would become a very significant part of my life, it would become my life, cowshit, below. As they lined up in the stanchions to feed on the hay and grain that had been laid out for them, we locked in their heads.

Only now did I realize that Siggi and I had traveled this far to milk cows. Wet and significantly dirty cows. We had arrived in the greener pastures of the Evergreen State, but our future did not look rosy any more. I quickly learned that it would be significantly sticky and pervasively green. It would become my *significant other*, it would be a shotgun wedding because I was forced to be married to it. Fullo would not allow me to bathe or shower.

Perhaps because we live today in the *New Age,* in a *New World Order*, a more efficient, more greedy, more anarchistic society, or simply because in sympathetic remembrance of my slavery days, in order to fertilize the fields around us, once or twice each year, someone drives giant manure spreader trucks along the city street by my house, thoughtfully, to more or less plaster and pave it with this *significant other,* to fertilize it.

Houwke instructed me in the fine art of milking. To do so, I had to bow down between huge, warm, wet bellies and wash a *nutrient* mixture off the udders, with a rag soaked in a bucket full of hot chlorinated water, which after a few washings transmogrified into appealing *manure tea.*

My Lake Titicaca, my dream.

After washing a cow, I fastened a rubber belt around its multi-stomach blimp, suspended a vacuum extraction pail from it and sucked four teats into its rubber-lined cups. These massaged out the barnyard by-product, delicious milk. I used two such suction devices that I had to move from cow to cow until they were all empty. Empty of milk. In the meantime Houwke sat on a hard, little stool in between bellies and milked a few of them by hand. I would discover that this was her only hobby: squeeze, squirt, squeeze, squirt, squeeze…

After milking each cow, I removed the milk machine and poured its contents into the open buckets waiting in the middle of the barn. All of the cows aimed their backs to this area. This was significant, because intermittently they took turns decorating these pails and everything else with the color theme of this state. As turbulent as my life had been, I never had to dance around flying *nutrients* before. Even though I was now a cowboy in the truest sense of the word, in the movies I had never seen them wear boots of rubber and ripped coveralls. I realized that my present reality did not match my long-time fantasy, and that Fullo's outfit was much more practical here than movie boots and hats. I could not wear such because my hat would pop off when I had to squeeze between bellies, and I might slip and fall with the slick kind of boots.

When the buckets were full, full of milk that is, I carried them, two at a time, up the hill to the milkhouse where I emptied them into big cans, to be picked up by the creamery truck. Then I returned to the barn to continue to service cows until their udders were all clean and empty. After we finished milking, we let them out again, and when I had thought I was finished with the cows, Houwke told me to take all of the milking equipment back to the milkhouse and wash it. When I was done with this, I was to harvest the main product of their farm, in terms of stink, weight and volume, by myself.

She instructed me:

"Clean up the barn. Scoop up the manure and dump it outside that door. There's a wheelbarrow out there. There's lime in that big box. Spread it around the barn when you're done with the manure."

She pointed out through the big doors and said:

"Also scoop up the cow pies in the loafing shed. It's pretty dirty. Then spread some wood chips around in there."

She lead me up to the milkhouse where she continued her instructions:

"Wash the milk equipment. Put two handsful of chlorine powder into the water. To kill germs," and increase your risk of getting cancer she might have added.

"I will go and make breakfast," she continued.

"OK," I mumbled, intermittently and unenthusiastically to her orders.

Schitzma! How did I get into this? I can hardly wait to clean up.

Just a couple of days before, Siggi and I had arrived from another continent. Just a few hours ago we finished crossing a continent. We had been torn from our homeland, tossed around the Atlantic and traveled across America into the unknown. I had no idea for how long we would have to continue to work like this. To protect my soul, my mind focused only on the moment because our future appeared to be grimmer than ever.

What is Siggi doing? Hope he does not have to do this. Don't think about it!

After I finished my chores I went back to the house, instinctively left my boots on the outside porch, and went in. Houwke advised me to wash in the kitchen sink:

"Wash your hands. You must be hungry. I'll cook you an egg and some oatmeal. The girls are still in bed. They'll eat later."

While I was dutifully following her orders, Fullo, sitting at the kitchen table, kept glowering at me. *Why is he looking at me like that? What am I doing wrong?*

Finally he snarled: "Don't use so much water. From now on you'll wash in the tub outside."

"Ja," I mumbled obediently, instead of pounding the manure out of him.

I had noticed a pre-cast concrete laundry tub outside the back door as I came in. It would become my personal bathroom during my entire stay here.

Houwke served me the oat mush. I sat alone at the table, gazing at the food, forcing myself to take a bite. It tasted like cardboard. Instead of being famished, I felt nauseous. Instead of feeling like a proud, self-reliant American cowboy, I felt like the tattered, stinky Unknown *Guellefahrer*.

◆   ◆   ◆

Later that day Fullo asked me to ride with him back to the city of Everett. As tired as I was, I was curious to get a closer look at America. Along the way we passed a factory with big smokestacks, where the air stank and was pungent with acid. Fullo explained that this was the paper mill where he worked at night and said that as a steamfitter he also fixed things in the adjoining lumber mill.

I studied the surrounding houses. They were different from the ones in Germany where everything was built with masonry and cement.

"What are these houses built with?" I questioned Fullo who lived in a red brick house.

"Out of wood."

"What about the roofs?"

"Those are tar shingles," he explained.

"Tar shingles!?"

Most of these houses were grimy and needed painting. I was disappointed. Americans were supposed to be rich and these were not, although they owned so many big colorful cars. In town Fullo led me into a huge store where I admired the posters of cowboys with big hats, heavenly girls with big smiles and juicy red lips. Uncle bought me a pair of rubber boots, overalls and a couple of flannel shirts but not the cowboy clothes that I had dreamed about. And I was too shy and too intimidated to ask for some.

Upon returning to the farmhouse, I found Aunt Houwke and my cousins, Frauke and Jolene, in the woodshed outside of my room cheerfully rummaging through the two wooden trunks that Siggi and I had brought with us. Ma had them especially made for our journey, and they contained all of our belongings. I said nothing while they examined each item they removed from our boxes, and I even smiled weakly to accommodate them. I acted as if they were welcome to rob Siggi and me. I did not want to make them feel guilty since I could be stuck under their control forever.

They were in a jovial mood, as if they were opening Christmas presents. Out came a set of old china that had belonged to our grandmother and they claimed it. Little cousin Frauke needed a trunk for her summer camp and was ecstatic when she claimed Siggi's box for herself. It had survived the long journey undamaged, but the one with my stuff was smashed and almost useless now. It was held together by straps of steel, compliments of the shipping company. Frauke transferred Siggi's worldly goods into my shattered trunk and asked me to take his to her room, and I complied.

I did not realize at this time that Ma must have known that Siggi and I would be separated, or she would not have packed our stuff in separate boxes. *Who decided who goes to which farm? And for what reasons?*

◆   ◆   ◆

I milked early in the morning and again at night. During the days, I worked around the farm as Fullo assigned me various tasks, which I mostly did by myself since he slept until noon and later drove to his job in the mills. I had no contact with Siggi and assumed that he was also coerced to do much of the same kind of work.

One of my earliest tasks was to clean some old wood-framed windows that Fullo had brought home from work. He handed me some tools with the order to remove the paint that totally covered the small panes. I attacked it with a steel brush and scraper, but the paint refused to come off, mainly because I thought that I had to be careful not to scratch the glass. When it was time to milk that evening, this job was unfinished. The next day Fullo inspected my work, and with a grim expression, he demonstrated how to vigorously remove the paint from the glass.

"This is how you do it. I don't care if they get scratched. We'll install them in the new milkhouse. I want the paint off by tomorrow," Fullo ordered me before he left again for the paper mill.

During dinner that evening I did not speak a word, and a heavy air hung over the house. After eating, I went back out to finish my assignment. I heard Jolene ask Aunt Houwke why I had to work so late and she replied:

"He has to do *Strafarbeit*, penal work."

I finished my chore at dusk and went to bed.

◆   ◆   ◆

The following Sunday the whole family got ready for church. I did not want to go, and as an atheist Ma had never required us to attend, but during the few times that Siggi and I had been there everyone had worn nice clothes. I was bored with sermons and looked forward to having a couple hours of free time, two hours of personal time a week for myself, when Fullo handed me a suit.

"I bought this suit for you. It cost me twenty-nine dollars and ninety-five cents. I think it will fit you. Put it on and get ready for church."

I was dumbfounded for I did not want to go, and as always I was too shy to resist the orders from elders. He had scolded me on the first day for using too much water, and I did not dare ask him for permission to take a shower. So far I had not noticed him taking one either, nor anyone else. It was too clammy outside to wash anything but my face and arms in the tub. I had grown accustomed to the smells around me and did not realize that I had become a walking font of powerful nervous sweat and wonderful barnyard aroma.

I changed into my new salt and pepper sprinkled suit, added more dabwilldooya to my hair, and looked into the mirror. How ugly! My pant legs bubbled out at the knees the first time I sat down and remained that way. Self-consciously I rode in the back seat while my cousins teased me, deepening my consternation. When I should have been excited to be in America, I rarely spoke and only gave terse answers as always.

I followed my relatives into their church and down the center aisle. We were late. Frauke lead the way, followed in single file by her family, and I, the tallest, brought up the rear, studying the procession in front of me. *These are my relatives? I'm ashamed to be seen with them. But who am I? Am I their slave?*

Feeling hundreds of eyes on me, I fixed my stare on Fullo's feet trudging ahead of me. Chains far stronger than iron held me to my masters. Burning cities, head carvings and such had forged the first chains in my mind, sensitivity to fright and terror. With their incessant enthusiastic whippings Ma, Aunt Adele and some of my teachers had forged chains of timidity and submissiveness. Then Pa and his lawyers had forged one of intense poverty. Since arriving on the farm, my last chain was being made with links of social isolation, unique body odor and body painting, bowl haircuts, physical dependency, and its concomitant culture shock. Although I didn't realize it yet, it was mostly the state of my mind that would keep me confined in my new slavery.

I slid down into the pew as far as possible because I did not want to be noticed. The minister droned from the pulpit, and I only understood an occasional word of what he was preaching. Everyone looked proper, and I felt that I was the only one totally out of place. After the sermon, the worshippers gathered outside in front of the church where Houwke proudly introduced me:

"This is **our** big boy from the Old Country."

We shook hands.

"How do you like our country?" someone asked me with a big smile.

Instead of spinning cartwheels of joy, I'm in America, I'm a cowboy, I answered, "fine" and shrugged my shoulders. I did not yet know that, henceforth, I had to attend church every Sunday with my masters, but because I balked, they permitted me to stay home during the winter evening services that they attended also.

The symbols of my slavery were subtle, as well as obvious. Houwke had cut Fullo's hair for decades and did a nice job on his big block. But she always gave me unique bowl cuts that I would be uncomfortable with, to show the world that I was a slave. Nobody but I sported such a cut that also accentuated my customized ear.

Fullo's cows decorated me with a green color that he would not let me shower off. My décor and my mindset, my quintessence of a perfect slave, was a heavy ball and chain. I could not rid myself of it because I could not saw it off. It forced me to be comfortable with cows and kept me away from people who might be able to help me escape. This slave had no friends. Fullo was a Brahmin, even though he was a boor; I was a slave, even though I was a hero, and I reckoned that with Siggi it was much the same.

◆   ◆   ◆

Shortly after we returned from the church to the farm, Uncle Deepo's family arrived there with Siggi. During this visit, it became evident that he would remain on Deepo's dairy farm, and I was to stay with Fullo. Our uncles followed the basic military strategy of "divide and conquer" and kept it secret, because there was no discussion about this subject at all. Long ago, others had made decisions about us without our knowledge, and we meekly complied with their wishes.

Years later I would learn of the initial debate about our future from the letters that our parents had written. Ma had already considered sending us to America immediately after World War II, but Siggi and I were never informed about plans that were hatched for us over the years. I realized that we were trapped now and Siggi must have too. We had no money to leave our masters and did not discuss it during this visit or other infrequent contacts with each other.

Our lives had not improved by coming to America, and in many ways they became worse. We lost our freedom completely as well as our *Stadtmusik,* the music that we so loved to play. We had no friends. Now we had to rise early every morning, seven days a week, to work. To work until we were dead tired at night, without reward, without hope of escape, for the enrichment of others. We did not question them. How could we? We accepted our present predicament again with passivity. This was the only way we knew how to deal with our continued existence of hopelessness, rejection and undeserved punishment.

And now exploitation.

We had been with our father for only brief periods, and during those times he had almost totally ignored us and refused to support us in any way. Not because he hated his children, but because we were a restriction on his hedonistic lifestyle, and because he must have been in total denial about our plight. Our mother's main purpose had been to fight him in court to get him to live up to his responsibilities. Years after the war, when menial jobs were abundantly available, she refused to buckle under and get one herself. However, she fought for alimony and child support with unrelenting single-mindedness.

Our parents had failed us, and the court system had failed us as well, because it had not upheld the laws. Only the German school system had done its job and had done it well, although it had been difficult for us and had not made our lives easier. And in retrospect, were we not imparted with too much discipline, too many feelings of guilt, thereby adding to our miseries? Our submissiveness caused us to automatically do whatever our elders told us to do, even if it were only for their own gratification. *Should we have rebelled a little, Siggi and I? If adults could punish us for not doing our jobs, or even for doing them, why could we not clobber others just for the fun of it?*

The cows ignored our superb education and so did everyone else. At this time no one seemed to care that we were becoming ever more literate jet setters. The education that would really have helped us the most, to become independent, we had to learn through prolonged, painful, personal experiences, even on the simplest level. We were ignorant of such things as how to make long-distance telephone calls, and where and how to apply for jobs, or where to find help to obtain such knowledge.

During this Sunday visit there was no discussion about our future; there was only peasant talk: How green is my green, how soggy is my pasture! Siggi and I did not ask why were we imported to America? How long will we be separated? Will we have to do farm work all of our lives? Will we get enough to eat? Will we get time off?

I did not think about why our mother permitted Siggi and me to travel so far from home. We did not question anyone even though we were now of an age when important plans would normally be made. Goals had to be formulated as to our education, training, girls, jobs, etc. None of this even entered my mind because our parents never discussed things like that with us; we were not guided in this kind of thinking. But in Germany we had learned that America was "the land of unlimited opportunities," so all of this seemed not yet to matter much because there was some hope that somehow our plight might end.

In late afternoon, Deepo's family returned to their farm to drain their cows again, taking with them Siggi and his shattered trunk. They also scrutinized him for keepsakes and heirlooms and found our grandmother's ornately-engraved gold watch with its long gold chain that Ma had given him. Now Deepo's family took it. Many years later, Siggi would ask to get Oma's gold watch back but was told that it had burned when Deepo's house had gone up in flames.

◆   ◆   ◆

During the next two years, with one exception, the only time when Siggi and I would see each other alone was during the occasional visits between these two families. Every few weeks or months, they took turns visiting on Sunday afternoons. Why I didn't know because Fullo did not like Deepo. Fullo even told his family that after I was "gone" he would not visit Deepo again. I didn't know if he meant after I was dead, deported, drafted, enlightened, or how I would be gone.

After their ritual church attendance, one family would drive directly to the other farm and leave again in a few hours, in time to service their demanding cows. It was always the same, and Siggi and I had little contact with each other, or with the rest of the world. Unbelievable as it might sound, I did not even know how to use a telephone, and I was actually afraid of doing so. Besides, Fullo would get mad if someone made long-distance calls from his house, costing him money, so anyone rarely did. Siggi and I had never used a phone before, had no money to pay for such calls, and at the end of our long days we were too tired to write to each other.

◆   ◆   ◆

I milked cows twice a day. They lumbered into the barn to their respective stanchions which were identified by names chalked on little blackboards near the ceiling. Evidently these critters could read because they always returned to their own spaces to eat their feed, while I serviced them. Sometimes one of them would step on my foot, refusing to budge, while I tried to extricate myself. They obviously were in collusion, because the harder I pushed their masses apart, the more they pressed me between their bellies, and the more a hoof crushed my foot. Often I had no choice but to wait them out. While waiting, because I did not have French textbooks or Freud's works with me, I entertained myself by squeezing fat maggots out of the cows' backs, popping out nine millimeter bullets when these were in season, until the cows released me.

Besides a lot of milk, I became acutely aware that cows also produced a lot of soupy doodoo. After each milking I had to scoop this stuff into a wheelbarrow, roll it up a plank and out of the barn to tip it onto a sloppy big pile. Because my muscles were too weak, my wheelbarrow often tipped prematurely. Then I had to fork or shovel up this same stuff again under the principle, that if at first you don't succeed, try again. And again. During the winter there would be much more trying than during the summer because these docile beasts spent much more time in the cow *nutrient*-shedding shed where they often congregated to keep out of the cold and the rain.

Since I always had to be tested for everything that I was forced to do, but did not want to do, I unwittingly took the first part of my *Guellefahrer* exam when my feet sank deeply into the green, water-soaked pile, and the slop oozed over the top of my knee-high rubber boots. Fortunately I kept my balance by leaning on the fork to extract my feet back out of the test pile, but, alas, without my boots and without one sock.

Driving tractors safely was the second part of my test.

When the pastures were not too soggy, I had to grunt my forty-ton cow pie onto a spreader, using a ten-tine hand fork. Sometimes in the rain. Then I pulled this precious load with an old tractor, to spread *nutrients* over the evergreen pastures to make them evergreener. To get to the far end, it was necessary to drive through a creek. On my first trip, I learned that I could get killed by a very unique method. As the tractor was climbing up the bank on the other side, the spreader got stuck in this stream. I depressed the gas pedal in order to extract it, but instead of causing a forward movement, the "horses" reared up. The front end of the tractor rose toward the sky, and I almost fell backwards out of the seat.

"Fulloschitzma…"

I had no idea that this would happen, and if I had finished exclaiming my cussword, thereby delaying quick depression of the clutch, the tractor would have kept revolving backwards about its rear axle, burying me deeply in the spreader and under the upside-down tractor. Fortunately the uniquely unusual arrangement of the tractor being loaded upside down on the spreader, its big wheels racing above me, sooner or later, would have drawn the attention of astute observers to my uncomfortable squeeze. Hopefully someone would then have screamed, "oh, Schitzma," and then hurried to my rescue.

Over the years, farm workers, workers usually not included in the nation's general productivity statistics, unwittingly chose this method to commit suicide. They would be recognized, however, in another kind of statistic.

I passed these highly unusual and difficult tests and graduated summa cum laude. In spite of all this, I still remained mentally somewhat balanced, did not cuss with four-letter words and did not become pickled in *nutrient* or part of an important statistic. *Would Professor Asal have been proud of me?*

Even so, I was stuck in slavery.

Siggi stuck in slavery.

Mother stuck in heirlooms.

Father stuck with his devil.

And there was no one in sight to reap *Schadenfreude* from my *Guellefahrer* tests, scold me for my profanity, or present me with a diploma. Nor was there anyone to free me from my stinky heroism.

Siggi and I had never been allowed to say "shit" but were now forced to wallow in it. I could not understand why Ma had threatened to whip us if we spoke this word, and then had sent us to another continent to become an integral part of it. She knew about such matters because she had grown up in it. In her father's farmhouse even the kitchen must have smelled of it. Assuming that Oma had cooked, had she taken deep breaths before meals and schmoozed: "Mmmmm, Mama, your dinner smells. Smells delicious, like fresh country air."

◆   ◆   ◆

About a couple of weeks after I arrived on his farm, Fullo mentioned that I should enroll in high school. This surprised me because I had not thought about it and did not expect it. Our conversation was brief, as always:

"You should attend high school," Fullo told me.

"Oh, OK," I agreed.

"I will take you to school to sign up."

A glimmer of hope, that familiar feeling of uncertainty. *With my spare English, will I flunk most courses? Be a monkey in a circus cage?*

The next day we drove to Everett High School where he dropped me off. A student who knew German consulted with my counselor to decide what level of education I had reached in order to choose my courses. I enrolled in German to learn English and to earn a good grade as well. And after a few months in America, almost without realizing it, I would think and speak entirely in my new language.

I had had four years of French, one year of which I had to repeat because the teacher ruled that I had flunked it. When my advisor learned of my French fluency, he enrolled me in the last subject that I wanted to suffer again. But I was too shy to say so, even though I thought that if I flunked it now, I'd flunk out of school again. And for the final time. I was now enrolled in a course where I had to understand two foreign languages, French and English, and where no one spoke my native tongue. Even so, I managed to earn an average overall grade.

I discovered that this high school was much easier than the *Gymnasium*. I had little homework and barely had to study to maintain at least average grades. Furthermore, I could graduate in about two years instead of five. The *Gymnasium* could even take longer if I would have to repeat a grade. Or I could flunk out entirely.

I began to learn about American culture on my first day in school. When the teacher walked into our homeroom, I automatically rose from my chair to greet him with respect, but I quickly slumped down again when everyone else ignored him. German pupils always rose when greeting or addressing adults. When the teacher dropped an eraser, I retrieved it for him as I had been taught, while all other students ignored him this time as well, but not the monkey. The student sitting across the row from me saluted me with his middle finger and tried to do so unobtrusively. I did not know if he complimented me or insulted me; I had not yet learned the meaning of this gesture. But I could guess: You stand proud like a hero. I automatically rose several more times before I overcame my neurotic habit of showing respect for my elders, or whatever it was that caused me to respond automatically on such occasions.

I also discovered that the students in my new country had fun, much fun. In the schools of my old country the only fun that we had had was that we could gawk at members of the opposite sex with agonizing self-control, draw and paint in art class and go on field trips twice a year. As isolated as I was in my new country, it did not take me long to find that the fun seemed to be endless here. But for my fun I could only attend school assemblies. During one of these, the band played and we all sang that we rocked around the clock. I rocked to great heights, then dropped back into manure when the school day ended.

I observed others greatly enjoying themselves, but I was not allowed to do so. I watched boys kiss girls, go steady, and build and race hot rods. Everyone responded to raging hormones while I was forced to suppress mine. They saw movies and went to dances. Everyone seemed to play sports and games, belonged to clubs and wore school sweaters with pins and letters announcing that they were heroes and heroines with intellect, culture and machismo. I could only be an unknown hero and kept this to myself. I kept to myself because I was always plastered with Fullo's *dairy product* that nobody seemed to like, and I always had to return immediately to the farm after classes, to dive again into the same.

At the end of our school year all of the students signed each other's yearbooks. There were none such in the German schools, and I felt that yearbooks were a nice tradition to remember the past. They also seemed to be the culmination of yearlong popularity contests because some of the students had lots of clubs listed with their pictures, and they collected many comments and signatures therein from their friends as well. A *Guellefahrer,* however, could not be very popular, be very high up the pecking order. But next to my picture in the yearbook my affiliation was listed as "Boy's Club." I didn't even know what kind of club that was, what it did, but I had not joined it. *Had somebody lied so I'd feel good? I, a smelly square pig in a dizzyingly social round hole?*

◆   ◆   ◆

Communal nakedness was foreign to me because there had been no showering facilities in any of our schools in Germany. Showering was not academic in nature and had too few social and health benefits. And since these schools had no lockers either, we always carried our school supplies home everyday, and for our physical education classes we wore our sports clothes under our street clothes which we hung on hooks during these classes. Afterwards we did not shower because everyone, except Siggi and I, bathed at home about once a week, whether they needed to or not. This was probably because water, sewer and energy were very expensive in much of Europe.

In my American high school I also enrolled in physical education and was shocked when the boys completely undressed. When I changed my clothes I turned my naked jewels toward a corner to shield them from view, and I noticed that the other boys strapped on baggies to safeguard theirs. *Weak muscles or strong men? Never saw little balls bouncing around the* Gymnasium. *Wonder what Freud would say about this?*

After class everyone showered together. But I could not bring myself to crowd in with naked male bodies, yearned for female bodies, and I did not like the locker room aroma. Therefore I quickly dressed myself. The instructor asked me if I were going to shower or stink like someone who had died running a marathon. I explained to him that I was not allowed to get water into my ear because I suffered a chronic infection and showed him my beautiful scar which did not seem to impress him. Here was my one and only chance to shower each week, and I was too embarrassed to do so.

One of the students came back out of the shower and collapsed on the floor. His entire body was shaking, and I tried not to stare. Maybe he did some kind of ritual, a tribal manhood initiation, such as jungle-bungee-vine diving. His shaking shook me up too; I had a lot to learn and thought that I had made a wise decision not to shower. Oddly, everyone ignored this shaker, and I continued to wonder about the strange customs in America. His shaking also made me nervous since I might also be called upon to become a naked shaker on the hard, cold floor.

Later I learned that this student suffered from grand mal epileptic seizures. He was a quiet boy like I, and had immigrated from Northeastern Europe where he had witnessed terrifying events during the war. This had shorted out his nervous system, and since no one could help him during his seizures, everyone ignored him.

After I dressed again, on my way to another class, I unobtrusively took a breath from under my arms. *Keep pits closed during class. Air them out in between.*

◆   ◆   ◆

It was not long before our class was asked to take something that was called an eye cue test. *More American culture?* I did not know what an eye cue was. How could I be tested for something that I didn't know what it was? I was too timid to ask. There were so many things that I did not understand, and I would have to ask incessantly. While I listened to the teacher explain our instructions, I gathered that my brain was to be tested, but my English was not yet proficient enough that I could fully comprehend the examples on the test form. *Do my records still show that I'm a complete idiot?*

In my old country I had never heard of intelligence tests. IQ tests were built into each essay and each math test, because if you flunked you were dumb and if you passed you were smart. But test results could also be a measure of how badly a pupil's soul was battered and not how smart he was, and the teachers would probably not know the difference.

◆   ◆   ◆

The next time our families visited each other, I found out that Siggi attended Sultan High School. Fortunately he did well and would become so popular that he would be elected student body president during his senior year. But I could never join in any extracurricular activities. I was socially, spiritually, emotionally and physically isolated on the farm far outside the city where we had few neighbors. My slave masters did not encourage me to participate in anything because they knew that this would take time away from my work, and I would need their car and spend their money. I knew that gas was extremely expensive because Fullo always asked the station attendant for "two dollars worth of regular." This bought about half a tankful and money did not earn interest there. And worst of all, I might get connected to the world, and my masters had to get all they could from me while the getting was good and I would provide.

I was not allowed to use their car for myself, even after I received my driver's license long after my arrival. The only reason I was finally permitted to get it was to be the chauffeur for Fullo's daughters. Even though Aunt Houwke had been in the United States for almost thirty years, she had never learned to drive. Cousins Jolene and Wuebkea were too young to drive; Greetje had left home before I arrived here, and Frauke was too short to reach the pedals. Since the girls rarely went anywhere except to school on the bus, I got very little practice driving a car.

Once Frauke and Jolene wanted to attend a high school football game at night and my chief master, my *uncle*, must have been in a very good mood that day. Since they had no way to get there, they asked me to drive them to the game and then to some friends' house afterwards.

I was cruising down a dark, lonely highway when Frauke burst out: "Turn right here." Instantly I reacted, stepped on the brakes and turned right. In our headlights I saw another car stopped at this approach. Our back end swerved around towards our left until we were square with the road. We kept sliding sideways directly toward this car, but an invisible hand stopped us within inches of a collision. I glimpsed the terrified face of the other driver. Then all sphincters must have relaxed again, because we had performed this maneuver with such precision that only my guardian angel could have done it. But I took credit for it. I floored the gas pedal, to gun down the new highway as if it were normal to execute life-highlighting turns. With my greasy pompadour, I was cool, but my passengers, however, were shocked speechless, maybe because they might have suddenly lost some weight.

◆   ◆   ◆

Uncle Fullo was built like an oak barrel, somewhat like the ones that everyone buys halves of, to fill with dirt, to grow weeds in, and sometimes flowers. It was also filled with something heavy because the short legs under the cask bowed into an O. On top of this barrel was a round head, securely fastened with a stout neck, which allowed little motion. Once I touched one of the stubby arms that were stuck to each side of this barrel while we were reaching in to repair an old tractor. Oak was hard; therefore I was surprised that it was soft and warm, like humans, and I never resolved the riddle of how something that looked so hard could feel so soft. *Is he full o' himself?*

Despite Fullo's hard and inflexible appearance, he could be an agile orchestrator in the cow barn. His bowed legs gave him an unexpected spring. He proved this when he flew into a rage after a cow whipped her moist, green tail across his face while he was squeezing out her last drop of milk. I didn't know if she did this intentionally, but she aimed at the right target. Nor did I learn if Fullo ate it, or if he had closed his eyes and mouth during that critical moment, although, gracefully, he did wipe his face with his sleeve.

Somewhat green-faced, he jumped from his stool and yelled at the cow loud enough so that she would understand him. He emphasized his remarks by splitting his wooden stool on her hindquarters. After she had delivered him gallons of milk, numerous calves, mountains of money and manure, this cow was dumbfounded. Energetically she did airs above the ground, while green ammo shot out of her back and an agonizing roar exploded from her front, together with a long tongue and whitish slobber.

The herd produced a quick response. It had practiced this because it knew that this would happen again. Therefore each cow always kept fresh ammunition in her oversized chamber. Milk flow stopped, tails went up, and significantly, moomookakapoopoodoodoo exploded in all directions. Each cow quickly unloaded via a second tail, a transient green one, arching toward the ground. Blobs splashed off the floor, texturing everything, including walls, cows, people and buckets. It was flying everywhere even though there was not even a fan in this barn.

The oak barrel danced, flailing its stub-outs to escalate their tempo. It beat the cows and roared like a bull, confusing them further. Pandemonium rose to an ever-higher crescendo. Cows were bawling, bucking and kicking. Machines were crashing. Milk was spilling. Freshest of *products* were steaming up the opera barn.

Not enjoying this performance, I quietly stole away, lugging two open and newly decorated buckets filled with seasoned milk up to the milkhouse and emptied them into the shiny new milk tank. After the orchestra was exhausted, I returned to finish drawing white money out of green cows, while they initiated me into the bovine orchestra, The Evergreen Orchestra. During their last opus, final movement, the bovines had aimed at the hairy ends of their tails, to load them with proprietary color, and waited until I had to approach them. Then they vigorously whipped their brushes to paint me green, so I'd fit right in, and not stick out like I did in my *Stadtmusik* orchestra.

After the cows were completely empty, the oaken maestro disappeared and left me behind to continue my dirty work. Later I released the orchestra and commenced with the obligatory scooping from this vigorous pooping. Yet afterwards, significantly, I was still not allowed to bathe or shower.

◆　　　◆　　　◆

Since Fullo worked in the mill at night, he mostly rehearsed his orchestra on weekends. *Besides having a hot temper, was he also the stingiest man on earth?* I had heard him reprimand little Frauke for wasting money buying a toothbrush. A toothbrush was a waste, while spitting out teeth later in life was not. Halitosis would not matter. Even though Fullo owned a farm and several houses, I believe all mortgage-free, he bathed only once or twice a year, and then in someone else's water. This was also the frequency of my bathing and the freshness of my water. Since I was a shy, obedient slave, and Fullo had scolded me for trying to wash off cow smell before eating, I bathed only when I was told to bathe.

One day, while sitting in class I discovered unadulterated cowsh, oops, *pardonnez moi*, Ma, *engrais de vache* on the back of my **bare** arm. I would have bored into a funky dung pile to escape embarrassment had there been one. Nauseated, without saying a word, I swayed out to the restroom instead, where I dropped to the floor and hung my head into the toilet to barf. Strangely, after I took a few deep breaths, I recovered. I washed the orchestra's color from my arm and returned to the classroom but was too shy and ashamed to tell our teacher:

"Hey, Teach, s'cuse me for leaving class. Was sick. Had to refresh myself in the toilet."

I was seated directly in front of him, to better hear him, and I still remember him saying:

"In America people shower every day."

At this time I did not know why he said that because my masters rarely bathed and they were in America. I did not realize that he was talking to, and about, me because he was looking at the ceiling when he said that.

There was one teacher who suspected that I wanted to escape from something or someone and offered me help. *Is it my color, my silence, my fertilizer smell? Can he see my soul?* As always I sat near his desk. Mr. Wickstrom mentioned that he could employ me to work for him in his greenhouse. I just mumbled that I could not and did not explain that I would not be allowed to do so, and that I would have no means to get there.

Since it dawned on me that people might notice that I radiated a unique aura, I decided to leave the barn five minutes earlier in the mornings so I could purify myself. I became so pure that Fullo scolded me for leaving his barn too early. He wanted me to remain a dung beetle and did not allow me enough time to wash myself, so, under duress, I graciously gave him back my daily five minutes. In the mornings I had only about half an hour to hurry from the barn to the house, wash my face, hands and arms, change clothes, eat and walk to the school bus. It was no wonder that my empathetic cousins gave me deodorant and after-shave lotion for Christmas, with appropriate comments. Even so, Frauke's favorite color was green, and I will never understand this. Maybe she still liked it because she had never spent time in the opera barn during or after a performance.

Cousin Greetje, Fullo's oldest daughter, came to stay with us during her vacation. Her boyfriend, Jack, on furlough from the Navy, also visited for a day or two. Since Fullo was not home Jack had the courage to take a shower. While he was whistling in the water, Houwke admonished him through the bathroom door:

"Don't use so much water."

"What?" Jack said from the shower.

Houwke did not repeat her request. Because of a potential scolding from Fullo, the meter could have been running in her head, one cup, two cups, three cents, four cents,…

Although Jack probably could not believe her command, or had not understood it, he did turn off the shower.

◆   ◆   ◆

Thanksgiving was unusually cold, below freezing. In the morning, Aunt Houwke, Frauke and Jolene were beginning to prepare turkey dinner while Fullo and I humored his cows. He was ecstatic about his night off from the mill; I was not ecstatic about my day off from school.

I returned from the milkhouse to the barn with two empty buckets and placed them inside the door. I put my cracked, freezing hands into my pockets and walked to the other end of the barn to check a milk sucker machine. Uncle Fullo sat on a stool between two cows, pressing an ear against a belly, as if to listen to the rumble of its stomachs. His short arms were straining to reach the money spigots below, squeezing out the remaining drops of money after a machine had finished milking them. Was he the only dairyman in the world with this habit?

Evidently there was too little money coming out of this cow, Beulah, because when he saw me, his face flushed, and he jumped off his stool, dropping his bucket.

"Why are you standing there with your hands in your pockets?"

Crack! An oaken fist hammered my delicate skull bone. Stars flashed through the opera. Again I was startled that the barrel could move so fast. *Did it hit me instead of Beulah because I could not blast moo-mookakapoopoodoodoo all over the barn?*

"I wasn't standing. My hands are freezing," I stuttered with a trembling voice as I raced out of the barn toward the house. But this chicken did not cackle.

"Fullo hit me. I'm leaving," I announced there.

I wanted to call Siggi and ask him to run away with me from our masters, but I was still afraid to speak on a telephone because I couldn't look this plastic gadget in the eyes. My cousins, afraid of losing their slave, started bawling, did not help me, and talked me into staying. It was easy to do because I knew of nowhere else to go.

That afternoon the whole family sat down for Thanksgiving dinner. Uncle Fullo solemnly tore a page from the calendar hanging on the wall behind him and read its lengthy religious lesson for that day. Then everyone, including me, bowed his head and gave thanks to the Lord for his blessings. *Am I his blessing? Or are we cursed, Siggi and I?*

◆   ◆   ◆

Our slavery on the dairy farms continued for more than two years, seven days a week, three hundred sixty-five days a year, minus one day for me, when I was allowed to have some time for myself, to stay in bed and barf in privacy. I didn't know how many days Siggi was allowed to have, to have privacy. But I was grateful for this day, for we were in the prime of our lives and intellectually curious. We were of the age during which one washes thousands of teats and grunts around mountains and rivers of cow products. This was especially appealing during the Pacific Northwest rain that could drizzle from September into July, when cow bellies were caked with mud and dung, and their active paintbrushes also.

During the winter months, the low temperatures and chlorinated wash water split open some of the teats of the critters like overcooked wieners. These same causes, as well as my often-wet hands and cold metal equipment likewise unzipped my fingers. At times I could see my white bones and barely hold a pencil. When I told Houwke that I was ready to scream, she instructed me to "put on some bag balm." Therefore I embalmed my hands liberally with udder grease, and this helped heal them somewhat, even without stitches.

Milk cartons claimed that the milk came from contented cows and was grade A, but they did not stroke the egos of the milkers. They gave no credits such as "Painfully Harvested by Ami," or "Tenderly squeezed out by Siggi," and I didn't think that Fullo's cows were contented, at least not during his presence. One day when I was milking alone, I had a chance to test this theory. Blackie was a very nervous cow, and the only way she could be milked was by chaining her back legs together. I did not do so, and while talking tenderly to her, telling her that Fullo chained and milked me also, I attached the milk machine to her udder. Even though her eyes got big at the start, she never blasted me with her green ammo and her hooves.

◆   ◆   ◆

Fullo and I were in the barn. Again. I checked the udder of a cow to see if it were empty. It was hard, rock hard, and there was little milk in the machine even though it had been milking her for a long time. I asked my mentor:

"Why won't the milk come out of this cow?"

Fullo came over, lovingly stroked her bag, yanked and pulled a teat, forcing out a stringy chunk.

"She has mastitis," he concluded. "I'll milk her by hand."

He yanked her teats vigorously and when he was finished, he placed the resulting product by the entrance. It was always my job to carry the milk buckets up to the milkhouse.

"What shall I do with this milk?" I asked him later.

"Pour it into the tank."

"But isn't it unhealthy?" I ventured.

"Waste not, want not," the ancient wisdom came back.

His greed prevented him from discarding infected milk. I followed his order and emptied this strepto-bacteria-loaded milk into the funnel bowl that had a paper filter wedged over its coarse bottom screen through which the milk drained into the tank. Then I returned to the barn, and when I came back later, the funnel was still full of this concoction. Mastitis chunks and hair clogged its filter. Unwittingly I became an accessory to an immoral deed. I returned to the barn to inform my master:

"The filter is plugged. What shall I do now?"

"I'll show you."

He came up to the milk house, wrapped his stubby arm around the filter bowl to lift it, and expertly rapped its side with a piece of iron, hoping to dislodge the crud in it. I watched him beat it ever more vigorously, until I thought that he hit his pocketbook, although not his thumb, when the filter broke loose, emptying unmentionable additives into the milk tank. Since I was a pessimist, I stayed out of his reach. I was convinced that more than two hundred gallons of organic bone-builder were now ruined and he would take it out on me. But I was wrong. This was no problem for Fullo, even though he also was a pessimist. Optimistically he put a new filter into the bowl and scooped it through the milk tank to recover the stuff that was peacefully drifting in the pure-white milk. Afterwards he added a handful of chlorine powder and some water for good measure, thus converting *engrais de vache,* water and poison into money. *May I serve you?*

The creamery tested each shipment of milk for bacteria, butterfat and proprietary additions.

The butter wrappers said: "Color Added Seasonally."

Since I have color-confused vision, I could not be sure which color was added, although I had positively concluded after wearing, inspecting and testing it under myriad conditions, that one cow product was green. My masters also harvested milk for their own consumption, which I also drank, au naturel, unpasteurized, including their proprietary additives. I absorbed so many of these, as well as those from the chlorinated manure teas, that I developed a corrosive humor that would be with me for the rest of my life. And that's why I think I'm "full of it." Full o' Schitzma.

◆   ◆   ◆

Because I worked hard I lost weight. My ribs protruded and I was hungry all the time, and at six feet, I weighed one hundred-fifty pounds. Once after a dinner, Aunt Houwke asked Jolene to finish some peas that she declined. When Houwke offered them to me, I wanted to devour them but Jolene said, "I'll eat them because I don't want him to have them." That was OK, for unbeknownst to my masters, I robbed them to supplement my daily bread. I ate the grain of their cows, as well as the linseed and milk replacer for their calves. Evidence indicated that rodents were stealing from these sources as well. Fortunately, Siggi, however, was occasionally able to eat *day-old* baked goods that the bakery threw out by the barrelful, and which Uncle Deepo fed to his cows.

I figured that Siggi's daily routine was much the same as mine. He was not allowed to eat all he needed either, although he was still growing. When he came in from the barn in the mornings, he found his breakfast bowl already filled, thoughtfully, with corn flakes and milk that often was mushy before Siggi would get there to eat it. Usually everyone else had already eaten and the table would have been cleared. Siggi ate alone and could not refill his bowl, and like I, he was too shy to help himself from the refrigerator or cupboard. We worked without pay and were too timid to ask for seconds, because for so many, many years people had trained us too well to be humble and subservient.

Siggi was not allowed a single day off either and was treated almost as royally as I. Recently he told me that he once had asked Uncle Deepo if he could get a vacation.

"May I have a few days off?" Siggi had asked him.

"Why? Where do you want to go?" Deepo became worried.

"I just want some time to read in my room."

Siggi told me that thereupon Deepo had sighed with great relief.

He had asked a hypothetical question because he was never allowed one free day, not even one Sunday. Even so, our masters told us that it was a sin to work on Sundays. Fullo's rear window sticker even displayed: "Stop Shopping On Sundays." *Is it sinful to make your slaves work that day?*

Our family, that is Fullo's tribe, did take one extensive vacation in two years. Some Saturday morning, shortly after Fullo had bought a new, used car, we prepared for our trip by milking and shoveling out the barn. Then we all got into his car and drove to Yakima on the other side of the Cascade Mountains to return again to do our evening chores.

During our prolonged, relaxing five-hour vacation we never set foot in a restaurant because this might cost money. I believe that Fullo in his fifty-some years had never been in a restaurant. Oak barrels do not go to such places. Even so, I enjoyed my vacation with him because in my humble opinion he was enticingly crude, amazingly narrow-minded and brilliantly ignorant.

◆   ◆   ◆

Siggi did have a big change in his farm routine. During his last summer in high school, Maxo, the same Maxo who never even had to say, "Here kiddy, here kiddy," to entice us to come to America, used him on his tideland to help build a dike around several hundred acres. For this work Maxo bought him a forty-nine Ford for about two hundred dollars. This provided Siggi with mobility, a big step toward freedom. I did not find this out until weeks or months afterwards when he visited me one evening and we drove to a movie. The next day my cousins informed me that we had sinned. Long ago their church had received a memo, a revelation from God, classifying watching movies as a sin. We're sorry, forgive us.

Siggi earned at least a car for his work during that summer and made good use of it when Maxo became mad at him. He parked in a secluded spot by a river and slept in it one night. But the next morning he humbly returned into Maxo's arms because he did not want to go back to his underpaid in-the-manure position at Deepo's and needed to retain a shelter. Like so much about our family I would not learn about this episode until much later.

Siggi's visit was one of the few times that I was able to get away from my masters and do something enjoyable during my dirtiest two-year absence from life. At two other times some of my classmates would pick me up and rescue me for an afternoon. One of them was Pete who had had the epileptic seizure in the locker room. He lent me some gear, and we went fishing together in a small lake near Everett. While there, he tumbled to the ground with a seizure. I did not know how to help him, so I just had to let him shake, but I worried. After he finished shaking, he rose again, acted as if nothing had happened and did not talk about his illness.

Early on, before I had a driver's license, two other classmates, Bob and Richard, who were in the German class with me, had picked me up and taken me to the home of one of them. There we listened to records, ate hamburgers and talked until evening when they drove me back to the farm after dark. Richard asked me if I wanted to drive his car, and I wasn't sure if I would be able to. I managed to get into the first and second gears and tried to grind into third unsuccessfully. Since I did not have enough confidence to drive much faster anyway, I continued in second. I gripped the steering wheel and stared at the pavement ahead in our headlights. Our conversation seized because we concentrated so hard on keeping me from driving off the road or grinding up the transmission. Unfortunately I was able to return unscathed because otherwise I might have had a nice vacation resting in a hospital for awhile. I remembered that my clinic stay in Basel had been a great relief from my wonderful home life.

The only other fun occasion that could have been a lot more fun if I had been less soiled, and less shy, was when Frauke paired me with her girlfriend for a hayride. Thus I met Vera, whose black eyes were on fire when she looked at me. I could feel my eyes return her fire and little Frauke encouraged me:

"Kiss her. Come on, Ami, kiss her."

I wanted much more. But again I employed super-human self-control to prevent a long-term relationship. Or embarrassment. I needed to know if Vera would swoon from my intense and tender embrace or from my barnyard chemical makeup. My everlasting aura kept me from girls and fortified my shyness. *I'll save my fire until after a shower. After I normalize my brain about such matters.*

◆   ◆   ◆

In my English class I was required to present an oral book report. I searched in the school library for a suitable one to read, one that I might enjoy, and selected *The Wall* by John Hersey. But when the deadline for the report neared, I had only read part of it. Nervously I informed my teacher that because I had to work before and after school, I would not be able to finish it. I also read slowly because I was still learning English, and therefore he allowed me to report on only part of it. So far I had rarely spoken in class, then only under great duress and stress, had never presented oral reports, and now wondered if my German teachers would have allowed me to not complete an assignment and still give me a passing grade.

When I picked this novel I had no idea about its contents. It was written in the form of a diary but with a number of people contributing their experiences to the daily entries. I read many pages before the main subject came into focus, and I could not believe how this story developed because I had not yet learned of it. It was about the Nazis rounding up Jews in the Warsaw ghetto and hauling them off to concentration camps. This was too painful for me to believe.

I always had had stage fright. Now this imported, stinking, insignificant slave stood before his intensely staring victors, trembling, sweating and mumbling with a thick accent, stuttering about the evil deeds of his people. I will never know what I said, nor if anyone heard me or understood me, because I was in another world, in a terrifying world.

Since I had few useful thoughts and didn't know how to fry my brain, I continued to thirst for gratifying knowledge. I found another book, *Einstein's Universe,* and checked it out. I read it mostly on the school bus and during our vacation trip to Yakima. Boy, must I have confused others! They had never seen a stinky guy try to tap into a genius' insights before. Although I did not understand some of his theories, they fascinated me greatly, and I thought maybe I could become an astronomer searching for a relatively gentler life on another planet.

I also loved history. I had learned about the ancient Greeks, Romans, early Germanic history, peoples' migrations, barbaric invasions and crusades. I always felt that the history books were sterilized, with great importance being placed on learning names, dates and places. "Tiny the Great," "Giant the Magnificent," "Philosopher the Conqueror." Too often the biggest killers, the invaders and conquerors seemed to have been the ones to be remembered in our history books. When I had left Germany, my history classes had taken me to or through the European Middle Ages. I knew nothing about modern history, the most violent times ever, other than what we had personally experienced during World War II and its aftermath. I knew nothing of its eco-political causes. Germans did not dwell on this time period, their painful past, and I could sense this from their silence.

In my profuse readings in Germany I had rarely, if ever, come across the word "Nazi" and there seemed to have been a great information vacuum about this regime. Its literature and icons had been destroyed after the war, but as a toddler I had heard the word Nazi mentioned in conversations by adults. Allies and Nazis were something they had talked about in serious discussions that I did not understand.

Now my world history teacher dropped the final WW II bomb on me, twelve or thirteen years after its official end:

"The Nazis sent millions of innocent people into concentration camps. And killed them systematically."

Noooooooooooo!

After this class, in spite of my pain and shyness, I approached this teacher and told him that I did not know anything about concentration camps. So he showed me a photo of a mass grave filled with emaciated bodies. My heart stopped and my soul convulsed.

"This is what the Nazis did?"

"Yes," he said.

The teacher recognized my agony, closed his book, and said that he had to go to another class. I stuffed another painful memory into my brimming memory hole, to be locked away with all the others. At this time I did not wonder about what roles any of our relatives might have played in the Nazi schemes because I knew very little about either one of them. Everyone I ever met was mum about this subject, as if it had never existed. Even my American relatives never brought it up. Only many years later would I learn a little about how Pa had felt about Nazis from an undated letter that he had written to Ma shortly after the war:

"…When I hear from my fellow man about everything that is happening, it stirs within me my innermost feelings of deep thanks toward our God. He has kept us all healthy, saved our belongings, and not the least kept me away from the early Nazi influence."

He kept us healthy?

"Always and always, I have through innermost convictions recognized completely and correctly, with a direct prophetic talent, the entire Nazi methods, and therefore we are now not entirely severed from business and economy. Thank God and be happy together with me, be really affectionate and nice towards the boys, who are our greatest happiness of all.

"When I listen to the war crimes trials in Nuremberg and read in the newspapers about it, the redness of shame, anger and hate rise to my face to be a German, who for twelve years had to live with the craziest of all sadistic systems in the world. It is indescribable how these gangsters reigned and murdered..."

To protect my soul from other people's interest in me, I automatically tried to keep unpleasant thoughts from my conscious mind. It was their behavior and actions towards me that prevented me from focusing on the very creativity that could help me do well in school, and now, learn how to obtain freedom. Had I been able to think objectively, had I allowed myself to use my mind to search for useful knowledge, or to be counseled by someone who cared, I might have been able to improve our situation, Siggi's and mine. But I had not learned this because our parents had taught us little and, furthermore, it was their war and attitudes that always had put a damper on my thinking.

◆　　　◆　　　◆

During summer our workload increased greatly. As always, we started our days early in the morning with a kicking contest, man versus cow, and finished each day the same way. In between we fixed fences, made hay, delivered calves, de-horned them if they dared to grow frontal spikes, and removed balls to create neutral sex. Fullo and I chased his crop of bull calves into the barn and tied them to a post. While teetering on a milkstool, he twisted haywire around the scrotums of the critters. One of them became too wired and kicked the scrotum of his master. The pain that I felt for the poor critter neutralized what *Schadenfreude* I might have savored of what it did to my uncle. Birds of a feather, in this case the scrotumwreckers, do flock together.

After these bulls went haywire, fresh little steers gingerly tiptoed out of the barn and for days contemplated changes in their nature.

"Doesn't that hurt? What will happen to their equipment?" I questioned my uncle.

"Oh, they'll just fall off," he answered casually.

The masculine fall-offs arrived a week or two later when my canine friend, Sheppy, brought home some hard, black and shriveled pouches, reminding me that I always had to protect my own.

Like I, the cows were keen judges of character, and because of such treatment they did not like Fullo. In his presence they produced more green stuff and less white stuff, and I wondered if they could do this because they had control valves and sensors to adjust their systems to respond to his presence. But nobody liked Fullo less than Fullo, and his only purpose seemed to be to growl at everything that moved and to accumulate wealth.

Dairy cows are bred annually so they produce calves and more importantly, money. Presumably, breeding is pleasurable for the cow, the bull and especially for the farmer because it re-invigorates the flow of money into his bank account. That is if the bull didn't kill him first. Holstein bulls are huge and infamously aggressive. One spring day Fullo had one such delivered to his farm. Bully weighed more than two thousand pounds, excluding the ring and twenty feet of chain fastened to his nose. Thus equipped, he could raise this fad, body piercing, to a higher level to gross out the squeamish. He was allowed to run loose with the cows, dragging his chain with him wherever he went, whatever he did, but he was not allowed in the barn. He'd break out the floor to the haymow above with his big head when he tenderly thumped his cows.

When Bully finished his necessary duties after a few months, Fullo casually said to me:

"Take the bull back to Jones' farm."

"I am scared to," I courageously mumbled to my uncle.

"You old grandmother," he growled back.

Always remembering his oaken fist, his intermittent reinforcement to properly guide me, I had no choice but to return this stalwart bull by myself to a farm several miles down the highway. Stalwart Fullo told me that he had something else to do in the meantime. I went into the pasture, sneaked up to the bull from behind and grabbed the end of his chain that was dragging on the ground. Casually whistling, I led him through the gate onto the highway, like walking a dog. The bull plodded along obediently until we came to the other side of the barn when Bully's harem came running to the fence, singing in chorus. They ogled us with big eyes, and their ears propped forward, while they were shouting moo, moo, and mooooh. Since I did not understand their language I could only guess what they bellowed at us.

They must have asked Bully to return because he pulled me in their direction, presumably to do some sniffing, to check for *open* cows. I pulled vigorously on his chain in the opposite direction, to cool his desire, while looking for a safe place to get out of his way, when he realized that there might still be an *open* cow. I gathered that there must have been because he began to dig dirt out of the ground, while snorting spit and blowing his trumpet.

For his attack on me. And not on some *open* cow.

Quickly I wrapped his, or was it one of my chains, around a power pole and cowered behind it while he attacked it with his massive head. I feared for my life as Bully became madder by the minute. Enraged, he kept pushing his head against the pole while I tried to hide behind it. I was afraid that if I stayed there much longer, we might get hitched. A frightened slave might be hitched, together with an angry bull, to a pole that carried power. And there was no one in sight to witness this union, to shoot the bull, to save me, or to record yet another act of my reluctant heroism on film.

Siggi had told me that Deepo's bull had ripped his nose to get free from his troublesome chain. He did not like to be enslaved either. This could happen now and help Bully succeed in his revenge. Therefore, I carefully unwound the chain, and dragging it, I ran as fast as I could down the road with Bully in pursuit. The Holstein party in the pasture pranced, danced and cheered him on, giving him additional courage to invigorate his escape with me to our freedom.

I felt his chain slacken, his snorting draw closer.

My heart was pumping, my lungs were heaving.

Never say uncle.

As I ran out of breath, I jumped aside the instant before his head would have connected with my already abused behind. His mass moved past my ass and suddenly my chances for survival greatly improved. Blind with rage, he did not turn around to charge me but continued down the highway, dragging me along. Afraid of uncle, I desperately clung to his chain but could not keep up his pace. I was flying now. Bully tried to give me lift, the way I had run to lift my kites on wind-still days.

To hell with uncle.

Since I was now out of immediate danger of becoming *Suelze,* ground up bones, meat and gristle, my fear was replaced by rage. Rage directed at Uncle Barrel and not at his twin, Bully. I let go of his chain, not to be jerked around any longer. Bully kept on running toward freedom, dragging the chain between his legs. Relieved and exhausted I kept walking, while the bull disappeared around a bend in the road, and timed as if he had been watching us, Fullo drove up in his pickup.

"Where's the bull?" he asked grimly.

Breathlessly, I just pointed while he squealed away, leaving me to follow on foot. Uncle Barrel must have caught up with Uncle Bully, opened the gate to Jones' pasture and guided him to it with his pickup. When I met up with him, Fullo reminded me again: "You old grandmother," and I remember it well.

A chicken honored a torero as grandmother. *Can I get a* certificate of achievement *for this?*

◆   ◆   ◆

Besides farm work, I had to perform other tasks such as painting Fullo's houses and slaughtering his cows. I detested painting and I detested killing. I hated painting, mainly because I had to use solvent-based, oil-lead paints, and Fullo gave me few instructions or proper equipment to paint professionally. I assumed that one just slopped the paint onto the walls, doors and frames as fast as possible to reduce ones exposure to fumes that gave me headaches. The paint was too thick and did not want to stick; I could not get it into the corners. After adding thinner, it was too runny and flowed down my arms when painting up high and dripped on the floor when painting low. Skinflint did not buy me rubber gloves and the paint would not wash off my hands or spills. I had to clean up with solvents. *If I ever get ill from taking in lead, solvents, chlorine, rodent and bovine doodoo, should I award Fullo a* certificate of achievement?

As I said, I hated killing, but every year Uncle butchered one of his cows and graciously permitted me to help him, so I could quench my thirst for blood. When that day arrived, after milking and breakfast, Uncle and I returned to the barn to slaughter the designated cow, whose udder was almost dragging on the ground, plum worn out. He released this docile creature from her stanchion.

"Hold her head still. I'll hit her," he told me.

I hugged her head tightly. Poor little cow.

"Whack," Fullo clenched his teeth and hit her on the head, the way he had practiced this on me. But now he used a sledgehammer. I let go. I had never killed anything bigger than a fish, thinking that fish did not have feelings. This cow, Beulah, groaned as her tongue came out and her eyes rolled in their sockets. Beulah had feelings the same as I. But she now also had a headache, while I was getting queasy. She staggered but did not fall. Fullo humanely gave her another blow to further compress her brain. She dropped. We dragged her head to the *nutrient* gutter, where Fullo slit her throat with a sharp knife, to drain out Beulah's life.

When they could have been making blood sausage, the girls were home baking.

If I hadn't been as dense as everyone told me I was, I would have become bloodthirsty at this point. We hoisted Beulah up with a chain to hang her in her favorite yoga position, head down, in order to drain her completely and to lift her from the pristine lime-covered concrete floor. With a very sharp knife my master sliced open Beulah's largest organ, her hide, from top to bottom, down the middle of her belly. He gave me a knife also and ordered me to help undress her. He skinned down her left and I came down on her right. When we got to the bottom, Beulah looked very naked. Fullo expertly removed her head and gracefully heaved it out of the barn door with a grunt. Before long, my best friend, Sheppy, came running, and rudely dragged it around a corner.

We cut Beulah into quarters and carried out her hide and guts. I could give these parts a decent burial sometime later. At one time we would have eaten some of them, but now times were better. For now we left Beulah's quarters hanging in the barn in the company of flies, until Fullo took them to a butcher on his way to the mill, to have her cut into smaller pieces to be wrapped, frozen, cooked and eaten.

◆   ◆   ◆

Besides Sheppy, I did have one other friend, but did not want her to be my friend. She was a heifer that I had stolen from her mother out of the pasture right after she was born. Strangely her mother had not liked this and chased me off. After many attempts I was able to grab her still slimy calf, sling it around my neck and run as fast as I could to get to the safety of the barn. By the time I got there, her mother became confused or could not find us, and this calf bonded to me instead. Specifically, to my back.

This is what we should have done also, Siggi and I, when we were still slimy. We should have grabbed our father and never let go.

This friendly calf followed me everywhere and whenever she saw me she came prancing with joy. To get my attention she pushed her head into my back and continued doing this for months whenever we met. One day, when she had grown much bigger than I, as I was walking through the pasture, she came up from behind, and I was unaware of her. She rose on her hind legs and placed her front feet on my shoulders, hopping along behind me. Line-dancing through the pasture.

Since I feared that the whole herd might learn to participate in this, I had to convince this heifer that I was not her mother. I line-danced her into the barn, bribed her with grain, and put her head into a stanchion and locked her in. Then I cut off her horns with a big surgical tool designed specifically for this purpose. Since I was no surgeon, I cut too close to her head and a fine stream of blood spurted from each wound. I felt sorry that I did this, but she left me alone after our bloody experience.

The lesson then is, nip undesirable fads in the bud before they get out of control, unless, of course, you have the uncontrollable urge to squeeze some blood out of such turnips.

◆   ◆   ◆

Beef was not enough. Fullo also asked me to butcher chickens, some of the most innocent of all creatures. I was to butcher about six of them for freezing. Of course he assumed that I knew how to do them in because you didn't need to tell a "grandmother" how to kill chickens. I laid one down on a board, stretched out her neck with my left hand and chopped with my right. I had read books but not about this, and I was not a skilled mountain man and worried about my hand. Fullo must have too because he advised me that my technique was dangerous. *Am I insured?*

"Hold her by her legs, upside down," was his advice for my next victims.

"What if she moves her head?" I questioned.

Her wings fluttering vigorously, I clutched my victim's yellow twigs, inverted her, and let her head rest on the surgery table. This calmed or scared her into complete limpness. One little round eye stared up into my eyes. Blink. You don't know what a quick wink from a little round eye can do to a six-foot man. I blinked. Chop. I missed her neck; I missed her head, chopped off her comb and before I noticed this, threw her away. Like the first hen, I expected her to bounce around and drain her blood. She did not do this but ran around the yard instead with all of her former friends chasing her, the rooster and I as well.

Each wanted her blood. Like some people, they also knew that "you have to get them while they're down." With pain and guilt I raced around with the flock trying to catch my crownless victim. Flapping wings, screeching and cackling confused us all, and I could not catch her. This was an emergency. This hen and I were in pain, and the other chickens were bloodthirsty. I picked an apple from a tree and aimed for her eye. The apple knocked her over, she twitched and shook, then did not move anymore. This relieved me greatly, and I laid her back on the operating table to sever her head.

Next.

I chopped off the remaining heads by the mountain man method, regardless of insurance. Then I dipped them all into hot water, plucked them, and with the help of my aunt, further prepared them for the freezer.

◆   ◆   ◆

As my high school graduation drew closer, I saw no options for our future. I was completely penniless and had only the clothes on my back. Since I had no car and lived out in the soggy country, I was unable to look for a job to escape my slavery, and there was not a single person in the world to help me. I felt as if Siggi and I were destined to spend the rest of our lives in the deepest of dairy doodoo. I had little social contact, even with our relatives, our masters. I had spoken little in the past and spoke even less now. Ma wrote to them after we had arrived here that:

"Ami and Siggi, especially Ami, have chronic silence, exactly the opposite from me…He would be a good Catholic father to take confessions, he is as quiet as a grave."

Ma! You should see me now. That's where I want to be. But my masters want me to stay. Free labor is impossible to find.

I was unaware about jobs and job training in America. I felt that it might be similar to Germany, where everyone followed one of two rigid systems of development, from school to apprenticeship, to journeyman status. Ma had chosen the other path for us, to attend a *Gymnasium,* to be followed by a university. In either case, along the way there were always rigid examinations, and I had no idea that in America anyone could easily get menial jobs and without much training or tests. Had I known this, I would have soon left the farm and never returned.

◆   ◆   ◆

One day I meekly announced to my masters that I wanted to take the grade prediction test that was offered toward the end of my last school year. It was required in order to gain admission to Washington's colleges. Even though I had no chance to attend one, and even though tests petrified me, my guardian angel decided that I should take it. It was to be administered on a Saturday, a day without school buses.

Coincidentally, Aunt Houwke and her daughters wanted to attend a church party on the night before this test and demanded that I drive them there. I courageously declined because I always retired early so I could get up early to play with the cows. I wanted to be rested, especially now, so I would do well on this test. But after some harassment, I consented to go if we could return by ten o'clock that night, and they agreed to this.

Ten o'clock came and went, and they showed no intentions of going home. Enraged, I went to the car, started it, squealed two-hundred fifty horses out of the parking lot and through the city as fast as they could run.

As a perfect slave I didn't think of it.

Without booze or any other kind of external stimuli, my supportive relatives lingered past midnight and were the last ones to leave the party. *Did they stretch time intentionally to tire me out, or just decide to become party animals because they had never had such an exhilarating sensation?* During the two years I was with them, they almost never left the farm in the evening, probably because it would cost money, except that on rare occasions the girls had stayed overnight at a friend's house. When I drove home that night, I was more worried than mad, and my passengers probably knew this because no one spoke a word. Were their thoughts the same as mine: "Mission accomplished"?

The next morning, while I was hurrying from the barn back to the house, Houwke shouted after me:

"Don't think you can have the car after you drove on two wheels last night."

I said nothing.

She had not said this at midnight because I had driven within the speed limit. Teary-eyed, I kept on walking without looking back. At the house I washed off any visible body paint, changed clothes and walked to town. I would be late and was tired, hungry, stinky and depressed. Fortunately a classmate, Bob, who was also heading for this examination, stopped and offered me a ride. I did not tell him about my predicament because I kept my problems to myself. He was very friendly, and I did not know if he could smell me, or smell my dilemma.

◆   ◆   ◆

I did not think that I did well on this test, and my scores confirmed it. They foretold that I would fail college English and do poorly in other subjects as well. The day I received my scores in the mail, I went down to the barn as Frauke waddled up to the house.

She yelled down at me across the highway, "How are your test scores?"

"Not very good," I replied glumly.

A smile lit her face.

"Now you can't get into college, ha ha, ha," she cockily returned. Those were her actual words, and as Dave Barry says, "I am not making this up." But like so many before her, she would be wrong about my abilities and my future and happily thought that now she could keep her servant forever. Or she could have been wallowing in *Schadenfreude*. I could not foresee my future either, but when you're only a *Guellefahrer* slave…

*Life **cannot** possibly get worse!*

5

THERE'S NO END TO THIS LIFE

When will we be free?

◆   ◆   ◆

On my high school graduation Sunday, Fullo and I were sitting in his living room, when with great concern for my future, he casually asked me:

"Would you like to continue to work here?"

I wanted to shout, "Are you full o' it?"

"I guess so," I mumbled instead, while shrugging my shoulders. *Did I just seal my fate for life?*

I had no choice, either stay here or secretly live in a barn somewhere, to feed with cows. But that would not be much different from what I was doing now. I was still too intimidated to ask how much he would pay me or about anything else related to my employment. For my two years of work for him, he'd never paid me one cent, except twenty cents for school lunches and dimes for the church collection plate. He even had stolen what little German money I had brought with me and had displayed it at the county fair, along with Houwke's vegetables, to win a blue ribbon. My only reward from him had been minimal room and board and an occasional whack on my head. In addition, I was also allowed a few days to pick beans and strawberries at nearby farms so I could buy some clothes and school supplies for myself.

Siggi and I did not even know who had paid for our passage to America. It was very doubtful that it had been Pa or Ma. Many years later Maxo would tell Siggi that he had paid for it, and that Fullo had pressured him for me to reimburse him for my trip. This was akin to a plantation master asking his slaves to pay for their voyage into the unknown after their arrival there.

In some ways, Siggi and I were worse off than the earlier slaves because we were completely alone in a new land. We were isolated and could not draw strength in numbers from companions in suffering. Like them, we were torn from our homeland, had to work hard without pay and could not escape to freedom. And we could not derive hope from an underground railroad or a war that might liberate us.

We became slaves in a foreign land as a direct result of our Progenitors' War. When our parents should have supported, counseled and guided us, they were fighting each other. And against us. Pa never paid any attention to us; Ma's whip paid too much attention to us. By the time our war would end with a bizarre peace in the mid-sixties, Siggi and I would be strafed in the crossfire of at least **twenty lawsuits**, involving at least **two dozen lawyers and judges** that I someday would identify by name. The foundations of our lives were not cemented with friends and family ties or fortified by religion. Missing were the steel re-bars that prevented the collapse of concrete buildings during earthquakes. *Will the constant tremors someday collapse Siggi and me?*

I still had no money, no car, no friends and no means or a place to which to escape. Fullo never suggested a wage and nothing more was said about this subject, so my status quo was maintained for the time being. I did not know if Siggi had any plans or if someone had made such for him after he graduated. However, a few days after Fullo's generous offer to me, his brother Maxo visited us. He had hooked Siggi and me with delectable virtual bait to land us in America and now needed somebody to work for him. *Was this why he had acquired us in the first place?*

"Jiminy cricket, doesn't anybody want to work anymore? What is this world coming to? The Communists are corrupting this country!" expressed political Maxo. I learned that "jiminy cricket" was Maxo's favorite expression. He could cuss in a highbrow fashion because nobody would know what a "jiminy" was, and everyone would think that he flew to India to play cricket. He owned several thousand acres of tideland that his parents had bought long ago for pennies an acre from our distant relatives, the Bursmas. While we were still living in Simonswolde, we once had visited a Bursma family in the nearby city of Norden. I remember that they had given Siggi and me each one Deutsche mark so we could ride a carousel at a nearby carnival. Eventually Maxo became the sole owner of the tideland. When one stood at one end on a clear day, and had good eyesight, one could barely see the high structures at the opposite end of his land.

Every day the tides covered this marshland as they had for eons. Maxo wanted to farm some of it and the salty tidewater had to be stopped from flooding in. During the previous summer he had hired a nice man, nicknamed Bud, to build a dike around several hundred acres with his dragline shovel. Bud had dug clay out of the ground to build it, and in the process created canals on both sides of the dike. However, during the winter, the fierce storms and high tides had eroded it substantially and had washed a long section of it out into the bay. *Did this require an environmental impact study? Or qualify for taxpayer-sponsored disaster aid?*

This washed out dirt and the sediments coming down from the rivers and shorelines helped build up the undiked portion of Maxo's tideland, thereby enlarging it because it was officially recorded to extend out to the waterline of the lowest tide. The more sediment that built up on this mudflat, the further into the bay moved its boundary. Since it was so flat, it did not require much rise of the land to extend the run a long ways out into the bay.

Now Maxo wanted to fill in this gap in the dike and strengthen it along its entire length. He and Fullo agreed that I would help with this project. I suspect that this was their arrangement from the very beginning, but they had left me clueless. Slaves, like children, do not need to know what is planned for them, especially since such information might encourage rebellion. But for obvious reasons I was ready for a different kind of work.

Siggi was already working on the dike when I arrived there, and he and Maxo were staying in a little old house on Freddy Bursma's farm. I was sure that by moving there, I would increase my chances of gaining freedom. We had little money but were allowed to pump gas from Maxo's tank for Siggi's car. Sometimes he even would give us a few dollars so we could see a movie.

But now Siggi and I worked harder than ever, mostly building a new bulwark of lumber on the outside of the dike to protect its clay from erosion. Bud drove pilings into the ground with a pile driver at regular intervals. In the areas where the dike was the lowest, Siggi and I pushed posts into the ground with Maxo's bulldozer. During high tides, which also occurred at night, we floated truckloads of boards down the nearby river to intermittent places along the dike. Floating was the best way to transport the great quantities needed to build this two-mile long revetment because trucks could not easily access this muddy area. We spent most of the summer nailing planks to these posts and pilings. Afterwards Bud filled in the resulting space behind this board wall with more clay from the borrow pits.

We also cleared the big tree roots and trunks that had been deposited over the years and had gotten stuck in the mud. We sawed them apart and blasted them with dynamite to be able to bulldoze them into piles for burning, because the ones outside of the dike could be set adrift to damage it again during subsequent storms.

On hot afternoons, Maxo brought us ice cream cones to boost our blood sugar in order to sustain our production. Even though we worked hard, I did not mind this so much because we were mostly without supervision and could smell the sea air and often bathe in sunshine. Mud was better than manure, and we could eat all we desired. Maxo was a good cook, compared to mother, and fed us a lot.

Uncle Deepo's son, our cousin Willem, also helped us for several weeks and Maxo paid him one dollar per hour. Had I known this, and had I had the courage, I would have requested to also be paid a specific wage on a regular basis.

Later in the season after our work diminished, I did occasional yard work for Bud and his wife. She made a note in her cookbook that "Ami will make good someday." Years later, I would visit them again with my bride, and Bud's wife would show her prediction to us to confirm that she had been right.

◆   ◆   ◆

One evening we were having dinner in the unfinished basement of Freddy's house where Maxo prepared our meals. We discussed our progress and what we had to do next. He had a sample of his cooking stuck to the corner of his mouth, where he usually kept a specimen until it fell off. Frequently he also decorated his shirts and pants with various soups, sauces and beverages. His designs were arranged in an artistic fashion on his shirt and around his zipper, where his fly advertised that he peed more often than he re-zipped.

After a greasy dinner our talk became serious. Our bellies were full, and Maxo savored his usual coffee but shouldn't have. His blood pressure increased to the point that it created a pink patch of a map of his tideland on his balding forehead, at a scale of twenty thousand to one. He acted like a jet setter, leaned back in his chair, pensively drawing on his cigarette much like a plantation owner would smoke a cigar. He talked importantly about politics and drew upon his vast education and experiences to observe that Washington D.C. was corrupt. There were goons who were interfering with his freedom to build a dike, to develop clam beds and also were stealing the fruits of his labors. There were mysterious events happening in the nation's capitol. When we asked him for specifics he became nervous and vague. This indicated that there could be some basis for his claims, or he could be paranoid, since he never mentioned names but always referred to everyone as "they." He traveled to the East every winter but always was very secretive about what he did there, so I asked him directly, "What do you do in Washington, D.C.?"

"I work for the State Department."

"Doing what?" I questioned him further.

"Oh, I travel to Eastern Europe and write reports," he answered, looking at the table as if it had asked him that question, while the map on his forehead became more defined.

He was always so nebulous about his employment that people teased him that he worked for the CIA. He never denied it because he liked to play the spy role, as well as the professor role and implied by his demeanor that this might be the case. This image was reinforced in that he never smoked before he left but was always very nervous and smoked heavily upon returning. We could tell that there was something troublesome in the nation's capitol. Was it its politics or was it simply the rat's race of its traffic, especially because he was a very inattentive and inept driver? Whenever Siggi or I rode with him, we worried greatly for our safety because he ground gears, drove too slowly and drifted out of lanes. But after a few weeks back on his tideland, he would always quit smoking and calm down again, although his driving would improve little because of his lack of attention.

◆   ◆   ◆

That summer Siggi applied for admission to Washington State University and was accepted. I had no idea how he could pay for it, did not ask him, and gave little thought of attending college myself. The scores from my grade prediction test were too low, I never had much confidence in my academic abilities, and I had no money. In Germany only the elite attended the *Gymnasium*. We had been lucky in that respect, even though we had to struggle to meet the academic standards, and I more so than Siggi. I also thought that only the elite attended college in America and dairy cowboys were not quite the elite. After Siggi entered college my desire for freedom intensified, and I told Maxo that I would also like to get more education.

"What can I do for a living? Should I go to college?" I asked him, instead of "how much will you pay me?"

I watched Maxo's face grow dark while he gazed at the food that he was preparing. My instinct told me that I had said something unpleasant to him. He continued to fix his stare on his work while the electrochemical activities inside his skull increased dramatically. He appeared to be thinking:

"How can I tell him that I want him to work for me forever?"

Instead, he humanely told me that I was a little lazy and stood around a lot. He expected me to wrestle and pound more vigorously, and to emphasize his remarks he continued that Willem also had that opinion. *I weigh one hundred and fifty pounds. My hammer is heavy. Reward has nothing to do with one's drive to succeed in slavery.*

Then he cheered me: "Let me see your grade report."

Obediently I dug out my final grades from high school and showed them to him.

Then he landed his final punch, such as I had suffered before.

"You are not smart enough to go to college."

My heart dropped into my dirty shorts, then bounced back into my dry throat. I believed him and had no reason to think otherwise. Often I hesitated before responding to others, to fill in the words that I had not been able to hear clearly, to construct the meaning of indeterminate sounds. When you don't hear well, stupid people will conclude that you are stupid and some will also tell you so.

For as long as I could remember, a heaviness hung over my soul, but I could not define it. I did not know what it was or where it resided. A blackness often burdened me and interfered with most cognitive thoughts, but I did not realize that this was so, and that most people did not suffer from such a state of mind. I did not recognize my SSS, Scorched Soul Syndrome, which surely must have contributed to my poor performance in school.

◆   ◆   ◆

One day during late summer Maxo had another brilliant insight:

"Why don't you buy your brother's car to help him with college?"

Maxo paid me intermittently only a few dollars, and I didn't know how much per hour, or if my pay were in arrears. We did not keep time sheets, and he was always vague about our work, our pay and our future.

"Help with what?" I shot back at him.

"We'll work it out," said Maxo.

"I don't want to buy it. The tires are bald and the springs are sagging."

"You should help out your brother," Maxo insisted.

He had a strange sense of humor, had no clue about reality, knew too much about reality, had a perverted thought process, wanted to exploit me, or a combination thereof. My net worth could not have been more than twenty dollars, he probably had more than a million, and Siggi worked for him and not for me. He did not explain how I was to help Siggi. His plan was to retain me permanently on his new farm. He did not tell me this at the time, but oddly enough, he told me this when he visited my wife and me long after I had left his tideland. He knew that an ignorant slave was easier to manipulate. To give hope in lieu of pay, he dangled virtual carrots before us with vague promises of help. He was single and often lonely and retained a few friends and relatives in contact with him by implying that some day they might inherit some of his wealth. His method worked quite well because it attracted them like, ouch, I bit my tongue again, honey attracts flies.

As it had been on the dairy farms, Siggi and I did not know if we'd ever get paid a fair wage, and we did not even know what a fair wage would be. I was still held captive with invisible chains, while Siggi was quickly loosening his. I worked without complaint and was ignorant of such basics as wages, paid vacation, health insurance, and Maxo kept quiet about tangible compensation for us. But intermittently he made insinuations about future rewards. Since Siggi and I were isolated from the outside world, his vague suggestions were singular, powerful incentives for young people with little hope in a foreign land.

I had no means to help my brother with college. We never received any help from anybody, expected none, and did not know if and where it was available. Our mother's court battles with our father had always provided insufficient means for our living, and therefore we knew how difficult it was to get money. Ma had fought for it like the devil, and our labors on the dairy farms earned us not even enough food. Now, as before, the one I lived with and worked for kept me intentionally isolated and ignorant.

◆   ◆   ◆

That September I drove Siggi across the state with the old Ford to take him to college. The question of its ownership was not resolved because it was still registered in Maxo's name. Long after this, Siggi told me that I never paid him for it, and I insisted that I had not bought it. I did not pay him personally and Maxo apparently did not pay him enough on my behalf. At this time I had signed no transfer papers for this car. The vague idea of its ownership was part of Maxo's manipulation to keep me befuddled and tied to his land, while at the same time making me think that he was paying me a decent wage by implying that the Ford was part of my wages because I was allowed to drive it.

I did not know how much Siggi earned from Maxo. Since neither one of us received a regular wage, I thought that the Ford was a reward for work that Siggi had done during the previous summer. Now it became my reward. Occasionally Maxo gave us some money in the spirit of making a *gift*, which it was not. We more than earned his *gifts* with our hard work on his tideland. Nevertheless, Siggi and I appreciated whatever little he paid us because otherwise we would have continued to have nothing.

◆   ◆   ◆

Before he left for his annual trip to the East, Maxo drove with me to the employment office in Everett to find a job for me. Or so he said.

"What kind of work would you like to do?" he asked me on the way.

I did not tell him that I wanted to be an astronomer and count the stars to compute the size of the universe because I did not know how to go about becoming one. I did not know what I was or what I could be. I was dumbfounded because I had not given this much consideration. I mainly had had experience in cow and *nutrient management* and spike hammering and lots of it. I barely had had any outside contact and was not the world's greatest listener or conversationalist.

"I don't know," I shrugged.

"Would you like to be a grocery clerk?"

"Maybe," I answered uncertainly.

I felt uneasy about having to work with the public. It meant having to smile politely, cluelessly, when someone asked me a question that I did not hear well enough. It meant being ignored when my slow monotone speech put someone into a trance. A future friend would tell me that I sounded like actor Peter Lorre. I was born on the edge of the Black Forest; he was born in the shadow of Dracula's mountains in Hungary. He had a low voice and a slow speech also. Even so, he became a famous movie star, and therefore there might be hope for me also.

Maxo led our way into the employment office.

"Do you have a grocery clerk job?" he asked the officer.

The bureaucrat searched his files.

"No, we don't have anything around here, but there is an opening in Pasco."

"Is that in Texas?" I inquired hopefully, confusing it with El Paso from a Western song.

"No, it's in Eastern Washington, one of the Tri-Cities."

I felt ignorant, I was ignorant. It was one of the worst traits in a human being, to be ignorant. But I did not know this because I was ignorant.

Maxo did not ask about other types of jobs or what other openings there might be, and we filled out no papers. If he really wanted me to get one, he would have told me to apply for the Pasco job or for anything else that was available that I would be able to do, no matter in what city or state it might be.

On the way back to the tideland, he informed me, "I have to fly to Washington D.C. next week. I want you to stay on the tideland and keep an eye on the dike."

"OK."

"Also, I want you to take my mother from the nursing home twice a month and drive her for a visit with Uncle Deepo."

"OK."

Freddy's house where we had stayed for the summer was located several miles from Maxo's land. Now he informed me that he wanted me to live on his tideland and drove me to the abode that he was going to move there. By now I had learned not to expect too much in my new homes. Rather than getting hyper again, I acted disinterested. Unlike our homes in Rheinfelden, this one was not a mansion. It was not a mobile home, trailer house or cozy attic. It was a shack. I had never seen such a dilapidated hut in my whole life even though there had been severe poverty and a great housing shortage in Germany. This contraption was built of pressed fiberboard decades before and had expired long ago.

It was to be my American Dream but became my German nightmare. I felt severely homesick because it was so much like my sick old home in the attic. It had no electricity, no water, no telephone, and worst of all, there was not even an outhouse. My father didn't think that his children needed a toilet, so there was no reason that a slave should expect to have one.

After we hauled my new home to the tideland, we placed it behind the old dike on the neighbor's field. We placed it exactly square with the world, so it would not look so out of place, so there'd be a hint that an architect might have designed it. This location would also provide some protection from the frequent southwestern storms and serve as a scarecrow for destructive hunters. Maxo wanted me to observe his dike during the winter, not only because of Mother Nature, but also because humanoids, euphemistically honored as *Vandals,* were destroying his property. In the past someone had thrown dirt into the fuel tanks of the equipment, and hunters had either mistaken his boat for a spruce goose or had wanted to titillate themselves with *Schadenfreude.*

After we protected my new *mobile home estate* with *Lifetime Warranty, Gold Bond* quality roof covering, I moved into it with my keepsakes. To go potty, I just went out to the frequently wet and/or muddy field and let it all hang and fall out, au naturel, always cognizant of which way the cold wind was blowing. There were no bushes or trees where I could hide, and unlike our attic, I had no neighbors whose toilet I could use now. As in the good old days, I could not wash my hands or take showers. To get fresh air into my new home, I kept the windows closed because they leaked so generously. Although I had moved yet again, I still felt so much at home.

All winter long I brought in drinking water in an old milk can, timed between storms, when I could spin and slide the Ford all the way to my in-the-mud hut. My standard of living was now lower than ever, when I had been sure that this would have been impossible. Now I was a lonely, powerless, waterless, toiletless stick stuck in the mud. I thought that I had reached the zenith of my accomplishments when I had belonged to the virtual Boys Club in high school long before I grew facial fuzz. And as yet, I still did not have to shave even though I was almost twenty years old.

◆   ◆   ◆

I was getting desperate about earning an income so I could become independent and begin my life. Anyone would be desperate in such a situation unless one was like Mahatma Ghandi. I was not, or not yet, and I wanted to discover what I could be. I now had a car that I could drive and a little money that Maxo occasionally "gave" me. This allowed me a taste of freedom. *Do I have enough confidence, intelligence to overcome my lack of guidance, knowledge and support to escape to freedom?*

After my eighteenth birthday, Fullo had taken me to a draft board to register me for the Selective Service. I could be selected to be drafted because I was classified 1-A, the category to be called up first during man-made crises. From my perspective from the mud flats, I saw no other employment options, so I visited the Army recruiter who smiled from a poster. If I had to work, I might as well earn some money and serve my new country as well. The recruiter wanted me to serve inside a tank of a tank corps. I knew that I'd suffer severe claustrophobia inside a tank because it would be a mobile bunker, but nevertheless I agreed to enlist.

I rode a bus with a group of draftees to the Seattle induction center for the required examinations. There we had to take written tests and fill out lots of papers that also required our health histories. The soldier in charge said that anybody who lived in the Seattle area should add "sinus trouble" as an existing ailment. Since coming to the Evergreen State, I had had a lot of bloody snot that continued to worry me a lot because I had never had such before. I even had told my secret to Aunt Houwke, and she had assured me that this was normal, and I had seen daily Dristan© ads in the newspapers that made me wonder if everyone had to sniff it in order to keep breathing.

I was not sure of all the diseases that I had had as a child, but there had been many. After completing our paperwork, we prospective servicemen were herded into a big room, told to shed all clothes and assemble in a queue to be inspected. In this queue were thin ones, fat ones, tall ones, short ones, and some with short ones and some with long ones.

I stared at the floor. *This place stinks like a high school locker room. How can a mass of flesh, such as this, annihilate other masses of flesh such as this? And for what? Land? Power? Tomatoes? The rules of the Geneva Convention have to be amended that all wars be fought by naked men. And naked women. I'll volunteer without pay...*

"Bend over!" came from behind.

I snapped my butt to attention.

This was not worth fighting for. I squeezed shut, fearing to offend the inspector of the assembly line.

"Spread your cheeks," he ordered me.

A man I had never seen before ordered me. I was stark naked and yet he ordered me. Everyone always gave me orders, whether I was fully dressed or stark naked.

"Good. Next."

I straightened up again, blushing. Blood had rushed to my head from bending over. Down the line came another orifices inspector and stuck a funnel into my left ear. Shone a light through it.

"OK. Right ear."

"Jees!"

You mean cheese, Mon?

He removed the funnel and replaced it with a clean one.

"You have a problem," he advised me as he made a note on his clip-board and continued his inspection down the line.

Later a Uniform mumbled something to me.

"Pardon me," I asked. He was authority.

He did not repeat what he had said to me. Important men do not repeat; they can throw tantrums. Uniform threw the papers to the floor. He must have asked me to take my papers that he had handed to me. Naked, I stood under the gaze of naked men. Befuddled, not having heard his request, I said nothing, nor did I pick the papers. Uniform did and gruffly handed them to me. This lesson was not lost on me. I had disobeyed an order, but only because I had not understood it. I did not have to obey everyone, not even Uniform.

After the physical exams, our herd dressed again and was led into a corral without windows where we had to wait. Sometime later a herdsman wearing a spiffy uniform and a snow-white cap arrived with the results of the tests for which everyone was anxiously waiting. The first call came.

"Neuman." That was I.

"Here," proudly I rose, waved my hand and stood at attention.

"Get your ugly face out of here," is how this important man shocked me.

Only Germans had insulted me in such a manner before. No one had ever done so in America, except my uncle Fullo. I will remember forever what he had said to me because he prevented my escape. Unfathomable wisdom had to be remembered, to be passed on down through the ages. Maybe someday someone will find the answer because I have not yet discovered the association between what was in my orifices and my appearance. *Was it only because I was ugly that I could not escape?*

When I was told that I was ugly, the draftees cheered because they hoped to receive this message for themselves. They didn't care if they were ugly as long as they did not have to kill or be killed. I came here seeking a job, even though I might have to scrub latrines in the service of my new country, as I had scrubbed my adoptive cows. Since this man had called me ugly, I remained in the corral to see if anyone else would be ugly because I had to wait for my bus anyway. But he found no one else to be so. Oddly, after he called up most of the names, he called me again, and I again raised my hand.

He said to me: "I thought I told you to get your ugly face out of here."

I had learned enough now, so I traveled back to the womb of my pressed-board shack. Back to my homestead with hair-trigger dynamite under my bed. I had never entertained the idea that I could use this dynamite to express myself to get people's attention. If I did, people dumber than I or less experienced in heroism than I, would just think, what is wrong with this boy? Is he crazy? Not, why is he blowing up the world? Who caused him to do that? What drove him to desperation? Who should be punished? Who should be sued?

◆　　　◆　　　◆

A few weeks after Maxo left for the East Coast, he wrote me the following:

"I was sure happy to receive your letter and hear that everything is O.K. and that you are still going strong in spite of your troubles. I remember when I had my first car. It was an old jalopy, and needed many repairs, but I found later on that I knew a lot more about the cars after I was through fixing them."

I feel such kinship with your struggling soul. I'm thankful that you let me drive your jalopy.

"You mentioned that the road had not been graveled. My plans are to close all of the hunting and the travel on the road, if those people using it do not put gravel on it, as they promised.

"If no one comes by the first part of December, you may let me know and I shall write to Tiffany to put on enough so that you can get in and out with your car or truck. If I have to put gravel on, then you should put up 'No Trespassing' signs where my road starts. To the devil with the hunters if they want to treat us that way. That will end the hunting in years to come too."

*Treat **us**?*

"I can well imagine you cannot do anything with the Caterpillar, and it may be best to let it go until the weather clears up."

If you can imagine your bulldozer getting stuck, why can't you imagine me drowning in mud?

"However, if there is a chance to make some cedar fence posts, you could try and split a couple hundred. Only if you are out of work. I would like to have you clean up the tracks on the cat and paint them with used oil to keep them from becoming rusty. Perhaps you have done it already. Then take out the batteries and throw an old canvas or plastic or something around it for the winter. I believe Uncle Deepo can help you get an old canvas. Then it is just about in as good a shape as if we had it in a shed.

"You mentioned what should be done with the dynamite. Ask my sister how much of the dynamite she wants and take it to her, and take a little extra down there in case we need some. If there is any left, let Mike have the rest. He can also get the black powder that is in Freddy's shed. The powder is dangerous because it takes only a spark to ignite it. However, I am not aware that dynamite is that dangerous. Dynamite should not be thrown around…

"Now with Siggi. Your brother wrote me a letter saying that he was well and coming along well in school. Do you think he should go the next semester to school (if he does well)?"

Since when have you asked me what we need or think? Are the natives getting restless?

"Would you want to help him out if he does not have enough money? Maybe he should work after the first year and help you get started, if you want to go to college? Actually he should find a fair job, if he does well in school. I will let you think it over and perhaps you should talk it over with Siggi."

Just tell me how much you are willing to pay me.

"I see where you had an 11.7 ft. tide at 6:46 this morning. (I have the tidebook lying next to me.) Have you had any storms? Has the revetment been hurt any? I am interested in this and in you. Please write as soon as you can.

"Give my regards to Freddy! Do you still have food and money? If you lack you should talk to my sister."

Shall I ask your sister to build a road, install water, shower, electricity, cookstove and a refrigerator?

"I will try to get a pair of binoculars to be used on the dike. Would this help you?

Sincerely your Uncle Maxo"

Have to research the "uncle" part.

Since Maxo H. H. Schitzma thought that dynamite was not that dangerous, I was not too concerned about it. I kept it under my bed because that was the only place where there was room for it since my hut was the only shelter on his tideland. However, this dynamite became so mushy that I could push a finger into it. I assumed that the watery pearls on the surface of the sticks were condensation because of the damp air in my cold hut.

The hut had an oil stove next to its exit door. This stove had a three- or four-gallon tank attached to its back and was located about three feet from my mousy arsenal bed. But I rarely fired it up because, like my groceries and drinking water, I also would have to bring in the fuel oil. It was just too troublesome, especially when I had to carry it several

hundred feet over slippery mud when it was raining and that was prac-
tically all winter long.

In my constant struggle to become civilized, I mostly wore pajamas
to bed instead of muddy clothes. One night I woke up freezing, so I
attempted to light the stove. To do this I opened a valve to drain some
oil into its firebox. It was too dark to see if, and how much, oil entered
it, so I had to guess how far and for how long I had to keep this valve
open. Intermittently I threw lighted matches or burning paper into this
oil that was not very volatile because it was so cold. Frustrated that it
would not light, I stuffed newspapers into the stove and lit it. After the
fire finally started with a roar, I adjusted the flow control and returned
to bed.

The stove and pipe began to thunder, pop and crackle and became
very hot. I jumped out of bed, shut off the oil valve and dove out of my
hut. Outside, roaring, flickering shadows told me to keep running.
How hot can stovepipes get? How hot can dynamite get? When I turned
around I saw that the chimney was a giant torch lighting up the night.
Barefoot and shivering at a great distance, I did not return to bed until
the stove burned itself out.

Because of my warming experience in this cold night, I thought it to
be a good idea to carry out Maxo's request, so the following day I carried his dynamite to the trunk of the jalopy. To do so I had to embrace
the box to hold its soggy bottom together. Getting it to the respective
parties required me to drive on a bumpy road. Only years later did I
learn that I might have been dancing with the devil, when the following article in my local newspaper enlightened me:

"MOSCOW, (IDAHO) (AP) Andy Shemline did not want officials
burning his barn to dispose of old, possibly dangerous dynamite. So he
took care of it himself…

"Latah County sheriff's deputies spent most of Thursday searching
for Shemline and the dynamite…

"Shemline said he decided to tell deputies what he had done Friday. But he made detectives sign a form saying they would not prosecute him if he revealed the whereabouts of the dynamite.

"Sheriff's Lt. Vern Moses said officials thought the public safety factor was more important than charging Shemline.

"The decision to burn the barn was made after explosives officials from Washington's Spokane County advised Moses that it would be dangerous to move the dynamite.

"'No one wanted to burn the barn, but compared to risking an explosives technician's life, there was no question what we had to do,' Moses said.

"Instead, Shemline disposed of the dynamite by dousing it with petroleum to neutralize it and then removed it from the barn and burned it, he said. He went to the University of Idaho to research the matter and learned how to dispose of the dynamite himself."

Maxo, do you know how close you came to sending me to the attic in the sky?

When I told Siggi about this article, he confirmed that one could wipe off the drops that formed on aging dynamite sticks and fling them to the ground to make them explode. The liquid beads were not moisture but highly unstable nitroglycerin. He also informed me that during his first summer on the tideland, while carrying a box with dynamite on his head, a not-too-distant explosion that was set off by someone else shook him.

Our guardian angels had protected us as they had so many times before. They had saved us from bombs, bullets, head-rot and Ma's high altitude boiling. They had safeguarded us during many serious illnesses and starvation, from our father and his Teufi, from our bomb making, from spoiled and E. coli-charged foods and unwashed fingers. They had protected us on a raging ocean, from raging bulls, and who knows how many other attempts to reduce us to dust. And now they had protected us from ignorance. *But why had they blessed us with so many lawyers?*

Our send-off to heaven would have been in such a unique fashion. Blow our bodies into little bits, sending them flaming into the sky, to rain back down like brilliant rockets on the fourth of July. But we would not have been wasted because our stir-fried parts would have landed in big circles to feed our little friends, the mice, foxes, ducks, geese, crows and magpies.

All of this was nearly accomplished without forethought. But what a thrilling afterthought!

Although my life was spared again, and I could not shower on the tideland, I did take an unexpected bath that also could have done me in. After it had been raining heavily all night, I was driving to town and crossing a big hump in the road that was part of an old dike, when my car splashed into a swirling sea of muddy brown water. Unbeknownst to me, the nearby river had risen over its banks. I waited and pondered how I could continue my journey. Because I grew impatient I put on the rubber hip boots that I always carried with me in the car, entered the flood and continued float-walking, trying to follow the submarine roadway as best as I could. But the current became too strong and I floundered into a hole, immersed to my armpits. Afraid that I would be sucked down the river, I struggled back to the car and drove home to dry out again. *Is there no end to **this** life?*

◆   ◆   ◆

Although I had missed a lot of chances to depart from Earth, I observed others coming down from the sky to lose their lives during another brief relief from my boring existence on the tideland. While I was returning there late one afternoon, I observed a large airplane descending into the mountains far from an airport. I kept watching it until it disappeared over a forested peak, barely missing it. Since it appeared that this plane was in trouble, I turned toward the direction of its flight to investigate further. I reasoned that this plane was unable to control its path because it did not change its course to land in the open pastures at the bottom of the foothills.

Before long, the car radio confirmed that a Boeing 707 on a training flight had just crashed. A couple of vehicles with "Press" decals passed me at great speed, and I tried to follow them, thinking that since this was a very low-population area, they were also heading there. Although they left me in the dust, I later found them parked by the edge of a forest, along with a few other cars. I looked for a road or trailhead but could not find any. So I took a chance and simply went straight into the thicket, in the direction the vehicles were facing, to struggle through the underbrush, hoping to find the crash site. Within a few hundred yards I came to a clearing, a huge disaster area around a small river. Only a few people had arrived here as yet. Like everyone else, I was browsing around the widely scattered debris when a sheriff announced that anyone who was not with the press or on official duty had to leave this scene immediately. Dutifully I headed back into the woods to where I thought I had entered. But night had settled quickly, and I encountered such a dark forest that I could not even see my hand in front of my face. I felt and beat my way through thick brush. There were no lights or stars, and the only sound that I heard was my thrashing about. I had no idea if I remained on a straight course or if I were just struggling through a random pattern to be lost forever. Strangely, I did not worry about this, or that I might fall off a cliff, and miraculously exited the forest within a short distance from my car.

◆   ◆   ◆

Maxo's apparent concerns for Siggi and me in some of his letters were part of his scheme to keep me on the tideland under the guise of actually wanting to help me. He only hinted about helping us but always evaded my probing questions with his own questions. He advised me only superficially and did not do anything useful to help me. His artificial concerns were like Pa's occasional interest to fool

someone. Maxo, like Pa, had a few words of support but never followed them up with concrete actions. Siggi told me that during his first
summer on the tideland, Maxo and he had had long discussions about
various subjects. Therefore I decided to impress him with my intellect
and simply asked him:

"How does a person think? Does one ask questions?"

His face formed the same worrisome expression and the pink map
appeared on his forehead, just like the time when I had told him that I
wanted to get more education, and he just mumbled:

"No. I don't think so."

That was the end of our debate, and I could tell by his demeanor
that he did not want to talk about this subject under the principle of
"let sleeping dogs lie," let slaves be ignorant. Again I read his thoughts:
"I can't let him start thinking."

In his letters he wrote me that he was worried about the storms
destroying his dike. Coffee intensified his worries because it stimulated
his nerves and brain enough to create vivid nightmares. He once told
Siggi that he had never slept through an entire night for as far back as
he could remember. I confirmed this problem years later when I stayed
with him in his house for a few nights, and he would wake me with his
shouting dreams.

I followed Maxo's suggestion and enrolled in night school at a jun-
ior college, now community college and soon to be a university. Eventually it might become something that hasn't been thought of yet,
maybe something like intergalactic super-cyber university. I enrolled in
mechanical drafting and descriptive geometry and did well in these
subjects.

One evening, during my commute to the intergalactic super-cyber
university, I thought that my steering felt soft or wobbly. I inspected
my tires and discovered that one front one was worn through and its
inner tube was bulging out. I did not know for how long I had been
driving on air, and it was a miracle that it had not blown out, especially
at highway speed. Although it was getting late in the day, a stranger

stopped to help me. Since I did not have a spare tire, he drove me to the tideland and back again, and when I offered to pay him he refused to accept anything. He told me that if I'd help someone else, he'd be satisfied.

◆　　　◆　　　◆

Often the field to my shack became impassable because frequent rains turned it into sticky, slippery mud. After the jalopy buried itself to its axles, I pulled it out with Maxo's Caterpillar. This packed clay into the very tracks that I had cleaned and oiled so well. From then on I parked the car at the end of the gravel road and changed into rubber hip boots to be able to walk back and forth between my hut and car. Mud would ball up on my soles and travel up the sides of my boots. At times the wind would howl and cold rain would blast me when I returned home from school late at night. Inside Villa Schitzma-in-the-Mud, mud accumulated faster than I could sweep it out. I quit brooming and shoveled it whenever it became too deep because it would dry into concrete-like slabs or wear into a fine powder.

I noticed that I did not live alone because the decor inside my villa was further enhanced by the black rice that my mostly invisible little pets generously sprinkled over everything, including on my bed and *kitchen* surfaces where I prepared uncooked, straight-out-of-the-can, gourmet-type meals. So far my little decorators had always scurried into hiding whenever I entered, and I did not realize until the darkest of winter that I also did not sleep alone. One morning I opened my eyes when a mouse bolted away from my face. Thereafter I was determined to kill them immediately, vigorously and mercilessly before they pierced my ears or other sensitive organs. But I could never stop them from coming.

Besides furry pets, I also had feathery friends that were afraid of me. There were dozens of swans, hundreds of ducks and thousands of snow geese. They did not want to be shot out of the sky, so they landed on the tideland only at dusk or during great storms. Sometimes I'd sneak up to the geese from behind the dike and slowly peek over the top so as not to scare them. It did not take them long to spot me, however, and then their racket would start. With honking and screeching that could be heard for miles, acres of white, flapping and fluttering feathers rose to circle the fields, rising ever higher to sail away into the sky.

◆   ◆   ◆

To provide me with companionship, Maxo thoughtfully had left me an old car radio and battery before he departed on his annual winter trip. But within a day or two this battery went dead. I resumed reading and occasionally visited Freddy's in the evenings to watch television. Maxo also bought me a subscription to *The Christian Science Monitor* and sent me a paperback book, *Ethics*. I did not know the meaning of this word and found it puzzling that he expected me to read or understand these publications. *Was he looking at me as a college man or as a slave master?*

I read these publications religiously with a dictionary close at hand. Initially I was unable to comprehend the meaning of *Ethics* but doggedly worked my way through this book, underlining the words that I did not know. I looked them up and reviewed them later so I'd remember them. From the *Monitor* I learned the words "ultramontane" and "insurgents." I felt that I should become one but did not have the courage to be a lone rebel.

At night, a camp lantern provided a gloomy light in my shack. It was more luxurious than a candle, and I didn't like candles anymore, especially at Christmas time. But this lantern was supposed to be used only outdoors because it produced a lot of soot. In the black deposit on the ceiling, I traced with my finger "HOME SWEET HOME." My deeply ignored message went to the *sanitary landfill* when Maxo discarded my sweet home after my escape from it. *Great health benefits far in my future?*

◆   ◆   ◆

One day I was driving the Ford across a single-lane bridge when a farm truck came onto it from the other direction, and we stopped bumper to bumper in the middle. Since the driver was very beautiful, I did not back up to let her pass because I was still not civilized. She smiled, I waved, and she backed up her big truck to let me through. I noticed the name of a food processor on the truck's cab and later called there to find out her name. A voice at the other end of the wire told me that they didn't give out information about their employees, and I wished that she hadn't smiled at me because I never saw her again.

Occasionally I went to church with Maxo's sister near Monroe. There was a tall, blue-eyed, blonde girl in attendance that I had to meet. After the sermon I inquired about her name and wrote her a letter to ask her for a date. She accepted and we dated for a couple of months. I was almost in heaven until I found out that she was still dating her old boyfriend as well. Keeping a girlfriend was as difficult as earning a dollar. What could I expect, I didn't even have a toilet. To acquire a flushing toilet and a shower with warm water became the goals of my life.

◆   ◆   ◆

Maxo did not communicate well verbally, even though he had almost earned a master's degree, having completed everything except his dissertation. His verbal discourse could be very ambiguous because he'd use pronouns without identifying the person or object referred to, as in "they did this," "he did that," causing the listeners to wonder who did what. Frequently this became even more confusing when he did not introduce the subject matter or changed subjects without transitions. Often he also spoke while walking away from the person he was addressing or did not finish his sentences. A banker once told Siggi that

Maxo must be very intelligent because so often he could not comprehend what he was talking about. His unique method of bamboozling people could be as confounding as legal and insurance documents, and it did not require much intelligence.

Maxo's friend Mike asked me to help him build a loafing shed for his, gulp, dairy cows. They both had given me the definite impression that they had an agreement about this. I wanted to get paid every week but did not receive anything from either one of them. I mentioned this to the carpenter whom I was helping on this project, and this started a grapevine that eventually reached Maxo in the nation's capitol or beyond.

Up to this time Maxo had written me friendly letters because he worried that his dike would be destroyed again and wanted to make sure that I quickly repaired any damage. It had cost him, or the Unknown Taxpayer to whom a monument has yet to be built, a lot of money to restore it after the previous winter storms. He wrote me instructions and demanded that I inform him weekly of the status of his dike, tides and weather. But I did not write him often enough because I did not like to write, as words did not come easily to me. I was struggling with my soul and the forces of nature, constantly repairing his dike by filling hundreds of sacks with clay and driving hundreds of stakes with a sledgehammer, often in the wind and rain. In December, after Maxo learned that I was complaining to someone about my pay, I received a letter from him, wherein he skillfully tugged my chain to make sure that it still was secure, while intimidating me with the most powerful method available to him:

"Apparently you don't find it necessary to write me a letter to tell me about the project, and how you are getting along at least every second Sunday (taking mother along and back to Snohomish). This was agreed between us and you could and should talk over the problems and difficulties you have with my sister. Instead you act and do towards my friends as if I were responsible for your troubles, etc. This is something that Americans (and good people in Europe) don't do either. I am not going to stand for this. Actually you act like a boy, when you should act your age. For this reason I am telling you in all seriousness to do the following, or else I am through with you. If you don't do the following I will write to Uncle Fullo immediately and you will have to go back to him. He is your guardian and he sponsored you to come to America. He is responsible for you."

Slaves are sponsored? Like athletes? Can I get paid to be on TV? Wish I had a TV.

"…So now it is up to you; either you do the things you agreed to and follow directions, or I am through with you and you go back to your guardian.

"Sincerely,
"Maxo Schitzma"

No more "uncle."

Earlier I had written him about his concerns, and that I was working hard to protect his dike, but our letters must have crossed in the mail. I also sent him photos showing some of the eroded areas of the dike. After he received them, he wrote the following letter to his protégé but in a different vein from the previous one. He seemed to be more concerned about my happiness and offered me greater virtual rewards than in the past. What he had learned from me greatly worried him; the dissipation of his dike and the possible escape of his slave:

"…and going often to my sister and discussing your personal problems with her. I have made arrangements with her as I told you before, and she can help you. You must not keep things within you, because they work themselves up to a regular explosion of bitterness. I like your last letter particularly because you tell me a lot about yourself and the dike. As you know you can get up to $50 a month from my sister, and your tuition, gas, food, etc. This is all I can afford at the present, but I think you can help prepare yourself for life by studying and at the same time look out for my interest. **You can be sure, if you look out for my interests there, I will do all I can for you.**

"I want you to eat well and get your meat and eggs from my sister and let her buy you canned goods. You should become a fine cook, and by eating well you'll feel better especially on the work on the dike. Eat meat, eggs, vegetables and milk every day, and plenty of them and not so many sweets."

Keep food fresh without refrigerator and cook without stove? Lick dishes clean like a good mother? Are you as deeply in denial as my father?

"Now as to the dike. The pictures shocked me when I saw them and it is probably more serious than you realize. If one or two storms did that what will happen when the storms come between Christmas and the 20th of January?

"...By all means do a lot of visiting, when invited, and in Monroe also go when not invited. I would like to have you go there every Sunday, if you can. Santa brought you something here, and I am going to send it to my sister, because you will probably spend Christmas there. I hope you like it."

What could it be? An electric shaver. A used electric shaver. A used electric shaver with used shavings in it. But where is the 2-mile long extension cord?

"Now see that you get the revetment in order, and write me every week how much progress you are making.

"Sincerely, your uncle,
Maxo Schitzma"

"Uncle" again.

The tone of this letter was opposite from the one before because he knew that his dike was disintegrating, and he needed me to repair it during the continuing storms and high tides. I was cheap labor, and in my humble opinion, greed and hypocrisy seemed to be the primary traits of the Schitzmas. Another growing season would be lost if his land flooded again with saltwater. Even though he was wealthy and expressed concern for me, suggesting what I should eat and finding a girlfriend, he made no effort to improve my living conditions.

Although some of the hairs on my head now seem to be growing in a reverse direction and are pushing out of other places, I am still waiting for Maxo to help me all he can as he had promised. When he died recently, I hoped to reap my reward, to receive the pay that I had earned so long ago and was happy to learn that a lawyer had prepared a will for him. *Will he reimburse me for my labor and my deprivation of a toilet and other civilized conveniences?*

I did my best to do everything that he requested me to do. I inspected the dike frequently, especially during storms and high tides. Since most of it faced squarely into the prevailing winds, the waves assaulted it with great force, washing it out in many places. The sea rolled in from the open bay and crashed abruptly against the boards, blasting through the gaps between them. The highest tides also washed over its bare top, diminishing it somewhat in height. I worked alone filling hundreds of gunnysacks with clay to plug the holes in the dike. I did so by hanging these sacks in a wood frame to hold them open so I could shovel dirt into them. After tying them shut, I dragged them, and dropped them into the washouts behind and in front of the lumber bulkhead, some of which I had to re-nail first because it had been smashed from the pilings.

And so I continued to live and work from day to day, alone on the tideland, miles from nowhere. Deepo, brother of Maxo, came to visit me. Once. I was glad to have company, any kind of company, but he did not help me, offered no help, and therefore I was not very hospitable. I did not offer him lunch and did not demonstrate how I had to prepare food in my fine gourmet kitchen: gracefully wipe black mouse rice from the counter, plunk lunchmeat on bread with flair, and pour milk down my gullet from a carton. I could not be debonair.

◆　　　◆　　　◆

Since Maxo had ordered me to take his mother to Deepo's farm, I picked up my date at the nursing home and drove her there. She was in her eighties, had dementia and often did not recognize anyone anymore. She sat next to me in my jalopy and just kept staring and smiling at me, and strangely, seemed to like me.

One early spring day, while returning from such a date, I drove past the pulp and paper mills in Everett and almost impulsively turned down the road toward the plants. They did not look or smell very inviting, and I wondered why anyone would want to work there. But I was curious about the myriad buildings, tanks, pipes and machinery from which all the smoke, steam and stink were coming and was stopped at the guardhouse at the end of its entrance road.

"May I help you?" asked the guard, the dreaded authority.

"I am looking for a job," I replied uncertainly. I did not anticipate being stopped and questioned, so I gave a legitimate reason for entering these premises.

The guard gave me directions to the office, and I went in to fill out an employment form. Again I was required to supply the health history and therefore was sure that I would not get a job here. *If the Army won't hire me, why would anybody else?* Ma had sent me the health history that I had requested, and I dutifully recorded everything: whooping cough, measles, diphtheria, *Rotsucht* (red craze or rash), *Nesselsucht* (nettle rash) and mumps. And of course the chronic middle ear infection and long-term exposure to tuberculosis. I could not remember having had consumption per se, but when a doctor in Aurich had looked at my lungs with a fluoroscope, he had reacted with an enthusiastic good-grief-like comment because my lungs appeared to be scarred. Even though I must have been a potential corpse, the factory hired me.

◆   ◆   ◆

At the age of twenty I had my first paying job. Hurrah, hurrah! I decided to move out of Maxo's shack and into an apartment in Everett close to the mill. It had a bathroom! My first and my own real bathroom! Hurrah, hurrah! To pay for the first month's rent, damage deposit and expenses, I applied for a seventy-five dollar loan at a nearby bank, which was more money than I had ever had at any one time.

The bank teller advised me:

"You have to see that loan officer over there."

I walked over to his desk where he asked me to sit down. I felt uncomfortable in the opulence of his office, his *Herrenzimmer*.

"I would like to borrow seventy-five dollars."

"What do you have for collateral?" the loan officer asked me while handing me a form.

"What's collateral?"

"It is something that you pledge as a security for your loan."

"Nothing," I said.

I could read the banker's face. "Where did this guy come from? I wish he would get out of here."

"You mean absolutely nothing?"

"These clothes here."

"Do you have a job?" queried the banker.

"Yeah."

"Where?"

"Screech and Stench Pulp and Paper."

"How long have you worked there?"

"I am starting next week."

He phoned the company to confirm this fact, thereby implying that I might be a liar, little did he know, and wrote me a check. I was elated. I had made one of the biggest decisions in my life, a decision that was not made for me by other people, to borrow money, had acted on that decision and gotten results.

That weekend, feeling exuberant with new freedom, I visited Fullo's family where Aunt Houwke served tea. I announced that I now had a paying job, and we caught up on important family news that was worthless for me. But it was not long before Fullo asked me if I could help him for a minute. "Sure," I said magnanimously. I was independent now and could not be chained again. Besides I was wearing nice clothes, so I could not get too deep into Fullo's ubiquitous doodoo.

He led the way down to his slaughterhouse barn. Again. When people lead you to their barns, especially if they don't tell you why, watch out. I didn't because I was becoming a trusting soul again, or was still a shy one. There he picked up a pitchfork and handed me a shovel. As we walked over to the milkhouse the air decayed. I suffocated.

There it was.

My spirit decayed.

There was a mass of crawling, wiggling maggots reveling in the putrid carcass of a onetime cow. Fullo had butchered her weeks before and had ostentatiously left her leftovers near the milkhouse by the highway. *To advertise his business?* In the meantime these leftovers had come back to life. When life got out of control, he must have been overcome with doubts, and therefore asked me to help him bury life.

An opportunity was knocking on my noggin that I could replace my nausea with the greatest of joys, *Schadenfreude.* To permanently cure his habit of exploiting defenseless imported slaves, I impulsively grabbed Fullo with a chokehold, flung him to the ground and sat on him. Then I pushed his face into the stinking, squirming remains and vigorously pounded it repeatedly into them, in order to squish a lot of maggots up his nose and ears. And into his soul.

But I didn't because I didn't think of it. Instead I held my breath, dug a hole as fast as I could to bury the squirming carcass.

Again, as always before, he did not thank me for helping him because he couldn't get a life, but fortunately, I was almost beginning mine.

◆   ◆   ◆

The personnel officer at Screech and Stench did not interview me, nor tell me what I would have to do, and I didn't ask him. But I was impressed that his company paid a doctor to give me a physical exam and a hearing test, free of charge.

I reported to work on a Monday evening because I chose to work swing shift as it paid a few cents, a lot, an hour more. After I was asked to buy leather gloves and a long leather apron, meaning that I was not going to work in a Musak-enhanced, climate-controlled office, Boss led me deeply into a huge windowless building, into the bowels of screaming hell. I followed him up and down various levels, through a labyrinth of posts and beams, cranes and stacks of lumber. Slabs of tree trunks were screeching through saws and screaming planers. Wheels were spinning, chains and belts were squeaking; thousands of boards were resting, stacking and moving hither and yon.

I resisted the impulse to run back out. *Not here, God, please not here.*

We neared the other end of the building; I could see daylight ahead. I was relieved when we went back out and into a long open-sided shelter covering a river of boards, laid side by side, on a set of moving parallel chains bringing them out of a dark cavern at the far end. Except for the squeaking of the chains and the clapping of the boards, it was quiet here. Men scurrying along the riverbanks were pulling them from the chains, to load them onto stacks, by length and grade. My guide stopped here and spent a few minutes explaining to me the various grade marks on this lumber. Since I was a quick learner, I needed no further instructions for my lifelong career. I was to catch selected boards from the river and stack them on the riverbank behind me. This was the extent of my training, and he did not introduce me to the others because they had no time to stop wrestling big ones from the cellulose river.

I took my station between two human robots that paid little attention to me. I donned my gloves and apron, strapping down its leggings, feeling armored and invincible like the knights of medieval Europe. I lifted the end of a board in order to pull it onto a stack. *Are these made of iron?*

It was heavier than any board that I had ever lifted, and I had lugged hundreds of them for Maxo's dike. This board was full of sap, rough-sawn, and had been part of a log not too long before. I lifted the twenty-foot long two-by-twelve over the rollers mounted at the edge of the waist-high platform, pulled it off, guided it unto a stack and dropped it with a clap. Turned around, grabbed the next one, pulled it off, threw it into place, turned around, dashed to the left, pulled it off, smashed it into place, dashed to the right...all night long.

When the sun set that evening, it dawned on me that I was working on the "green chain," which I had heard about in high school as being the toughest job in town. But what I despised most in my new profes-sional life was the lack of interaction with the robots around me. While I wanted to be friends, to enlarge my tiny family circle, they did not talk.

When will I become a robot? Will my brain shrink in proportion to the swelling of my muscles? Had shrinks studied them? Should they reproduce? Yes, yes! For the good of the shareholders. How do I become a shareholder?

When my body-morphing, character-warping encounter was over at two o'clock in the morning, I followed the robots out of our disassem-bly plant. As soon as I reached level ground without obstacles, I ran to my jalopy even though I was dead tired and my legs were rubbery. My arms felt inches longer, my legs somewhat shorter, and my back crooked, ready to break. When I arrived home I fixed dinner: five bowls of corn flakes with milk and sugar. While I ate, I read, because I thought I had wasted the night, for I had not yet rejoiced in the night that the Lord had made.

The next evening I returned to my station on the wooden river, and I was doubtful that I could last very long doing this heavy work. My body was aching. The boards never stopped coming. At times I could barely keep up with the flow, running back and forth along the river, lifting boards, while making male guttural grunts, at various locations to remove them. I was using every cell in my body, all but my brain cells, which were cocooned as always.

These boards were sawn from beautiful trees ripped from the balding mountains. Trucks had brought down their corpses and dumped them into a mass-grave pond at the mill, whence they traveled on a chain to be denuded. A giant arm moved along them, blasting them with jets of high-pressure water, to explode off their bark. The pale, naked trunks then moved single file into the sawmill and through giant saws with dragon teeth. Butchers pushed buttons, moved levers to shuttle them back and forth to rip them repeatedly. After each cut they decided how to turn the remaining trunks for best economy, to send them back and forth again to cut more planks. These then traveled to the "green chain" for the historic event, to be sorted by robots, the first humanoids ever to touch them.

And so the weeks dragged on. Night after night after my shift, I ran back to my jalopy, no matter how exhausted I was, because I could not wait to get out of **this** hell. I wondered why others did not run out also. *Are they crazy? Or am I? Can they not run anymore? Had their hopes been sawed to dust?*

◆   ◆   ◆

Siggi returned from college for his summer vacation and moved into my sparsely furnished apartment. We finally had our own apartment, freedom and toilet. It had not been easy to acquire this.

And we had motivation.

After I arrived home from work at night, I always wolfed down cereal while reading, then fell into bed at three or four o'clock in the morning. Siggi would be asleep, and we saw each other only on weekends because he had a day job for a generous one dollar sixty-eight an hour in a camper factory far outside of Everett. Besides earning a few cents an hour more, another advantage of working nights was that it was cooler then. Sweat was a by-product of my labors, therefore the Screech and Stench salt mine company supplied us free salt tablets from vending machines. Candy bars cost a dime.

Again our bed sheets changed from white to gray but not as much as before, a hint of old home style. We were too tired and too independent to waste time, effort or money to wash them regularly at a self-service laundry. Nor were we making much effort to cook or do dishes. When we were thirsty, we drank out of a milk carton. When hungry, we opened a can of peas or beans, warmed it on the stove and ate directly from it. I often had four Danish rolls for dessert. Or six. Our diet was as routine and junky as our work. Ma never had cooked but once, so we had no interest in it, and our spare time was too precious to do more work that we did not like.

Our small apartment on Broadway in Everett was the top of a two-story shack with a flat, black roof and dark brown siding. Or it could have been cowy green. The rising summer sun quickly heated it to afford us the ambience of the tropics. Humid heat often woke me in the mornings, and my muddy sheets would often be tangled around me. This was the setting of "On Broadway" that we listened to on the radio.

I usually rose by noon and was home alone because Siggi was at work. We could not afford a TV, so I got a quick fix for my anomie by reading and eating. Again, while reading, I devoured cereal, boiled eggs and drank from Hi-C cans or paper cartons. We never drank soda or alcohol because they were too expensive, and we had no peers who pressured us to do so. We had not yet found friends here with common interests and the same concerns for the problems in this world, and the papers said there were many. During these days people built shelters in the ground for a possible atomic war, and I thought this to be silly. I did not want to bury myself alive in a bunker because I had done that before, and I didn't like it. If the missiles came I wanted to be their first target.

"To the citizen or the police;
We must love one another or die."

◆   ◆   ◆

After several weeks on the green chain, I was transferred to the planing mill. This was the last place I wanted to spend eight hours a night. This was where I had asked God to keep me away from when I passed through here on my first day on the job. Here I had to do the same kind of work, pulling and stacking boards from conveyor chains. These did not weigh as much after having been trimmed, kiln-dried and planed smooth, so my work became somewhat easier, but my torture became much greater, although I was harpooned by far fewer slivers. I was now totally immersed in the one hundred-plus decibel shrieking of wood planers, music from hell. It was louder than jets during take off, as painful as the screaming of air raid sirens that had been stretched into one continuous, unwavering note, evoking the unending, soul-piercing agony of yore, nights of shuddering tremors.

Inside our huge bunker several jets shot out wooden missiles in ceaseless salvos. Their noise joined with that from other machinery to send vibrations that quivered every molecule in our world. I could not escape from them. They quivered every cell in my body, and I could hear them without an ear; I felt them in my bones. To talk, we robots shouted directly into each other's ears but mostly communicated with a simple, crude sign language that was punctuated by the *bird*.

The Company did not provide us with ear protection because this did not yet exist. *Or did it?* I never saw anyone wearing earmuffs. To dampen hell, I stuffed a wad of cotton into each ear, which made no difference in the sound exploding inside my head. After leaving work, I always removed waxy cotton from my whistling ear, rotten cotton from my silent ear. I always checked this cotton to assess the state of my health, to assess how rotten I was. The nightly cacophony would diminish my hearing acuity considerably later in life, gradually being replaced by permanent whistling instead. Now I continuously hear the screeching of tiny planers, distant echoes from hell, with my only and withering ear. In lieu of a gold watch, this was my fringe benefit from the Company for my faithful and outstanding service.

Most of the lumber we produced was a nominal two inches thick, but occasionally three-inch thick beams came down the chain. These had sharp edges and were dripping wet. We also had to remove them from the conveyor and drop them skillfully onto stacks like all the other boards. To do so, I had to let them slide through my hands to be able to keep up with the production, and before too long, their knife-like edges sliced through the rubber gloves that I always had to buy myself, like my leather gloves and aprons, pickling my hands with preservative or pesticide. *Can I be preserved until I die and long thereafter? Can I remain forever with King Tut, or better yet, with Nefertiti?*

I worked overtime every chance I had in order to earn enough to attend college in the fall. Therefore I once rearranged tons of lumber for three and a-half consecutive shifts. By the time I finished my second one, I could barely crawl. On Saturday morning, on my way to my final shift, after about three hours of restless sleep, I put on my boots and staggered out of our apartment to another off-Broadway performance. Siggi bid me adieu with an intensely serious face, "You walk like an old man, Neuman."

I was going back into the bowels of hell and, therefore, needed a lot of encouragement.

Rare were the signs, "Warning. Ripping Dragon Teeth" or "You May Get Squashed Like A Bug Area." There were so many hazards that there would be signs everywhere. Some robots might spend their entire shifts trying to read them all and produce nothing.

Over the time that I was drawn nightly to this mill by my desire to further my education, while keeping a toilet, I observed differently modified robots. One occasionally rotated through the nearby "You May Get Squashed Like A Bug Area" area. A crane had dumped a load of lumber on him and broken his spine, which had been repaired with bones cut from his legs. This shortened them and when he walked, they appeared to move in a rapid rotary motion under his rigid spine.

At this stage he was still not wearing a hard hat or visible back support. Not many robots did and neither did I.

A few weeks into summer I witnessed another robot modify himself. His job was to cut defective portions out of the boards that the lumber grader diverted to him. He pulled these from his left side and placed them squarely in front of a constantly spinning circular saw. To make a cut, he stepped on a button on the floor that caused this buzzing saw to jump forward through the board. And finally through his fingers. Panicked, this robot stumbled around. I became almost paralyzed and could not help because I did not know how. I could not even become a gawker because I could not leave my station at the lumber conveyor. Fortunately several robots were hunters and helped him; they had practiced with sawed off bones before.

The wooden rivers never stopped flowing because there could be no slowing of profit. The highest standard of living in the world had to be maintained and what are a few digits of a robot? If one becomes useless, we can always get another, and he'll be thankful to work here.

◆　　　◆　　　◆

Since I was a chip off the old block I was horny. A bleached blonde who had had to get married at the age of fifteen, bore twins in Texas and divorced at seventeen, was living next door to us. In the afternoons, the three of them sometimes came over to sit on the lawn with me. Her little girls called each other "peehole." I was not used to such loose talk from someone so young, although I heard much worse from robots.

Blondie was also horny as well as aggressive. One afternoon she visited me, and we started kissing on the couch. Oh, did I want to. Oh, did I have to. And she even more so because before I knew what was happening, she unzipped my pants and grabbed me around my muscular chest and said... *What did she mean by that? Was that a compliment?*

Apparently to encourage me, she continued, and her exact words were, "The only time I'm ambitious is when I'm pregnant."

Even though another body part was in total control over my actions by now, oddly, my brain kicked in. My conscience would not allow me to create another "peehole," one that I could not support, or she would not love. I wrestled her to re-zip, she wrestled me to unzip, and so it went until it dawned on me that something could get caught in my zipper or somewhere else. Therefore I ran out of the apartment before I got caught or lost control over myself. Wearing only her bra on top, and I can't remember what on the bottom, she followed me out into the alley. Flipping me off, she yelled after me, "You *expletive-deleted expletive-deleted*," for all the neighbors to hear and to see. Fortunately she was chasing me, or they might have thought that I had attacked her. *Would anyone ever believe that she was trying to do me?*

◆   ◆   ◆

I worked at the planing mill until fall. In the interim, I had applied at Washington State University and much to my surprise was accepted. In the middle of September, Siggi and I drove across the state to Pullman in the old Ford that neither one of us owned. We carried no insurance for the jalopy, or for our bodies, but for now it was mine to keep. It was still in Maxo's name, and Siggi still thought I had not paid him for it. I never owned it, never signed any papers, and I had not been paid enough by Maxo for my work on his tideland. *Was he also encouraging real brotherly love?*

We took turns driving across the state and after several hours when Siggi was driving through the middle of nowhere, I said to him: "Stop a minute, I have to get out."

He stopped, I squirted. Before I could get back into the car, he drove off. He stopped. I ran after him. He drove off. He stopped, he laughed, we laughed. He drove away. I walked. Finally he let me back in. It was a happy time under the expansive blue sky of America, and we were off to college.

We arrived in LaCrosse and Siggi was still driving. Suddenly, as we approached a stop sign, our car swerved around and screeched to a halt, almost square with the road.

"What did you do?" I asked frightfully.

"Nothing. I didn't do anything," Siggi replied with worry.

We got out and discovered that a steering arm had come undone, causing our front wheels to cross in LaCrosse.

"Wow! If that'd happened at sixty, we'd be dead now," I philosophized, feeling that our guardian angel was still with us.

We found a service station and the mechanic who fixed our steering told us: "You are lucky guys."

We've always been lucky??!! I wonder what the future will bring.

Ami and Siggi's mother with her parents and sisters. The left side of this photo, which depicted her two brothers and grandfather, had been torn away. Ma never spoke of them.

Ami was born in top left corner apartment which was subleased from Mr. Doebele who also lived there. He suffered from advanced tuberculosis but the hospital had dismissed him. To keep Ami a healthy baby, Ma placed him in the sun in one of the windows. He suffered a heatstroke and was almost cooked. His first stroke of luck.

Pa, Aunt Adele, Oma and Ma with Ami and Siggi (sitting) in front of the Simonswolde house. At times up to four families, mostly refugees, lived simultaneously in this small home. Pa took this photo with a self-timer during one of his few visits. He always had enough money for film, luxury cars, alcohol, cigars and women while his family had to literally scavenge for food.

Pa took this picture of Siggi and Ami while visiting them in Simonswolde. Ami is wearing leather pants and scratchy homespun, knitted wool
stockings that were held up with garters. Their leather pants were the only
new clothes they ever owned up to that time and for many years thereafter.
They were much too big for them when Pa bought them, but by the time
Ami and Siggi outgrew them their bottoms had worn through.

Siggi and Ami dressed as cowboys, with homemade cardboard hats, during the Mardi Gras holidays in 1952. After having lived in deep poverty, they had just moved into the brand-new luxury home of their father, and for a few months they enjoyed the best times of their lives. But after a judge evicted them and their mother, the three of them became squatters in a stranger's attic without heat, electricity or water. Fortunately, during that time, kind neighbors allowed them to use their three-story-high privy.

Siggi and Ami with their cousin Friederle in front of their new home. The scaffolding was for the application of cement stucco to the concrete block and clay tile structure.

Siggi and Ami on their way to the "MS Berlin" to sail to America. On crossing the Atlantic they were thrown off course because of a hurricane and a damaged propeller. After traveling across the United States by train, and within hours of their arrival on the farms of their relatives, they had to milk cows. Only days or weeks later did they realize that they were slaves and could not escape.

Ami not long after his arrival on the dairy farm in America. Little Frauke asked him to pose on the telephone. He is totally deaf in his right ear! Never having talked on one before, he was almost afraid of and too nervous to use it.

Ami, with scar behind ear, taking a test in his high school driving class.

Ami measuring Maxo's dike after Siggi and he had spent a summer nailing two-inch thick lumber to the pilings. This revetment was to protect the clay from the waves of fierce storms.

Maxo's dike washing out. Ami spent one winter, by himself, re-nailing missing boards and filling hundreds of clay bags to keep the dike from breaking through again.

SEP • 59 •

Villa Schitzma without any utilities, and significantly, without even an outhouse. Ami lived here alone while repairing Maxo's dike. He had to carry in his drinking water in an old milk can and was unable to drive to his villa during rainy periods.

While Ami was a slave, Pa and his single employee designed and supervised the construction of this hotel complex. It was known as Porta Germanica, *Gateway to Germany.*

Ami and his bride's "honeymoon" apartment, where they lived during their last year of college. Even though he was a fifth-year architectural engineering student, he was unable to determine which architect had designed this cozy building, temporarily embellished with a dust mop.

One room in Ma's apartment in Rheinfelden. At that time she lived with her boyfriend in nearby Switzerland. Every room, including her kitchen and bathroom, were furnished in this fashion. During our visit we could not find the bathroom fixtures because they were buried.

THE IRONIES

o o o o o o o o o o o o o o o o o o o o o o o o o o o o o o o o o

He giveth strength to the weary; and increases the power of
the weak…They will soar on wings like eagles; they will run
and not grow weary, they will walk and not be faint.

—Isaiah 40:29-31 NIV

6

THE LIBERATION

o o o o o o o o o o o o o o o o o o o o o o o o o o o o o o
Paranoids are the only ones who notice things anymore.

—Anatole Broyard

Am I paranoid? Or am I living under a rock of grim reality?

◆   ◆   ◆

After Siggi and I arrived at the university near the Washington-Idaho border, we moved into separate rooms in a dormitory and took care of our paperwork. Since I had spent little time here before, I explored the campus and its surroundings. Pullman is an island in the rolling hills of the Palouse, where in the summer golden grain grows in waves from the eastern horizon into the sunset. In winter the hills are brown or covered with snow.

The tree-lined streets and red brick buildings on campus radiated an academic atmosphere that thrilled me. I was proud to be a part of it and felt a sense of belonging. And there was no slimy mud or soul-wrenching screaming anywhere.

Up to this time I had given little thought as to what I wanted to study and didn't know enough about the available choices. While slouching on my bed, I perused the course catalog to see what studies were offered. In less than an hour I decided to major in architectural

269

engineering because I thought that being creative would offer me the greatest satisfaction. I hoped that this subject would quench my creative curiosity. I also remembered Pa's lifestyle. He had been his own boss, had a lot of fun designing and supervising the construction of many buildings, while earning a lot of money in the process. My decision would cost me a lot of money, two inches of finger, and eons of office boredom.

I had made very few major decisions in my life and those had been mostly on the spur of the moment; all others had been made for me by higher, or lower, authorities. The big decisions that I had made so far were as follows: In Simonswolde, one, one, one…, will I able to jump across this ditch and not fall in? Yes, maybe or no. Always, two, two, two…, will my life be a blast? Always, not yet! Three, our decision to come to America was without a thought. The strong gravitational pull generated by books and movies, combined with our unending abhorrence in the bosom of our family, caused us to respond instantaneously to Maxo's trap. Four, I found my first paying job out of curiosity about the stink of the place. Five, borrowing seventy-five dollars helped in my final escape from slavery. Six, the decision to attend college was a spontaneous firing of the synapses in my brain that might have been inspired by my guardian angel. Now seven, what should I major in?

I was doubtful about all of the mathematics required in my pursuit of happiness and therefore went into denial about it. It had always been one of my weakest subjects, but maybe it would go away if I ignored it long enough.

In the past, my imagination had offered me an escape from mother's and father's important activities and their consequences. I liked to draw, was good at it, and had always wanted to know about the inner workings of everything. By the age of six or seven, I had disassembled clocks to discover time. I took apart radios to learn the results of not reassembling them correctly. Over the years I destroyed many an object with my curiosity but also fixed some that were broken. In Simonswolde I researched our world on a globe which had a dime-sized compass built into its base. I rotated this base back and forth to figure out why the compass needle always pointed to the same direction. Finding no solution, I pried off its glass cover and forced it to go my way. But it always insisted on returning to the same bearing. While this little needle had an unwavering aim, our family floundered through its mortal existence.

When I was little I always had asked Ma, how, why and where? She remembered my curiosity in a letter:

"You always wanted to know everything and even asked me, 'why do flies have legs and worms don't have any?'"

Why do I have so many questions and so few answers?

◆   ◆   ◆

When I showed the results of my grade prediction test to my academic counselor, he did not roll on the floor laughing his belly off, but kindly asked me to enroll in "bonehead" English, even though I was a hairy beast. I did not tell him that I had only recently been delivered by boat but told him that I had a good command of the English language and should not have to take a remedial course. I also did not inform him that when I took this test, I had been very tired and had been highly decorated with grade A moomookakapoopoodoodoofroufrou, because he might have misunderstood me and thought me to be quite witty.

I surprised myself that I had countermanded a professor since he represented the authority that had always frightened me. *What had happened to me?* Authority had made me stutter and stammer and had often punished, whipped or oppressed me. Then I was even more surprised that he granted me permission to enroll in English Composition as I desired. There was another big lesson in this.

By this time I had dated girls only a few times. Now that I was in college, I was slowly dissolving the chains that imprisoned my body and mind, and this was a period of confidence building for me. In my new freedom I could try to identify the ghosts from our past that might be dwelling within me, and it would take years to realize if there even were any because they were not easy to find. I had escaped from my exploiters, was able to shower, make friends and did not have to be lonely anymore. The tourniquets on my heart and brain were loosening also because no one told me anymore that I was stupid. I tried to make up for lost life and did not need a lot of material things to catch up. Being able to do what I was doing in college was all I desired as long as I didn't flunk out.

No one could ever intimidate or abuse me again, and I would never have to work without earning a just reward for my efforts, even though in the interim it might still be hard labor at Screech and Stench. There were a lot of nice people in this world after all. I spent hours sitting in the Student Union lounge that was such a vibrant place, watching and visiting, often with girls. Students sat in booths and crowded around tables. We joked, smoked, sipped Cokes and listened to the jukebox. On weekends this building was usually packed with teachers and students and was pulsating with talk, laughter and music. Some of the songs from the jukebox never changed; "Scotch and Soda" and "Georgia" will always be on my mind.

Although I never realized it until many years later, Siggi and I never talked about our ordeals or about our father and mother, nor would we do so in the future. At this time we still had two big challenges to deal with, earning enough money for college and achieving good grades.

◆   ◆   ◆

Twenty-some years later, my wife and I would return to visit our alma mater. I was anxious to relive an hour or two in the Union Building where I had spent some of the happiest times of my life, but we would be disappointed the minute we walked in. *Who died?*

The main lounge was morgue silent. The booths and tables we used to crowd into, up to eight at a time, were no longer there. Randomly arranged tables with two or three chairs had replaced them. The few students present looked sad and all seemed to be strangers to each other. The same jukebox was still there but the music had changed, and I didn't like it. Oddly enough I still found "Scotch and Soda" and put a coin into the machine to play it. But it was not the same; the old spirit was gone.

In the lobby I perused a telephone book because I wanted to connect with someone, or something, from my mostly happy college years. The first section of listings therein was printed on blue paper. Blue made me feel good; it was my favorite color. But my mood would change quickly when I read the list for services, agencies and support groups unknown to me. Sex Offender Support Group, Suicide Helpline, Pregnancy Hotline and Alcoholics Anonymous, as well as numerous other official and volunteer groups. My unhappiness intensified.

Are these students more devastated than the tortured masses of World War II? Didn't their parents love them? If these organizations had existed when I studied here, could I have eased my ghostly pains by being a raving alcoholic maniac? Could I have been a sanctified victim? Could these agencies exist if this campus were not loaded with victims?

I reflected upon my college years and back-sighted mentally to past markers as I had learned in surveying. I remembered when I had stood by the window in our dilapidated second floor apartment in Everett and had looked down to observe two girls. They had seemed strangely lost in our rundown neighborhood. They wanted to be positive and popular, and they would be labeled pessimists for pointing out unpleasant truths because so many people could not deal with disagreeable facts and therefore ignored them.

While thinking about these blue telephone pages, I took a mental foresight and projected the trend from my backsight ahead into the future. I could see America's social fabric unraveling. I guessed that this could be the trend in all wealthier societies to varying degrees. Generally, people need humbling and loving experiences to stay the course.

Siggi and I had had a few of the former, and if we gritted our teeth and continued to crawl upward, we could find success and happiness in life. But through my foresight I worried that our new country itself would backslide and pull us back down with it.

◆   ◆   ◆

We didn't start drinking booze in college until after our first year and then only to flush out stress after a difficult test. After one such, two of my friends, who were not quite old enough to drink legally, asked me to buy some beer. We drove to Moscow, Idaho, where the legal age was nineteen instead of twenty-one, and I bought a twelve-pack of Coors. On the way back I was driving the Ford past the campus police station, when blue lights flashed behind us. I tried to ignore that familiar sinking feeling in my belly while the policeman informed me that one of my headlights was out. Then he asked me to open my car trunk where he found our beer. He took it and asked the three of us to follow him into the station where he told his chief why he'd stopped us. The chief checked our driver's licenses, warned us not to drink on campus, and dismissed us since our beer was unopened, and we were still breathless.

Even though I did not drink much, I did get drunk. Once. Involuntarily. Totally. Siggi and I went to a New Year's Eve party hosted by our friends, Richard and Amir. They lived above us on Lombard Avenue in Everett during the time when we had to skip one semester to earn more money for college. As we entered their apartment, gracious Amir offered me a drink, a glass full of orange something. It tasted mildly alcoholic, and after I finished it, it finished me.

The last thing that I remembered was that I announced to the party that I was flying to the moon and departed. Since I passed out quickly, I didn't know how I got there. At about four o'clock in the morning, I slowly woke up and was so cold that my teeth were rattling uncontrollably as they only could on a cold moon. But I was not there; I was lying on my back on our living room floor and could not move. Strangely, Amir was no longer my friend. I heaved, shivered and chattered weakly:

"Bbbb blankkket," but no one heard me since I was the only one there.

Did I get space sick and lose it on my way to the moon?

Had I barfed, I could have drowned myself; I would not have been the first person to suffocate in vomit. I wondered how I'd gotten from the moon back down to our apartment, so when I recovered, I asked our friend, six-foot-four Richard:

"Did you carry me down to my apartment?"

"Er! No, I pulled you down," he responded.

"Pulled me? You mean you grabbed me under my arms and dragged me?"

"No, I pulled your feet."

"Even down the stairs?" I wanted to know.

"Yeah," he confessed, "your head bounced nicely down the steps, ha, ha, ha."

See Mr. Lindeman, I do know how to use my head.

A year or so later, Siggi also flew to the moon, along with a lot of others. Fortunately my girlfriend and I missed the flight on that rocket. We arrived at the off-campus launch pad at about eleven o'clock at night and wondered why there were no lights at the party house, inside or out. I opened the front door and turned on the lights to expose lifeless astronautettes and cosmonauts scattered all over the place. *Houston, we have a problem!* They were lying on the floor, on beds and couches, singly or in bunches. I checked all the flight compartments to find survivors and found one in the bathroom. Siggi's girlfriend sat on the floor and was the only one who had not passed out from space sickness. She was tenderly holding his head in her lap, face up, because he was unconscious like everyone else. He told me later that he had not passed out at all, and that intermittently boys and girls had come into the bathroom to empty their bladders. He could hear them tinkle and talk about privacy, but his girlfriend had assured them that he was not in this world, and I was also sure of that because he did not respond to my prodding. My girlfriend and I were glad that we had missed that moon flight.

◆　　　◆　　　◆

Although I had now started using my head, Richard didn't always use his; at least not when he cleaned his .22 and thought that it was empty. While I was visiting him one day and was standing at the open window, contemplating the symbolism and geometrics of the Star of David on the synagogue across our street, he banged a bullet into a wall behind me. Instead of reacting in terror, like diving out of the third-floor window, as I would have when I was younger, I ignored the sudden ringing in my ear and calmly turned around to see the most surprised man ever. After my adrenaline level fell back to near normal, I wondered how far this bullet had traveled, whom it might have killed, and realized that this might have been illegal. Therefore I hurried back to my apartment below, pretended to be intensely studying Shakespeare's *Henry VI*, *what's this about lawyers?*, in order to establish an alibi in case the police came looking for the guilty party. But no one ever came to investigate.

Then came a time when none of us used our heads. Richard, Siggi and I felt bored and longed for adventure, so we rented a small boat and cruised around a nearby bay. When we were far out, a gale rose to rock us around exuberantly, so much so that we became afraid and decided to return to shore. I was the captain operating the outboard motor, and while I was looking ahead and turning our craft around, I felt its control stick pull away. Instinctively, I gripped it firmly as our motor fell into the sea. It hadn't been secured well enough and the vibrations must have worked it loose. We lifted it into our boat but could not start it again. Without control we bobbed around, to and fro, for what seemed like hours before the rental agent came to find us, maybe because he might have thought that we had stolen his boat. Fortunately the gale did not strengthen, and we did not capsize, but years later one of my roommates would drown under such circumstances.

◆　　　◆　　　◆

Occasionally I went to a nearby self-service laundry in Everett to brighten my bed sheets, to brighten my outlook. One time, "Uncle" Maxo, whom I had not experienced for a long time, came in and darkened my outlook, and we exchanged information. After I had left his tideland, he had had trouble finding someone else to work for him, at least for the wage that he was willing to pay. He hired Lloyd, a retired neighbor, part time, and when I met him later, I found him to be a very, very kind and alcoholic man.

Maxo asked me what I was majoring in, and I told him that I was studying architectural engineering, a five-year curriculum. I knew that this would make him happy, and sure enough, his face lit up in the way that I had anticipated, which told me what he thought:

"Good, you'll flunk out. I'll get you back again."

He saw the old Ford, and with a faint hint of a smile, he said to me, "Ah, you got a new car!?"

"No, we just had the old one painted."

"I see," he replied.

Siggi and I had the Ford painted, for thirty dollars, to stroke our egos, because it had looked like a wreck. Its hood had blown up, obstructing its windshield at sixty miles an hour while I was crossing a very long two-lane bridge. Gripping the steering wheel, gritting my teeth. Over the years we had replaced a fender and the trunk lid also and had bought all of these parts from genuine junkyards, so not much had matched in color, like my colorful, color-blind personality. Nowadays we might not be able to buy *pre-owned* parts from junkyards because we seem to have fewer junkyards. Miraculously many of them have evolved into *classic auto malls* and *antique car* supplies. *Are junk-yards also rising to a higher level, like Siggi and I?*

Every time I would see Maxo over the years, he'd say, "You got a new car?!" But this was rarely the case. Even when my wife and I would visit him much later, he'd make such a statement. We owned, and I mostly repaired, a *Cougar*, the kind made of plastic and metal and without tail, for more than sixteen years. It was always the same color and he'd still exclaim, or ask, if we'd bought a new car whenever he would see our wild animal. He was always counting dollars, ours, always hoping that I would have to come back to his tideland because I might not be able to find or deal with other jobs or people since I had been such a loser. *Is he hoping that I'd go into debt and default on my payments?* His facial cast, his brain waves, his statements, his body language, all signaled that he had hoped this to be the case. Long ago I had developed a sense for survival that also could read the thoughts, feelings and the true and false signals from certain people.

Siggi, who got to know him much, much better than I, told me that he thought that Maxo was envious of people who were successful or did things that he was not able to accomplish himself, such as relieving himself, big time, on a wide-open tideland. Yodeling in a rainstorm. Puttin' on the Ritz.

◆   ◆   ◆

As I progressed in my college courses, I continued to gain confidence in myself and my abilities, especially when I earned an average grade in my first semester English Composition and an excellent one for the following semester. These were two courses that I was to fail, but instead, I had finally shattered my own and certain expert opinions about my intelligence. They had tormented me, and I was finally proving them wrong, even though most of these people would never learn about the dramatic ballooning of my intelligence, after they permitted me to loosen some of the *Knoten* in my brain that they had created.

I earned good grades in architecture as well but barely passed the mathematics courses, and during subsequent semesters I discovered a repeating cycle. I did very poorly on the first exam because I was extremely nervous. I'd stare at my test paper, sweating, scribbling and erasing. Toward the end of the test period I often would be wrung out and figured that I'd flunk now anyway, and that there was no further need to worry. Then my pencil and slide rule would race to beat the clock, and when the test period was over I would feel as sticky and relaxed as if I had just come out of a hot Swedish sauna, without the benefits of the hot, the Swedish or the sauna.

As the semesters progressed, my confidence came ever earlier during the test periods, and my scores would improve. The more I learned in a course, the more confidence I gained; mathematics was not so difficult after all. The ghosts from my past would play evil games in my mind, but I would stubbornly refuse to let them gain the upper hand over me, no matter how much pain they would inflict.

◆   ◆   ◆

Over the years I would banish my more obvious ghosts. I would completely rid myself of this evil math test ghost long after leaving college, when I changed my career from architecture to highway design. My employer would teach me my new occupation, which included a three-day course of trigonometry. The night before the first day of this course, my firebombing or some of the numerous other interesting experiences combined with the early morning alarm clock ghost to trigger the midnight ghost to wake me at night. Exhausted the next morning I called in sick. I stayed in bed most of that day, dozing off and on between reading newspapers and magazines. Over the years I would miss work only infrequently and almost always because of this midnight ghost.

Before noon I answered a telephone call. A court clerk asked me to appear for jury selection that afternoon, and I told her that I was in bed because I was not feeling well. When I returned to work the next day, I was still tired but, strangely, in a good mood. Jim, the instructor who taught this class informed me:

"You might as well not come back since you missed one-third of this course."

"But I want to," my guardian angel replied. I could not have said this because I always ran away from math tests if I didn't have to take them.

"OK," he responded and his face portrayed his thinking that this would be hopeless.

At the end of the third day I had to again attempt to slay my math test ghost during our trigonometry test. As usual I sat in the front row so I could hear the instructor more clearly. I concentrated so hard on solving the problems that I was oblivious to my surroundings, and that I was the last one to finish this test. When Jim gave me back my graded test paper, it had only one red mark and it read 100, the only perfect score in that class in many years. When my boss asked Jim later how I had done, Jim simply shook his head, answering:

"Boy, that Ami's really somethin'."

He didn't know that he'd just paid me one of the biggest compliments that I had ever received in my life. Neither he nor I told my boss that I had a perfect score and this in spite of missing one-third of the course. Jim did not want to swell my head, but I was proud that I had finally laid to rest one of my most agonizing ghosts.

My employer would also help me slay another one, fright of public speaking. I remembered how terrified I had been when I stood before the wall in high school, waiting to be shot, while reporting about *The Wall*. In this class, however, my fright would slowly dissolve somewhat when I watched some of the other employees shake at the lectern before it was my turn to show them how well I could tremble. After I presented my speech, I gained so much confidence that I volunteered to give an almost impromptu speech to this class the following year. For that one I listed a number of subjects that I knew something about and wrote them down on slips of paper that I put in a box. Then I asked a student to pick one out, and I spoke about inflation, a perfect subject to dazzle everyone with bullokaka...

◆   ◆   ◆

Because of ghosts and my desire to keep my grade point average high enough to be able to remain in college, I had to drop a course early during one semester when I was not doing too well. I dropped physics almost three weeks after its start, hoping to enroll in it again during another semester, and substituted a math-less one, literature. Shortly before the end of that semester, Professor Krieger gave us copies of a poem called *September 1, 1939*. I did not read it, much less study it, and we never discussed this poem in class. Maybe I was to have studied it as a homework assignment but had not heard, i.e. comprehended, this instruction.

Again I had that familiar sinking feeling when one of the essay questions on our final exam was to discuss this poem. I had to fake my way to a correct assessment of its contents, and its deeper meaning. You could always find deeper meanings in the words of poems. I thought that September 1, 1939 must have been the date when Hitler had invaded Poland, but I was not sure. It was at the time I was born, and I had come into this world with a bang. I knew little about this big bang history even though I had been in it. In my test essay I described what I thought this poem might be all about and wrote about the evils of Nazism, relating them to the probable context of this poem.

Since it was the end of the school year, and I left Pullman for my summer job at the West Coast, I did not get back this graded test and did not know if my assessment of this poem had been correct. It could have been about floating the Amazon River in a bathtub. When I later received my grades in the mail, I was amazed that I had earned an average grade in literature. Since I forgot my analysis of this phantom poem the minute I finished the test, and I never received it back from the professor, I have been wondering ever since what this poem was really all about. So when I began writing this memoir, I thought that it might help me discover part of the dreadful history into which I had been born. I searched and discovered Auden's poem on the Internet. When I read it I was surprised how closely the punch lines of each verse related to my own life.

◆   ◆   ◆

My very good friend, Gale, and I took a structural engineering class together. One morning I woke up with my last ear plugged with wax and I felt desperate. I needed all my senses to earn a passing grade on the test that we had to take that day, and I knew that I would be haunted again by my math test ghost. Gale and I arrived at the classroom at the same time, at the sound of the bell announcing the beginning of my hell. The professor was already handing out test papers while giving verbal instructions. I saw his lips move and heard muffled sounds. Gale and I sat down next to each other, and I nervously whispered to him:

"I can't hear the prof. What's he saying?"

If we talked, the professor could accuse us of cheating. For that reason I did not want to say anything more to Gale, to get a clue as to what was happening. He pointed and motioned to me, but I did not understand his message; maybe he told me to be quiet. I felt as if I were drowning and no one would help me.

Not being able to hear well would cause me frequent problems throughout my life. Unbeknownst to me, the screaming of the saws and planers at Screech and Stench would slowly destroy my remaining hearing acuity. In noisy situations I would always feel that I was missing something because I could not fully participate in conversations.

I not only wanted to destroy my ghosts, but I also had to fix my ear; I had to stop the rot in my head and restore my hearing. In later years I would buy two hearing aids, but they would help me discern spoken words the least when I needed them the most, namely in noisy surroundings. Conversely, I imagined that I could get sucked down a toilet when I flushed it because it sounded like Niagara Falls. Therefore I've kept my hearing aids in a drawer because they are too expensive to throw out, yet. *How many hearing aids are lying uselessly in our nation's drawers?*

A few girls tried to teach me to dance, but I had always been a klutz without rhythm. One day I discovered why. I turned up the music so loud that my girlfriend plugged her ears. I heard the beat of drums; I felt the rhythm. I had seldom heard the right vibrations, so I would bounce around to the clarinet or whatever instrument I could hear best, resulting in my counter-culture dancing. I started a new jig, and to this day people in much of the world still dance my way. It is a loose kind of dance, left arm in, right elbow out, step toe left, then hop around without embarrassment.

But it was not only the beat of the music that was too vague; it was also spoken words that could confuse me. One time I ordered a sandwich at a lunch counter. The cute girl taking my order asked me, "Breed or bite?"

Even though I hoped that I had heard correctly I said, "Pardon me?"

"Breed or bite?" she repeated.

I was confused, as I had been so many times before; the light in her eyes did not match her question. A basic instinct wanted me to breed right there, and I thought she gave me that choice because I was a handsome stud. I wanted to tell her that he'd be more than happy to breed and would not bite. But then it registered in my brain that she must have asked me, "wheat or white?" because I was in a fast-food joint and people normally don't breed there. I pawed the ground, snorted with disappointment, and told her uncertainly "wheat." *Had I told her, "let's breed," would she have served me instantly? With a flying pie?*

◆   ◆   ◆

During my early days in college, Siggi's first-year roommate invited me to live with him off-campus in his trailer that had a stick-built bedroom addition, which became my room. I accepted because he'd charge me far less for room and board than I had to pay for living on campus. I paid him a fixed monthly sum and this included about seventy-five cents a day for my food.

When winter became really cold, this fixed sum did not include keeping me cozy, so I used a floor rug as a blanket on my bed. When it became colder still, I also asked roomy's dog, Rusty, to sleep on top of it to keep me warm. But he was heavy. I continued to strive toward becoming civilized and insisted on clean bedding, so I bathed Rusty. Since I did not want him to freeze I dried him off, and since I did not want to fuzz up my towel, I used the salt and pepper suit that Uncle Fullo had thoughtfully bought for me. I'd worn it only a few times, and after I dried Rusty with it, I thoughtlessly threw out this expensive keepsake.

I discovered that my roommate had a somewhat different view of the world than I, and this did not enhance my mood, because he was moody. He would sit at his desk for hours brooding over his studies without saying a word. But later in the semester he lightened my spirits when he placed an ad in a German national magazine advertising for female European pen pals. He received over three hundred replies, including portraits, from several countries.

I corresponded with one of these girls and enjoyed this long distance romance. She was an actress in Munich and said that she knew the Pirzers who owned the dancehall/beer cellar where we'd lived at the end of the war. Then she informed me that she did not mind sleeping with older men, and I wondered why she wrote me that because I was not much older than she. In her next letter she suggested that we should get married as soon as possible, even though we had never met.

I concluded that she was pregnant by a forty-some year old man that she'd written about, so I quit writing her and began to write to several more pen pals from my roommate's fine collection.

Because of the lack of food at my room and board establishment, I failed to score high enough in my physical evaluation tests: push-ups, sit-ups and chin-ups. Therefore I was required to take "bonehead" P. E. during the following semester, when I moved back into Sherwood Hall where I could eat in a dining room and always fill my belly. I had plenty of muscles from working hard, but they did not function too well during this time. But with sufficient nourishment I became one of the best athletes in that class and wondered what I was doing there.

◆   ◆   ◆

Sherwood Hall and its twin dormitory were two-story, flat-roof wood structures adorned with old, gray tar or asbestos shingle siding. They were built at the end of World War II to house GI's but only temporarily and were still "temporary" in the sixties. *Should they be classified as hazardous sites? Or be placed on a national register of historic buildings?* Some of the dormitory's occupants unlocked each other's doors with knives that they borrowed from the dining hall. They also removed walls to enlarge their quarters, and one of the students even kept a live turkey in his suite. The walls were so flimsy that I could hear simultaneous, poorly syncopated music from my neighbors that sometimes interfered with my studies.

I had worked very hard to be able to live in this dorm. I resided there for several semesters, during some of which the combined grade average of its occupants dropped below "2.0." Once or twice with my help. Our motto could have been: "We'll all flunk together when we go!" Before we do, we would like to thank the janitor for always keeping the floors and bathrooms spotless and shiny and our sheets and towels so clean.

286 Heroes from the Attic

Nowadays people have become much smarter than we were, because more than half of the students in many colleges are on the honor roll. I read that more than eighty percent of the graduates of one famous college now finish with honors. *Had I been born a couple of decades later, would I be smarter, or dumber too? And with a lot less pain?* These students achieve this even though many of them now sleep on top of each other. Boys on top of girls, or vice versa, or some such combination. If I had had my choice of where I could have slept, I would have flunked out before too many semesters. But we were deprived because our girls were always locked in for safekeeping every night in their own separate buildings. We did not dare return them to their dormitories after their curfew because they would be punished, and then they might not allow us to date them again. But unlike the girls, all the boys were allowed to be out all night. *Because they couldn't get pregnant? Didn't need protection? Discrimination? Or was I befuddled?*

Today I could not only be smarter, but I could also live in greater style. Near the center of a town not far from my present home is a beautiful brick building with immense skylights. It is also surrounded by a luscious green lawn. Its *victim residents* don't pay to reside there. I do, along with many other fools. They live in comfort, study law, pump iron and watch movies. One of its occupants wrote a letter to our local newspaper saying something like, "I've been in jails all over the country and I want to thank your community for the finest facility I've ever stayed in." Even though this jail was built only a few years ago, it is already bulging and new "portables" had to be added. These are surrounded with a shiny, high, chain-link fence, topped with coils of razor wire, in order to blend in with the aesthetics of the adjacent beautiful rose garden.

"Mismanagement and grief:
We must suffer them all again."

◆   ◆   ◆

Siggi and I enjoyed the international flavor of Pullman, the quiet university town. There were students from all over the world, and over the years we socialized with, or befriended many of them. There was an Untouchable doctoral candidate from India and shy Bamadele from Nigeria who lived across the hall from me. I liked them because their black eyes reflected their lives; they showed that they were heroes also. There was Chaim, a master's student from Israel, who would later discover the agents that caused aging in plants, and Siggi played a lot of chess games with him. Hans von Randech, the son of a Nazi general who was executed for disobeying Hitler's orders, taught me sociology. A very good friend was Khadja Mohammad Fuad Softar Ali Butt, an architecture student from Pakistan, who could recite Shakespeare from memory and daily drank several glasses of milk that he reinforced with two teaspoons of sugar. This caused him to carry ever more weight. When Fuad had first arrived in Pullman, he thought that he had landed in the wrong state, because he expected to arrive in Washington D.C. and not in the empty hills of Eastern Washington. Over the years I learned some of the differences, attitudes and beliefs of these cosmopolitan students, and I respected them and enjoyed them greatly.

Siggi was an excellent chess player and beat most of his opponents most of the time. Sometimes he played on behalf of the Cougar Chess Club, which invited him to become a member, but he did not join. He also played against our mutual friend Steve and me and won almost all of the time. But after losing too often, Steve, others, and I quit playing him because he bruised our egos too much. He would sometimes even win after turning the chessboard around toward the end of a game to continue playing our losing side. And as if that weren't intimidating enough for his opponents, he spent little time pondering his moves and sometimes even read a newspaper while waiting for his turns.

Argh!

He did not play chess according to the conventional wisdom of planning his moves in advance. He played like Napoleon played his battles. While his enemies were pondering their strategies, he'd pounce quickly to gain advantage and attack with full force. Likewise, Siggi usually brought his queen into the battle as soon as possible. It caused great damage to his opponents in the very beginning of the game. He studied history and tried to relate what he had learned from the past to the present, and I imagine that he applied this knowledge to fine-tune his chess tactics.

◆   ◆   ◆

At the start of a new school year, we moved into a new dormitory, Goldsworthy Hall, which faced the loop road around campus. By this time I had overcome the chronic shyness of my youth, and when I was in a really good mood, I would even become feisty and adventuresome. For example, one day when new snow covered the ground, I was returning from the dining hall when I had a brain drizzle. *If I roll a big snowball, will others push it onto the street?*

I rolled one as large as I could, placing it next to the curb, and went to my room where I broadcast my brain waves, waiting and watching the setup below. Amazingly, within minutes a group of boys responded and rolled my snowball bigger. They created new ones and placed them across the street, eventually blocking it. Ever more volunteers joined my party, and a festive mood spread over the belly-filled, but booze-less, crowd. But soon I lost control over my revolution when my rebels began to ignore my brainwave broadcast and were breaking off traffic signs to embed them in the snow wall. This worried me because it was destructive and could lead to traffic accidents and hurt innocent people. I was relieved when a police cruiser arrived, although it was unable to push through the snow to clear a path.

My relief was short-lived, however, when my roommate who would later drown, dropped a big snowball from a pedestrian overpass onto the hood of a passing police car while yelling, "Cops hurt." The police officer became enraged and spun away. This titillated my rebels, so they feverishly continued to add to my wall, and in the end they crowned it with a porta-potty stolen from a nearby construction site.

The seed of my idea blossomed into a barricade across a major road and into a leaderless riot. The police returned with a pickup loaded with snow for extra weight and attempted to push through again. It became embedded instead. The mob cheered, jeered and booed until several more cops arrived and dispersed the revelers, chasing them into dormitories and into hiding. Now I worried about undermining the authority of the police, because every act of insolence leads to further such acts. And if unpunished, leads to popular criminality.

Ami's Avalanche Axiom. The implications of this theory could be enormous. An imported ex-slave started a riot, and only he knew why and how it began. Yet his nasty little idea and small effort had great consequences; his little snowball grew almost spontaneously into an avalanche of civil disobedience. He gave no verbal orders, informed no one, but achieved far-reaching results without great effort on his part, taking no credit, no blame for its consequences.

Could I have expanded this riot to the campus in Moscow? Could I be interviewed on television? Could I have sold spectator tickets and membership dues? Could I exploit this game for my personal benefit? Can anybody? Does anybody?

◆   ◆   ◆

In college I caught the zest of life as much as my meager resources would allow. I dated girls and one of them was the epitome of hedonism. Nothing seemed to bother her. Everything was fun and funny. She was from Germany and was burdened with few studies because she was a live-in maid for a professor. I met her while attending a party at another professor's house. While I was engaged in a conversation, she walked in, six feet tall with big sky-blue eyes. She played it cool and I had to meet her because a man chases a woman until she catches him. It did not take her long to catch me, in the middle of the night, in her basement bedroom, where we pursued one of man's primeval instincts. And woman's also. I had never had so much fun before and realized why half the people in the world could be the unintended outcome of such fun.

At three in the morning, euphorically and quietly I sneaked out to the Ford, coasting it downhill before starting it. I did not want to wake the professor because someday I might take one of his courses, and he or I would be embarrassed by what went on under his bedroom at night. When I arrived home, my roommate Bill assumed that I had spent another long night slaving away in the architectural design lab, which I occasionally did to meet deadlines. This night had been different, but I never told him.

◆   ◆   ◆

At about this time Ma wrote me the following to enhance my zest for life:

"…Monday I read in the newspaper that Herbert is building a fifty-meter high building with twenty-four apartments, businesses and underground parking near the German border by Basel. Have you received any payments from him?"

No, but I'm glad Daddy is doing so well.

Ma wanted us to know that he earned lots of money or should have, or could have, but was always scheming to avoid paying us. While reading this letter, I was resting on my bed while Bernard, my roommate at the time, was studying at his desk. I rose quietly, walked out of our room and went for a long walk. I was looking for a guilty party that I could pound into pulp but could not find one.

Years before, a court had ordered Pa to pay seventy-five marks a month to maintain his two sons. This amounted to less than twenty dollars apiece. Over time, because of Ma's stubborn pursuit, this sum was increased somewhat. But this was immaterial since Pa paid his obligations only infrequently. A penny to his children was a penny that he could not turn into body fat, smoke or alcohol. Fine cigars were necessary to fumigate the aphids on his roses; fine wines were necessary to deal with the families that he had created, but I didn't know about the usefulness of his fat.

It was Teufi who almost exclusively would enjoy the rewards of Pa's talents as an architect. After all, that's why she had married him. Ma continued her court battles to keep the early court orders in force, to enjoy the rewards of Pa's talents also. Since they differed so much, I didn't know why she would have otherwise married him.

I rarely thought about our past. I never wrote to our relatives in America, Germany or Switzerland. And I seldom wrote to Ma. But she kept writing us about our good old days and giving us useless advice. She scolded me and called me a scoundrel for not writing her more often. She even asked other people to encourage us to write to her. At this time I did not even want to hear, speak or write German. I forced myself to forget; therefore I wanted to avoid her intercontinental missiles because it would be easier for me to remain a hero.

But our past can be a boomerang, which, when it comes back to haunt us again, it's best to duck. In the summer of 1962 one such arrived in my mail. It was a registered document from the Consulate of the Federal Republic of Germany in Seattle. It was addressed to me at Washington State University and was forwarded to our permanent home address, Siggi's and mine: General Delivery, Everett, Washington. For too many years we resided in a box in this post office.

I wondered why the Germans were sending me such a big document. Pa had promised us that if we were good boys, we would some-day inherit his *Grundstueck,* and Siggi and I would certainly have exceeded his expectations, if he had any. *Did Buskohl die? Will we inherit his legacy? How did they find me? Did they want to draft me?*

I tore open the envelope and tried to interpret the fourteen pages of turgid gobbledygook of German sesquipedalian words and protracted sentences. In essence, the court summoned Siggi and me to appear, personally, for the first time ever, around the time of my birthday in October. Our father claimed that he could no longer support us. He owned nothing and worked for his wife for less than two hundred fifty marks, a little over fifty dollars, a month. He claimed that the defendants were now of age and had not made any claim for support since January of 1958.

This court summons did not state that under the law, Paragraph 1602 BBB, every father would be required to provide support for his children. According to the Support Rights Laws, unwed minor children are doubly privileged "...in that the children do not have to deplete their own possessions in the support of their parents and, secondly, in that the parents are at the risk of their own support in having to share everything with their children."

This summons also ignored that a father was legally required to pay for the education of his children until they obtained the same level that he had achieved himself, even if they were of legal age.

His complaint also twisted the truth in that we were gainfully employed in America and earned so much money that we even could afford to own a car. This claim was very misleading. The Ford jalopy had been in Maxo's name for many years, and we still drove it without insurance. Owning a car in Germany at that time still implied a wealthy lifestyle. An automobile was mostly a luxury there because the efficient transit systems reached even the remotest villages. However, in America a car was an absolute necessity, like a roof overhead with a toilet beneath, especially in the expansive western states.

We could not afford to fly to Germany to appear in court. We learned from Ma's past experiences that it would be futile to deal with, and through, the German laws or lawyers. Nor could we take time from our hell or our studies. At this time I commuted nightly to the planing mill on a single-gear bicycle without lights, that I had bought for ten dollars because Siggi needed the Ford to get to his job which was much further away than mine.

He and I did not respond to this court summons, as our enemies had undoubtedly anticipated, and thus we lost this case by default.

Poof! Poof!

There went another wad of our existence. And to those who were supposed to protect us.

Included with the documents from the German consulate was a letter written by Pa on the letterhead of "H & E Neuman, Architects," Herbert and Elfriede, aliases Buskohl and Teufi. Teufi must have learned drafting from Pa, if at all. She could not legally practice architecture since she had not studied it, and Ma's lawyer confirmed that she was not licensed. But the court accepted that our father was now working as an employee of his present wife, an impostor, to deny our support under German law.

These documents stated that Pa was now penniless. Teufi owned everything, we owned nothing. When I read this, I did not know if he were penniless only on paper or if he were now really a pauper. I knew that paupers lived in streets, attics and other idyllic places. Pa and Teufi had lied and twisted the truth so often that one never could be sure about the facts as they claimed them to be. Whatever the case, after I read these papers I placed them with my letters from Ma and promptly forgot about them. I saved them for a time when I might be able to face our past. I did not even discuss this with Siggi and did not ask Ma if Pa were now really a pauper. I did not care if he lost everything or became a multi-millionaire because I thought or cared little about our homeland and our family.

Only years later did I confirm that it was true that Pa had made himself penniless, and that he had paid an incredibly high sex-maintenance fee. It was true that Teufi had convinced our father to give all of his possessions to her so he could escape his obligations to support his children. Our father gave everything he owned to the devil in a Faustian bargain. He gave away his architectural practice, his luxury home, his Mercedes and his sweet little children. He bargained away everything but his clothes and received only heartaches in return.

Then Teufi divorced him.

Did Pa claim Siggi and me as deductions for his taxes? Was Teufi also claiming us? Had Fullo and Deepo? Maxo? Some of them simultaneously?

Deals like this forced people to cheer themselves with jokes:

A *Diplom Ingenieur,* an ear surgeon and a lawyer were sitting at their *Stammtisch,* drinking beer and debating what the oldest profession might be.

"The oldest profession must be medicine," said the surgeon, "because God was a surgeon when he took a rib from Adam and created Eve. Surgery."

"No. It must be engineering because God engineered the whole universe from chaos," said the *Diplom Ingenieur.*

"Who do you think created chaos!?" the lawyer retorted.

Two dozen hard-working jurists and two loving parents had created chaos in our lives, Siggi's and mine. They had pretzled our souls, had stolen our worldly possessions, and had sent us into dirty slavery far from home.

And furthermore, no court tried Teufi for practicing architecture without a license. No court convicted her and our father for obstruction of justice and for attempting to mislead the judge. They were not punished for committing perjury by telling monstrous lies under oath. For that matter, not one of their lawyers was ever summoned to be tried for obstruction of justice or for misleading the judges. Pa had impoverished himself so he would not have to pay his obligations and had even lied to the court to become a pauper. It thus came to pass that he was reaping what he had sown. *Did he still have humor left to joke about this fateful harvest?*

◆   ◆   ◆

Ma didn't send me any letters about this latest court case but sent Siggi at least two of them, in which she instructed him to write to the judge for this upcoming trial. She wanted him to paraphrase her letters, as if he had written them spontaneously, without any influence from anybody else.

Siggi and I did not socialize much with each other in college and did not even discuss this case. We reminded each other too much of the past that we wanted to forget. When we incidentally met somewhere on campus, one or the other would usually say:

"Did you get any mail?"

In other words: "I'm so lost and lonely. Did you find our family?"

Usually the answer would be no and that would often be the end of our conversation, and we'd be on our way. We frequently walked fast wherever we went, as if we had a purpose, always going toward a goal. Even with full bellies, we'd pass everyone strolling back from our dining hall. We were always hoping to find a family or old friends in our mailboxes because someday, someone might send us some nice relatives. Everybody had parents, roots and soul mates; therefore we must have them also, and all we had to do was to wait patiently for them to appear in our lives.

I did not know if Siggi followed Ma's advice and wrote letters to the judge. Her pro forma drafts were written to address His Honor but were a jumble of ideas and reminiscences. Her thoughts often shifted from sentence to sentence. Some seemed as if Siggi were to copy them for his letter to the judge, while others appeared as if she were only remembering the past, and he was to write to her instead:

"My Dear Siggi!

"It is certain that winning or losing your court process is dependent only on the letter that you will write...

"...think only about the 'beautiful' Teufi, how annoyed she will be, when she will have to pay you even a miserly DM100 per month. One needs only an enemy to be able to accomplish something. The law requires that a father of even an illegitimate child must pay a minimum of DM75 until it is eighteen years old.

"...It is a truly sorry democracy, where abandoned children have to sit in the corner and are mocked by their fellow pupils. Children are cruel as is well known, and their mothers in their loneliness and poverty do not know how to help. I will send the court documents via a law professor to the local justice minister. Ami is very upset to read in the plaintiff's complaint that 'both parties are guilty for the divorce.'"

Give me some air!

"I will return to Loerrach and tell the truth to that liar, Dorothea Duckmeyer (Teufi's lawyer), until she is blind and deaf. It must be a fantasy democracy where the fairy tales of swindlers are believed as being true and you as an honest, faithful, decent human being, who has never failed in her duties vis-a-vis our father and us, cannot receive an audience. I know it is only because of your good conscience through all these sad years that we stayed alive in spite of everything.

"Do you still think about the gallows humor in the cold attic about a judge of the orphan court, Blaersch from Saulgau. He evicted us from our house with the remark: 'Clear out immediately!' We did not even receive the required six weeks' notice. We should have set up our bed in the rain. Our father could have read in the *Bild* (a nationwide newspaper) how we fared after he threw us out at the bidding of his new hatmaker. How was it even possible that he sold his house and became himself a person on pension?

"What this pig and especially his lawyer, Dr. Brauer, were able to do to us! When I think about them and of others that have tormented us, I sometimes wish that the Russians would overrun this country to the Rhine River. Then they would also feel what unjust treatment is like. Maybe her shiny career will come to an end some day. We will come and storm the bar association in Freiburg…

"We were the ones that suffered. What we will never forgive is that the police never helped us when our 'father' wanted to kill us. Poor Ami has required years to overcome the consequences of this terrible intimidation. We should have publicized this immediately, that for more than a year and a half, we had to climb in and out of the window out of fear. Not even the pastors of both religions, with whom Ami pleaded for help, came to our aid. You say that you are no friend of heroism. But when we overcome the greatest concerns, then we will announce your heroism…

"If we knew the German laws, or if we could find a lawyer who knew the West German laws, we would be glad to relieve you of the burden of always having to appear before the forum of rightfulness. I believe we were eleven or thirteen years old when we had the courage to seek out the sorry judge Bender when our 'father' wanted to take us away from you. This man was without any idea and stuttered about a mistake that he had made. How many mistaken judges are being taken in by Teufi? When Ami pulls nightly, year after year, heavy boards from a conveyor belt, he will always remember this. Teufi has to fear this pent-up resentment."

More air!

"…The dictatorship of money is the worst kind. Our father could with all his money buy the president of the European council, and our innocent mother was declared to be also at fault in the dissolution of her marriage. We had to 'suck our thumbs' while our father blew his money on dozens of mistresses. And when our mother went to the police about this, she was told he could daily bring six women home, if they were over sixteen years old. This is the result of the new 'freedom'…"

Ma quickly followed up the above sample appeal letter to Siggi with a second one:

"…That you don't have a family that cares about you can be seen, because Uncle Fritz has kept all of the inheritance from his father for himself. He did not give Buskohl anything. He was at that time a mayor and was able to control everything so he could become the sole owner. Today he owns several stores in…

"…The Germans have become a compassionless and pitiless people. Teufi would have skewered us on a spit and eaten us at night, had it been allowed. Think about the constant shutting off of the gas main valve in the cellar for two months. She wanted to destroy us. We could not get one drop of warm water. (It was our luck that we could live

better on cold water than on cooked water with unhealthy sugar, which
ferments in the body, the acids which are formed destroy the teeth and
maybe also cause headaches.)

"When I had to come to the initial divorce court hearing in Nov.
1949, Pa told me he wanted to go with me for a walk along the Rhine
river after dark to talk with me. I have made the great mistake of never
mistrusting Buskohl. But I smelled the bait immediately at that time.
His invitation was so unnaturally friendly and excited. I told him,
'with you I will not go walking along the Rhine River,' and he
answered promptly, 'I am no murderer.' So, blitz-like, both guessed
the thoughts of the other one. It would have been a simple matter to
push me into the river. Afterwards he would have gone to Dr. Lupfer
who, as a drinking buddy, would have given an alibi. When someone
would have found me three days later in the power plant grating, he
would have said I committed suicide because of melancholy from the
divorce.

"Dear Siggi, do not take this seriously, it is all in the past. But do
not show this letter to Ami, because if he has to drive the old Ford to
Pullman he could have an accident because of this sorrow. Besides he
could become sick from failure of glandular activities, like the pancreas,
which can happen after grief. This slides easily off you since you are
slick as an eel. In the Hardtstrasse he had severe constipation, his intes-
tines became lame, his digestion ceased to function, because we always
had the same food. Keep an eye on him, since he has to drive and is in
great danger in the old car...

"...What one has not experienced personally, one cannot feel personally. I walked from Rheinfelden to Loerrach to the church on the
windy wedding day of Buskohl and Teufi, on 15th September
1953....I wanted again to see and hear this stupid performance from
the mouth of the otherwise very dear and nice Pastor Mennicke: 'Till
death will part you!' (That I don't have to laugh!)..."

These excerpts from Ma's very long letters were examples of Ma's
fuzzy, unfocused thinking, even after I edited them, to clarify her

thoughts as best as I could. She intended to write Siggi pro forma letters for the judge but digressed into his very most personal hygiene. She knew that I was not able to shower in America for extended periods and remembered our inability to stay clean during our past. Siggi never showed me these letters, but I retrieved them years later from Ma's apartment. He must have returned them to her on his many trips to Europe during later years, or maybe she had never sent them to him.

About a year after Siggi and I were summoned to court, Ma was so disgusted with the German social-judicial system and its treatment of the three of us that she wrote Siggi, who seemed to have a lot more correspondence with her than I did:

"…That is how Buskohl always does it. He builds himself houses, the one in Weil is already his third, and this one belongs to his wife, and the debts to him…

"…He presents a piece of paper to the court showing only initials, no addresses: 'Owed to H.C. 10,000 marks. A.K. 5,000 marks.' He claims he owes more than 70,000 marks. He uses this as an excuse that he can't support you…

"…Khrushchev recently said in East Berlin that he wants to sweep us away and all my acquaintances are glad about this and I the most. It cannot continue like this."

Besides long letters, Ma also wanted to send us clothes in America. And sometimes succeeded. She sent Siggi a suitcase with seven overcoats and several dozen socks. He kept one coat, gave the others away or threw them out. Ma still ate little, partly to satisfy her addiction to hoarding, but could not afford to mail us her presents for which I will always be grateful. In case Siggi worried that he did not receive enough coats from her, she informed him that this was not her fault:

"Because the postage is increasing, I asked Pastor Mennicke if he could pay it, to send you some stuff for Christmas. He said he did not have anything. The church had to build homes for cripples because of the many people who are crippled in traffic accidents. He offered me a fifty-mark gift for the postage. I told him to keep it since a one-time fifty marks was not enough for the postage for all the things I have to send. If I were to pass a law, there would not be so many cripples. (During frost periods the giant trucks are damaging the tar street...)

"Maxo told me that lately he had difficulties with you, but you were not at fault, but Aunt Helene. She treated you like a serf, but I wrote you this before."

◆   ◆   ◆

During my third year in college I was engaged to Wendy, and we had a lot of good times together. She invited me to a dance in her dormitory because my skills had improved enough that I did not crush her toes anymore. The band played and the *forum romanum* was crowded. Gracefully I danced Wendy into a pillar that caused it to bend in the middle. It was ready to topple. These pillars were made of split corrugated cardboard, that fluted Pompeiian look, wrapped around cylinders of chicken wire. When I tried to straighten this pillar, I initiated an earthquake. The pillar collapsed. All pillars in the forum tumbled, domino style, because colorful streamers were tied from column to column. The earth was shaking, girls were screaming, boys were cheering, while the band played on.

At the end of our school year, Wendy and I returned with our belongings to the coast in the old Ford. Since I did not have enough room to take all of my stuff, I threw out the architectural designs that I had painstakingly created in ink on expensive illustration boards for my architectural design courses. I really wanted to save them because I had spent so much time preparing them, and I also needed them for my résumé to obtain a good job in the future.

I stored my ancient typewriter and two old snow tires in the basement of my dormitory. But when I returned again for another semester, those items were gone. Somebody probably threw out my tires because they were worn out. We bought only used ones, although it might have been illegal to drive on them because they did not have enough tread left.

On our way to the coast our engine overheated repeatedly, and I kept adding water to the radiator in order to be able to finish our journey. Near Moses Lake, in the middle of Washington, I discovered bubbles rising from the coolant and guessed that the engine block was cracked or a gasket had blown. In either case we could not risk continuing with such a defect. There were so many problems that needed to be repaired that it was not worth fixing this car anymore.

"What I won't do for love," said Wendy to me. For her this was an adventure, but I kept ripping at the cuticles of my fingernails. What could I say? The transmission was ready to go out again, and I had already replaced it twice with used parts. Since I had no money to have a mechanic inspect it, I sold the Ford to a junkyard for twenty-five bucks. This bought a bus ticket for the rest of my trip. Wendy went home to Seattle, while I traveled to Tacoma where I had heard about a summer job with an engineering firm. Since I did not have a cent to my name, I walked from the bus station to the engineers' office. I arrived there travel weary and sweating from the humid afternoon sun. My hair was greasy, neatly plastered in place, my stomach was growling, and I felt befuddled and forlorn. In the reception office I asked the first employee who walked through the lobby if his firm would be hiring anyone, and he said no.

I went back out, bummed a dime, and called Mike Hanson, a friend from college whose father operated a molding mill at the Tacoma harbor. While I held the phone, Mike asked his father, who did not know me, if I could work for him. Mike told me that I could start the following Monday. I informed him that I would have to walk there, and that I could not afford to rent a room. He put me on hold again to consult with his family a second time, and when he returned said:

"I will pick you up. You can live with us."

A crushing burden lifted from me. That familiar sinking feeling in my belly dissolved almost instantly. Suddenly I became very hungry.

Without the Hansons I would have had to sleep under a bridge, eat from people's garbage and might have become homesick for the good old days in Germany. But maybe not because I found Americans to be more helpful than the people I left behind in my old country. I did not contact my relatives because I had not liked my previous experience, and it had taken too long to extricate myself from it.

◆   ◆   ◆

I did not know where Siggi went for the summer, or if he had found a job. After I settled in with the Hansons, I located him at a YMCA dormitory about fifty miles away. When I called him he sounded forlorn and nervous, and I worried. So the following weekend I took a bus to visit him, and he kept picking his thumbnail cuticles with intense absentmindedness. Some of his fingernails were rippled like a washboard and one thumbnail had dried blood crusted at its base. This confirmed that he was a nervous wreck, much worse than I. His worry gauge signaled a state of crisis. I checked my own indicators but could not yet detect an improvement in my own state of mind.

Ever since I could remember, whenever we were under great stress, Siggi and I had the habit of tearing away the cuticles of our fingernails, particularly on our thumbs. We probably started this habit while waiting out the bombings in the bunkers, because in dark, shaking bunkers, minutes became hours, and hours became days. This treatment of our cuticles created horizontal grooves at the soft bases of our nails that grew outward. The depth and spacing of these ripples were directly proportional to the intensity, frequency and durations of our worries, and I have never noticed anyone else with such a stress gauge.

Fortunately Siggi found a job during the following week.

I worked for the Hansons all summer, received union wages, and they did not charge me for room and board. Even so, by the start of the fall semester I had not earned enough for another year of schooling. The mill production diminished, and the Hansons did not need me anymore. Since I had no car, Mike's mother and two sisters drove me with my stuff to Everett where I returned to Screech and Stench which had promised to employ me again.

Unlike my father, Mike's father shed tears when we said good-bye. Unfortunately I have lost contact with this very generous family and have never expressed my gratitude enough for their kindness. If it had not been for them I would have been hungry and homeless, that is, had I decided to stick around. I lost Wendy because I had no car or money to contact her often enough to maintain our relationship a long thirty miles apart.

◆   ◆   ◆

By the end of the first semester of my fourth college year, life was getting too easy, so I rotted my right index finger. I worked all night to finish a model for a school that I designed for an architecture class. Since the architecture department thought that we should get some sleep, it often sent a policeman to evict us from the building at about 2:00 a.m., locking the doors behind us. But because of time pressure some of us, this time including me, hid in the building and continued our work after he left again. At about eleven o'clock the next morning, zombie-like, I went to the workshop to cut a piece of plastic. But three small saws had no blades or did not otherwise function. Since I was under great pressure to finish, and I could not afford a lousy grade, I groggily used a big table saw. It used me instead when it nicked the bone on the back of my finger.

I went back to the design room to complain about the dull saw blade and held my hand up to prove it. When the student whom I was reporting this to grew pale and his eyes bugged out, I realized that trimmed fingers might be serious. The professor took me to the hospital where I waited for about two hours before I received attention. By then I had lost a total of only about two or three drops of blood, not enough to worry about.

The surgeon sewed up my finger, placed it into a brace, and after a few days I was released with the instructions to come back again in a week for a checkup. During this time, to ease all my pains, I partied at night. We drank, in moderation of course, and danced to The Beatles at the house of Count von Randech. The next night I went to a party at Chaim's house where we revved our pulses by dancing to Israeli folk songs. And we drank in moderation of course. The party houses were bursting with students who were dancing, singing, rocking and bouncing. The walls and floorboards were thumping, and it seemed that the whole world had joined our rhythm. It was cosmopolitan time.

My date went to the bathroom. Another girl noticed this and quickly made her move. She disconnected her dance partner and came to embrace me, to hug me tightly, so she could extend her tongue into my mouth. Even though I liked this very much, I pushed her aside. You shouldn't take someone's man just because his date went to the can. That's what happens when you're not reeking of the dairy that seemed to have overcome my virile smell in the past.

I happened to be looking at my finger while the rubber band that fastened around the end of my brace suddenly snapped. I walked to the hospital and the doctor yanked it, ouch, to knot it back together and dismissed me again. Before too long, during one night my finger swelled to almost double size, became purple and was bulging out of the bottom of its bandage. I was in such trauma that I did not think of or dare to take off the bandage that was choking off the flow of blood and caused such intense pain. I also might have fainted if I saw the condition of my finger. I tossed around on my bed and tiptoed through the hallways of our dormitory most of that night, whimpering in agony, because my finger was crushed in a vise. I prayed, dear God, release me from this torment. I will never sin again and will always honor my mother and my father. At five o'clock in the morning, I tiptoed to the student health service to find relief. Walking intensified my pain. It was still dark outside, and the nurse told me return at eight when the doctor would arrive.

One hundred years later, when the doctor examined my finger, he said, "You have gangrene! I'll have to amputate. I'll try to leave as much as possible. See, this much," but he did not chop off his finger to demonstrate how he was going to customize mine. If I had known that he would have to remove the dead part of my finger, I would have chopped it off myself years ago because it would have saved me an eternity of deepest hell.

"Then I cannot practice architecture anymore. I won't be able to hold a pencil," I mumbled to the surgeon.

"You will be able to draw if you hold it like this," he responded.

I was tired, paranoid and doubtful. I had invested a lot of effort to make it this far in college, and in life, and now I felt that it was mostly wasted because I would have to change my major to accommodate my new digit configuration. And I still didn't know what else I could study, my choices still seemed to be limited, and I would need a lot more money to extend my studies.

While I was resting in the hospital bed after my amputation, the surgeon removed my bandage and asked me to dip my stump into an antiseptic solution. Even though I did not even touch the bottom of the bowl, my whole index finger felt as if it were poking through the metal. I expected the solution to run out, but my sensation was only imaginary. Since my mind and/or nerves created a virtual finger that could do anything, I wanted to drink the solution to acquire a virtual brain that could do anything, but the doctor did not recommend it.

I stayed in the hospital while my finger remainder healed again, although it continued to be very sensitive to touch for a long time thereafter. To prevent infections, nurses tickled me with needles, and I enjoyed their attention, so much so that I looked forward to them daily. The nurses, with or without needles, were the highlights of my hospital stay.

A week or so after my second admission, a nurse pushed me out of the front door in a wheelchair, per protocol. I walked away and did not know where I lived. I could not remember how to find my dormitory, but somehow I arrived there. It was the end of the semester, and I did not study for my final exams. I did not understand what the teachers were lecturing about, and my notes were so scribbly that I could not decipher them after my reality came back. Without being aware of it, nor when it happened, I drifted or snapped into amnesia from the shock, the drugs or the anesthesia.

I functioned, for I don't know how long, in a complete intelligence and emotional vacuum. I did not know how to find classrooms, restrooms, labs or lecture halls. I think that somehow I ended up in the right places, at the right times, most of the time. It was as if an invisible hand led me wherever I had to go. I crossed streets without paying attention to traffic. I went to restrooms without being aware of why I was there or what I was doing. I had no mind of my own. I was not responsible for what I was doing because I did not know who or what I was or anything else. Did I shower with clothes on or roam the dorm stark naked?

And no one seemed to notice that I was a brainless zombie. And no one seemed to care.

Afterwards I remembered that I had asked my physics professor if I could postpone my final test until later. I explained that I had recently been twice in the hospital and was still in great pain. But because he would not allow me to do that, I squirmed around in my seat for two hours, holding a pencil with my bandaged stump. I only wrote my name on the test paper, found it later to be illegible, and I did not grasp the meanings of the questions I was to answer, much less answer them.

During my final checkup, while I was waiting in an exam room for my doctor to arrive, I sneaked a peek into my medical file which the nurse had placed by the door. I found a note from a doctor to my surgeon, mentioning something about what the "interesting patient talked about." But I did not want to get caught reading my file, so I quickly put it back into place. I've been wondering ever since what secrets, or nonsense, I spoke *while under the influence* during and after my surgeries. *Had I babbled about Nazis or playing in doodoo? My love for lawyers or girls? Or had I boasted about the many ghosts in my soul?*

After I received my final grade report for this semester, and my brain functioned again, I figured out that my grade point average for all classes had dropped by one whole grade because I had missed or flunked some of my final exams.

◆   ◆   ◆

My self-mutilation started a tradition in this architectural school, much like sword dueling at the German universities of yore. It used to be a status symbol for their male students to have nice long dueling scars on their cheeks. My ear and my new stump were as prestigious and as heroic as any scar of those swordsmen. But no one realized this.

Our architectural design workshop was a real butcher shop, a dueling ground for the creation of status scars, a battleground where we built fine models. Exactly one year later, another student cut his finger, the same finger, on the same saw, during the same finals week. The same surgeon sewed his finger back together, and he did not lose any of it. But it remained scarred, rigid and bent backward. We compared index fingers and agreed that my shortened configuration looked more distinguished than his crippled one.

With one quick swipe with his sharp utility knife, my friend Fuad sliced cardboard as well as three of his fingers.

Another student committed amateurish hara-kiri. Gripping his utility knife in his fist as if thrusting a dagger, he pushed down hard while guiding it along a metal bar to cut cardboard. He came to the edge of the table it was resting on, before he came to the end of the cardboard, and jabbed the knife into his leg, severing the main artery. Since he did not have a hose repair kit, he went into shock and froze in place, while his pants became soaked with blood. Fortunately someone applied a tourniquet and took him to the hospital or he would have bled to death. Even after this event, we never received any verbal or written safety tips, nor thought of suing anybody because this was still the era before proliferate laws protecting humanity from itself.

◆   ◆   ◆

After Siggi and I were separated by coming to America, we grew apart and had little contact with each other. In Pullman we never roomed together and hardly visited each other. I did not remember that Siggi had visited me in the hospital, or if he even knew that another small part of me had returned to dust. When I reminded him about this years later, he told me that he had visited me twice, but both times I had been asleep. We were struggling to get through college and avoided pain. We were like so many people who are in denial of the existence of unpleasant, even life-threatening situations, and tried to avoid such mental pain as much as possible.

Often I knew that Siggi was nearby because on many evenings, after dark, he walked by my window while I was studying. He would shout, "Neuman hurts." I think he meant me and not himself, or maybe both. I still do not know why he did this because he won't tell me; we felt no animosity toward each other; at least I felt none toward him.

One evening he sent me this message for the last time. He had borrowed my old bike and was cruising downhill past my dorm room. Again I was studying and heard, "Neuman"…Crash, scrape, tinkle. I looked out, and in the streetlight I saw Siggi dragging my old bike off the road. Its handlebar had broken off where it had been welded, and this had caused him to crash.

This reminded me of another one of Siggi's bike-sailing experiences. We had taken a bicycle trip from Rheinfelden into the Black Forest, and as we were racing down a hill, his brakes had failed. At the bottom of this hill was a blind railroad crossing. Because he could not see what danger might be ahead, he had played it safe and had stuck his foot into the spokes of the front wheel, which caused him to sail expertly over the handlebars and land flat on his back on the pavement. Fortunately he was unhurt and only tore a hole on the back of his sweater. His front wheel and fork bent so much that I took his bike back home on the train, while he continued his journey on mine, accompanied by our friend who had come with us.

◆   ◆   ◆

Every summer we returned to the coast for our jobs. I simply walked into the office of the sawmill, hoping to be re-hired, and in the beginning years we always were. Siggi got a job at Screech and Stench as well, in the laboratory of their paper mill, testing the production runs every night. I spent one shift with him up high in the factory and watched his activities and those below. He started out by gathering paper samples, took them up to his lab, ground them up and reconstituted the resulting pulp back into paper. Then he conducted various tests, such as folding, punching and tearing the specimens, and we could not visit much because he had to concentrate on what he was doing.

In the factory a huge, long, rectangular box poured forth a wide ribbon of paper that spooled onto a giant roll. Whenever it was full, several men cut this ribbon and manually threaded it onto a new spool to start another roll of paper, while a bulldozer carried away the full one. All the while the unending ribbon of paper never stopped flowing from its iron womb.

By the end of his shift I was becoming very bored, when suddenly an alarm sounded. I looked down and was astounded by what I witnessed. A full spool had been removed, and the paper band continued flowing out of the machine. The new spindle had not properly taken up the new end, and the paper was now growing into a big, messy mountain on the factory floor. The bulldozer kept pushing this aside, while several men cut the paper umbilical cord, attempting to properly re-spool a new roll without getting buried under the growing pile. They had to work quickly because the paper kept coming at a steady speed and would soon bury them and the dozer. After repeated attempts they finally succeeded in starting a new roll.

Siggi did not have to work very hard physically and fortunately during my last summer at Screech and Stench, my job also became a lot easier. I did not have to do heavy labor anymore, and better yet, I did not have to suffer the constant mind-blowing screaming of the wood planers. Now I worked in the parts room and in the machine shop doing various tasks, including drafting machine parts and fueling the tall stack carriers that could straddle over piles of lumber to move them. I liked this part of my job the best because I could look down from great height while cruising around. At times I spotted for a welder with a water hose to squelch potential fires as he welded in various locations of a sometimes very combustible environment.

For two weeks I also worked in the machine shop during the day shift. The foreman told me to slow down my production or his crew would be expected to keep up this level of output. I could not understand why this should be so and as always continued to give it my best effort. This ethic was in my genes; it had been pounded into my soul. *Was this yet another ghost?*

Besides our summer jobs, Siggi and I worked in the dormitory commissary in the evenings throughout some semesters. In addition, every Sunday evening during one semester, from eleven until two o'clock in the morning, I enhanced my social life by cleaning and mopping the kitchen floor of the empty student union building for a generous one dollar an hour, less than half of what I earned at Screech and Stench. This late night carousing helped me stay very alert in my favorite class at eight o'clock on Monday mornings, "calculus and analytical geometry." Then my tiredness joined with my math test ghost to torment me almost unbearably whenever I had to take a test in this subject. I passed this course only because a classmate, who later became a successful commodities trader, and I studied together for one of these tests. He read our textbook, outlined all of the important formulas and theories that he thought might be on this test and wrote them down on paper, which I then solely studied. Because of his approach to absorbing the study material, I earned a good grade, which helped me pass this difficult subject.

My own method of studying had always been to try to load the entire textbook into my brain, being afraid that I might miss something, and thereby overloading it enough that I would do poorly on these types of tests. Someone had ingrained this habit in me. Actually it was more than a habit; it was a neurosis. I finally realized that the more I studied, the worse my grades could be. So before the next finals, I severely weakened this neurosis ghost by playing a lot of jolly volleyball in the courtyard of our dormitory, instead of overloading myself with extraneous info, worries and neuroses. I kept encouraging my teammates to get the ball over the net by yelling "over." Before long, both teams kept yelling "ova," imitating my accent, regardless of who had the ball. From then on, Ova became the mantra for all players. Ova improved my grades because I studied less and worried less. This was another example of how Siggi and I had to unlearn some of what others had pounded into us. Literally. We had so many ghosts to destroy.

◆　　◆　　◆

I think that Siggi and I have never knowingly told anything bigger than little white lies or cheated anyone, even if the truth would hit some people like an express train, or we'd shoot ourselves in the foot, so to speak. Although I needed to achieve good grades in all subjects to counterbalance the damage done by my ghosts, I would never cheat to raise my scores. For example, a classmate asked me if I wanted to study with him for an upcoming written architecture test.

"That will help us both," I said to him.

"I found a copy of the test in the waste basket," he whispered to me as we sat down.

"You mean the real test?" I questioned.

"Yeah, I'll show it to you."

One of my ghosts caused me to leave him sitting there by himself, dumbfounded, because I rose again, said good-bye and left the room. My honesty ghost would not even allow me to remain in the same room with him because I felt so strongly that by remaining near him, I would somehow be associated with his dishonest practice. Uncompromising honesty prevented me from improving my score. Throughout our lives, that particular ghost would even cost us money and more. It might be like François VI, Prince de Marcillac, Duc de La Rochefoucauld had said in 1678: "Honest people will respect us for our merit; the public for our luck." So far we hadn't had much luck in life. *Do we have any merit, Siggi and I?*

At one time I had been so desperate for money that I advertised to sell the Ford for one hundred dollars or less. After Maxo had found out about our experience in LaCrosse, he had let me register it in my name, but I could not afford to insure it. When Jon came to buy it, I had told him everything that needed repair.

"The front wheels need aligning," I had told him.

"The gears are really loose. Sometimes they lock up when you shift into reverse," I continued.

"I'll have to think about it," Jon had finally said to me.

No one ever bought that Ford at that time.

Eventually someone did steal it.

During a summer stint in Everett, I had come home one Friday night and by next morning the Ford was missing. I had reported this theft to the police, who then had found it a day or two later. It had been abandoned where it had run out of gas not too far from our home, and one fender was dented as a thank-you for its use.

◆   ◆   ◆

Although neither Siggi nor I told our roommates in college that we were impoverished, they knew it. I brushed my teeth with soap scraps that I found in the dorm showers. One day my roommate, Bernard, insisted that I attend a dress-up scholarship dinner in our dining hall. I was not interested and informed him that I did not have anything fancy to wear, thinking that he would accept that excuse. But sly Bernard ironed one of his white shirts, at two o'clock in the morning, so I could wear it to this function. Because of his efforts I felt obligated to attend. During dinner the master of ceremonies called my name and presented me with a 100-dollar scholarship check.

Siggi had been the first one to receive this award during the previous year. The boys in our dorm must have collected it specifically for us and did not want to embarrass us, so they contrived a scholarship to disguise their acts of charity. After two years this was discontinued, and as far as I know, only Siggi and I benefited from their generosity. Thank you immensely, Goldsworthy boys; you helped us a lot. I never applied for or received any other scholarships, and this one helped greatly to pay for my college costs, which amounted to an astounding all-inclusive 1,200 to 1,500 dollars a year.

These so-called scholarships and the assistance from the Hansons were by far the biggest help that we had ever received from anyone, except for the postwar packages from the Schitzmas. There had been two other instances, but they were part of an organized impersonal effort. For some months after World War II all of the children in Simonswolde had received free chocolate milk, compliments of America.

CARE had sent us a five-pound can of butter while we were squatting in the attic in Rheinfelden. The donor's name was listed as Mr. Northrup from Hollywood. At that time we wrote him a letter of thanks, but we did not know if he received it, or if he could read German. Thank you, Mr. and Mrs. Northrup for your kindness; there was no butter in our neighborhood garbage, and your gift was greatly appreciated.

Then there was my friend Fuad who smoked *Lucky Strikes* and always offered me one whenever he lit one in my presence. I always tried to quit smoking, but never could resist his offers because I was hooked. I finally overcame my addiction when I taped a few cigarettes to the inside of my room door. Whenever I passed through, I squirted them with a water pistol. The brown juice ran down the door and was disgusting enough that I was able to quit smoking and for the final time. Quitting was also made easier because I did not see Fuad much anymore. I began spending most of my free time with my future bride, Linda, who did not smoke, and therefore I was not directly tempted nearly as much.

I first met her in the dining hall when she sat across from me during a dinner. She was tall, had beautiful eyes and long, thick, shiny hair and I kept staring at her, which made her nervous. When I finished my salad I asked her if she were going to eat hers. When she said no, I asked her if I could have it, she agreed, and thus began our life-long relationship.

◆   ◆   ◆

In September, days before starting my fifth year in college, Linda and I were married in her hometown, and the many wedding guests astounded me. All of them except for Siggi were Linda's family and their friends. They gave us many presents and Maxo also sent us one, a silver tea platter with sugar bowl and creamer that were engraved with an old Frisian pattern. And on the bottom of the platter was engraved, "Best Wishes from Uncle Maxo." Three decades later I would introduce this present as evidence in court.

While we both completed our final year in college, we lived in a tiny, forty-dollar-a-month attic apartment that did not have a living room. It was located in downtown Pullman, had moldy bathroom walls and a miniscule kitchen. Some couples paid two hundred or more dollars for their rents but unlike many of them, we did not go into debt.

At graduation time my friend Gale and I finished our final examinations before Linda finished hers. While she was studying, he visited us, and he and I played "Sea Battle." For this simple game, each opponent drew his "ships" on a sheet of grid paper that we hid from each other, x-ing out an equal number of squares to represent them. We could arrange them in any linear fashion and could make them any length. The first player who blackened out his entire navy lost the battle.

After we built our fleets we started our naval battle. Gale said: "D12."

"Missed," I informed him.

"A1," I continued, knowing that Gale was smart and probably would hide one of his ships in one of the farthest corners of his ocean.

"Missed, J19," he answered.

And so we continued, missing and damaging each other's ships more or less at random.

Suddenly I got lucky. I had a number of successful hits in short order.

"K2," I said.

"Hit," Gale said in a cold voice.

"L4," we could send an additional torpedo for each successful blow. I blasted him repeatedly and could not control my laughing.

"M19."

"This guy is psychic," mumbled Gale as I finished him off to win the battle.

I was not. Had I been, I would not have believed how good my new life was going to be and in the not-too-distant future. Now that Linda and I had graduated from college, we were ready to conquer the world. Or at least travel around and enjoy its wonders!

7

FREEDOM AT LAST

o o o o o o o o o o o o o o o o o o o o o o o o o o o o o o o o
A successful person is one who can lay a firm foundation with
the bricks that others throw at him or her.

—*David Brinkley*

Did we have enough bricks? How would we use them, Siggi and I?

◆　　　◆　　　◆

After an eternity, a quarter century, my new life was almost normal
and ranged from office boredom to marital happiness but was interspersed with an occasional hint of my ghosts. For the most part, at this
time I was still not sure what these were, how many were hiding within
me, or that they even existed. So far I had suffered the math test ghost,
the speaking ghost, and long forgotten shadows of others. But I did not
think of them as being uncommon, as my personal ghosts, because I
thought that everyone suffered similar anxieties to varying degrees,
mainly because I had never enjoyed an easy life.

Siggi and I came into this world in a country at war with itself and
with many other countries as well. We had lived in deep poverty while
suffering through scores of vicious court processes. Our Progenitors'
War continued well into our college years, when mother still sued
father and father still sued mother. And Teufi sued all of us. After eigh-

316

teen years there was nothing left to loot from us, and true to a parallel timeworn cliché, this war would not end until the fat lawyers sang.

Someday there would be other such bands to enhance the lives of our families, Siggi's and mine, even though we would still be innocent creatures who continued to live within the law and tried to never harm anyone.

Before the end of the Progenitors' War, we were uprooted from our homeland and shipped to America where we worked in slavery. Then we struggled through college. In later years, when I would examine our past and would briefly mention something about it to other people, I expected them to query me more about our tribulations because these had been so prolonged, so intense and so out of the ordinary. I was proud that we had survived them, thrived in spite of them, and felt that Siggi and I deserved a little empathy and recognition for this. But people usually would not show much interest and simply reply that our struggles had built character. Therefore we must be robust characters and a part of the backbone of humanity. But we would also learn that such statements were often just lip service, and that there would be less and less demand for such backbone. We would learn that being a vertebra would too often result into what hundreds of web sites claim that "no good deed goes unpunished."

◆   ◆   ◆

Linda and I moved to Seattle and began our new jobs, she with an engineering firm, I in an architect's office. She finished four years of studies in three years, even while changing her major three times, and I earned a five-year degree with little financial support from anyone. My curriculum took me six years to complete since I had to skip one semester to catch up on my earnings, had worked during college, and had suffered a few setbacks in the battles with my unascertained ghosts. Early on we decided that we deserved an elevating experience since we both had worked so hard for so long, and it did not take us long to conclude that we wanted to travel.

As we formed our travel plans, we discovered that it would not take all that long to save enough for a trip around the world. And save we did. With this prospect, it was not too difficult to squirrel away all of Linda's paycheck and some of mine, if we bought only the absolute necessities. I had always survived on next to nothing, and Linda's ancestors had worn skirts and played bagpipes in Scotland.

♦   ♦   ♦

After Siggi and I graduated from college we became American citizens. Now we were worthy of it.

♦   ♦   ♦

As our lives were changing rapidly in America, those of our parents were improving as well. Siggi was going for his Ph.D., while Pa and Ma, bitter enemies for more than twenty years, had found new friends. Each other. Yes, each other! After all, they were born on the same day and that made them friends, even though at times, one had wanted to kill the other. One year after my graduation Ma wrote me:

"…I have to praise Herbert. He did only what he thought was right, everything else he did not care for."

Why don't I understand this?

"I have to listen every Sunday afternoon to his complaints about the unnecessary things that his Teufi is pursuing. He has only me and Dr. Lupfer, and no other place in this world where he can seek refuge from the horrors he has at home."

Horrors at home? Harvest time for Daddy?

"Now Teufi wants to get rid of him since at the present time there is little construction activity. She has already rented out the architect's office. He is supposed to leave the house because she wants to rent it out for five hundred marks. She does not buy any more food for him and he says he is very depressed. Since I am dependent on him I am very worried about him.

"He claimed before the court that his office was in her name and he only had an income of two hundred marks a month as her 'construction supervisor.' He paid taxes on this income but never received any of these wages. (Think about this!)"

This evokes my ever more favorite expression, Weird, weird, weird!

"According to the advice of an attorney, she is supposed to pay him twenty-one thousand marks immediately. Now it goes with him exactly like the three of us in the past. **He is living on the edge of a bed!**"

"I have to laugh but this situation cannot continue because it is very serious. And since he could not pay me my one hundred twenty-five marks for the last two months, I was forced to think: 'We four, you and Siggi, he and I, are sitting in the same boat, I mean according to the law. And I hope that this matter sinks into your consciousness.'

"Even though he was in bondage with Teufi for fourteen years and forgot about us, it serves no purpose to hold this against him. He has to be kept alive because he is a very capable architect, and Ami, you could learn more from him than any other person.

"Therefore I am pleading with you, since he is now having a difficult time, facing divorce and other catastrophes, to write him a nice letter here in Rheinfelden and not to Weil, so that he has some comfort, joy and support in his difficult days. Sometimes he is optimistic and sees golden mountains for the day that he is divorced…"

No, mother, we are not in the same boat. Soon I'll be on an ocean liner. Yes, mother, I'll forgive you and father although I feel there's nothing to forgive. But my thoughts cannot be with you often. I won't be sad anymore.

Ma also sent me the following clipping from a newspaper:

"Successfully Completed In America.

"Weil-on-the-Rhine. Ami Neuman, a son of the Weil architect Herbert Neuman, has completed his examinations as a graduate engineer with great success in the University Pullman, (America). Our best wishes to the young building master."

In this article, someone had subtly advertised an architect's business by taking credit for my success, to show the world how capable we are, we Neumans. Bring us your design projects. We are the best; we are international.

Through all the years, our parents had never gloated, "We forged our sons into heroes." Not once did they praise Siggi and me personally for our great efforts or congratulate us for our accomplishments. They did not ask, did we scorch your souls? Not once did they tell us that they were sorry for giving us such an interesting life. They did not ask, how agonizing was your slavery so far from home? They did not ask, did you learn anything?

As always, I read Ma's letters and paper clippings quickly and then forgot about them; it was unmanly to wallow in parental love and affection. It was too overpowering; I would get bruised. But there are always the reminders such as: "Johnny's going fishing with daddy." There are those yearly shopping frenzies with hints of religious tunes and colorful lights that cast such long shadows.

◆   ◆   ◆

After working full-time for one and a half years, Linda and I quit our jobs because we had saved enough to begin our first major trip. We made arrangements to cruise for two months to Europe by way of the Pacific, then travel there for three months before cruising home for another month across the Atlantic and back through the Panama Canal. In retrospect this had been a very wise decision, for nowadays it would be difficult for most people to save enough to be able to do this, partly because of the long-term devaluation of the dollar vis-a-vis many other currencies.

I announced to my office that I was quitting but did not volunteer our plans because I was still modest and did not want to show off. I did not want anyone to think that I was better off than anyone else. I knew how rotten life could be and did not want to gloat about being in any way superior to others. However, upon persistent questioning I revealed more and more of what my wife and I intended to do and was greeted with an odd reaction from a few of my colleagues. I did not realize that the basis of their reactions was emotional, one of envy. I did not understand this until much later, for strangely, I could not remember having experienced such a feeling myself. I only became directly aware of envy when someone felt my sleeve to check if my shirt were wool or flannel and observed that person's reaction. I was not bothered that Maxo owned the tideland, and I owned nothing in the sense that I felt that it should be mine. Maxo insisted that someone had paid for our trip or that we had borrowed it. *Could he have been envious, because he refused to believe that Linda and I had earned it ourselves?*

To this day I still don't know why I am devoid of envy. Maybe it was bombed, beaten and starved out of me and was replaced by different kinds of ghosts. I've also never felt really tempted to steal anything, except cow feed from my masters.

◆   ◆   ◆

As we were packing to move out of our apartment to begin our voyage around the world, Linda said to me:

"We are out of boxes. Could you please go to the store and get some more?"

"Sure Sweetie Pie, I can handle that," I told her and went out. I sat down to start our Volkswagen and wondered what I had to do. *What am I doing here?*

I drove away and somehow arrived at the supermarket. I could not remember where to find it, or how I found it, but somehow returned home with cardboard boxes. After we finished cleaning and packing, we started driving to Linda's parents in the fun city of Elko, Nevada. Eventually this gold mining and gambling town would be designated

"The Best Little City in America," properly advertised, complete with logo.

I was driving. My mind was empty. We arrived in Salem, Oregon, after dark and pulled up to a fast-food drive-in. Cars were buzzing all around us. I had a brief flash in my mind that these were kids cruising main street since it was Friday night, and that's what they do on such a night. They were searching for that elusive contact. Cruising was rooted in the ancient mating dance of the species, the American Graffiti. This insight came and left again seconds later.

"What are these people doing? Why are they just driving around?" I asked Linda from out of my fog.

She gave me a worried look, saying: "Are you all right?"

"Sure," I think I answered. I think I lied. I didn't understand the meaning of her question, or why she had asked it.

We bought something to eat and continued on our way south. I did manage somehow to stick a hamburger into my mouth and swallow it. Outside of town there was little traffic on the dark highway. I didn't know that I was driving and weaved down the road while crossing the centerline repeatedly. Linda asked me again if I were OK. I was once more in an intelligence vacuum because there was not a thought in my brain; I was barely aware of my own existence. In spite of her continued requests to let her drive, I blithely continued while barely paying attention to what I was doing. I was ignorant of her worries for our safety and told her that I was OK because I didn't know that I wasn't. Unbeknownst to me, my brain had shut down again the way it had after I came out of the hospital lacking two inches of finger. Like then, I somehow functioned but again, I did not know how.

Miraculously we arrived in Elko without an accident and stayed a few days with Linda's parents. I did not talk much and slipped in and out of lalaland during most of our visit. Linda's mother asked me to mail a package. I didn't know where to find the post office five blocks away, how I arrived there, or if I mailed it. To this day I still wonder why I did not drive around aimlessly until I ran out of gas or did not crash into cars and buildings. Linda's father took me to a pasture to look at some Hereford cows. As soon as we climbed the fence, they ran up to greet us. Befuddled, I thought they were going to attack us, so I jumped back over the fence. Later I didn't think that Charlie was impressed with his son-in-law's courage. Had I been in a lucid state of mind, I would have known that those cows were normally harmless. *Why did this happen again? Could it be a reaction to chemicals? Hope it's not my ghosts. They are difficult to find and harder to slay.*

Both times I had taken in foreign substances. For my gangrene there had been anesthesia, huge amounts of antibiotics and painkillers. This time it could have been the shots for yellow fever, typhoid, typhus, polio, etc. that were required for our voyage. We had to be inoculated numerous times over several weeks to be able to ward off these diseases.

Linda's parents drove us to San Francisco where we toured around the Bay Area and also visited Seal Rocks. There was a coin-operated scale at the visitor center that foretold the future. I weighed myself and read my fortune: "You are going to travel around the world." Had this scale been located at the pier, I would not have been surprised by this prediction, but it was miles away from one. *Coincidence or divine foresight by a mechanical device?*

◆   ◆   ◆

We embarked on our ship, the "SS Oronsay." Our stateroom, a tiny cabin much like a coffin just big enough for sleeping, rocking and barfing, was located below the water line. There was also a driveshaft spinning inside our coffin. This did not matter much because we were headed to many exotic places and planned to stay on the upper decks during most of our waking hours. We were scheduled to cruise to Hawaii, Japan, the Philippines and Hong Kong. Then we were to continue to India, the Middle East, through the Mediterranean Sea and on to England. But because of sunken ships from the Arab/Israeli war, the Suez Canal was closed. Therefore our itinerary was changed to bypass

India and the Middle East, two places that we really wanted to visit and were rerouted around Africa.

As we approached Japan we sailed roller-coaster-like through the fringes of a typhoon. My necktie on the doorknob was our rock and roll indicator; it seemed to swing with a more or less steady rhythm, thirty-some degrees to the left, likewise to the right. This was my second storm at sea, and I wondered how many more we would have to suffer through on this trip. Nightfall arrived. The tossing about of our ship caused me severe fright and such claustrophobia that I was able to stay in our cabin, a tempestuous bunker, for only brief moments. I felt as if our ship had been abandoned since I seemed to be the only passenger staggering around the lounges and hallways, while Linda stayed in her bunk bed below the pounding ocean. The doctor gave her an injection to ameliorate her seasickness. I wanted to comfort her but always had to leave our coffin quickly because of my fright, while she seemed to be too ill or too doped up to care if our ship tipped over.

It did not help my confidence that crewmembers were raising the doorsills to the outside with boards, to keep out the sea that was crashing onto the decks. To allay my fears and get some rest, I tried to analyze the action of the waves and the twisting of the ship to reach an objective conclusion about its seaworthiness. I figured that there was no way that it would not burst its seams because even the floor tiles were popping off the bending steel structure. Our ship creaked, groaned and crackled everywhere I went; there was no escape from it. Intermittently it bounced with an agonizing crunch that felt and sounded as if it had hit a mogul on a downhill ski run. I heard a crash. A piano ripped from its tie-down and smashed into a wall. Someone sailed from his top bunk, mattress and all, and broke his ankle. Breakfast dishes set up in the evening jumped the rails around the tabletops and were sliding back and forth in pieces across the floor. Lone crewmembers scurried about.

I spent most of that night stumbling around our ship feeling like a caged lion. I climbed the ship's ladders and experienced variable gravity. Climbing, while the ship went downward, I floated upward as the support gave away under me. I felt almost weightless. Conversely, when the ship rose under me my weight seemed to double. I was a tiny bug on a twig bouncing about on a raging river.

Not being able to tolerate my confinement anymore, dwelling in the agony inside our ship, I burst to the outside even though this was strictly forbidden. This little bug could get blown away and drown. When I opened the door to escape from my cage, an invisible force pulled it outward. It drew me out while sucking the air from my lungs as well. Ducking into the storm, while clutching the handrails, I worked my way toward the front of our ship. Screaming and whistling, it plowed through the night. I worried about my hair. Was it planted firmly enough or would my scalp be bare?

The bow smashed into a wall of water that rolled toward the stern. Our world tilted upward, then downward, as we descended into the valley to crash into the next mountain. Liquid thunder roared through the night. White water raced past our ship into the blackness behind. Intermittently twinkling stars rolled about in the black sky somewhere above. I tottered upward toward the stern. As I approached it, an invisible mountain rose into the black void beyond. I knew it was there because the gale ripped white water from it that reflected the glow from our lights. While I clung to the rail, I craned my neck to find the peak of this rising mountain. It blocked my view of the stars; it devoured them.

The bow dove down again as we plunged into the next valley, to labor up another mountain. Reversing directions, the stern rounded the top of the wave, and the ship shuddered as its propellers rose out of the sea, revving up speed as they churned the air. Before we schussed down the next slope of water, I stared down into the abyss where moments before a mountain had been, the next one emerging to lift us again toward the sky.

This was a roaring time to pray.

We were tossed through the night on a wild roller coaster ride. It gave me the greatest thrill of my life, while at the same time terrifying me as much as the conflagrations of my infant days.

But I did not barf.

However, I did propose to Linda that we debark in Yokohama, fly to Australia, from winter to summer, and meet the "Oronsay" there. But we quickly abandoned this idea since it was too costly, and we would miss many, many wonderful places along the way.

The next day the raging fury ceased and the sea calmed again. I thanked God that we had survived. A news bulletin reported that a lumber ship had broken apart not far from us. After a good rest the following night, our trepidation became a faded memory as we continued to steam toward a new continent.

In Japan we rode a bullet train, a rocket flying just above ground. We raced in taxis at great speeds and followed other vehicles much too closely as well. We learned why many of the taxi drivers strengthened their necks by lifting car tires with them. Linda left white-knuckle marks in their seats instead. We were overawed by the ornate temples of Kyoto and saw the three monkeys who heard, saw and spoke no evil. We toured the Golden Palace, admired Geisha girls, and savored exotic foods and sake.

We toured Hong Kong, a most vibrant city, in rickshaws pulled by barefoot coolies. We enjoyed a nine-course dinner while delighting in the dancing of glittering girls, fiery dragons and smashing gongs. There could have been some male dancers also, but I don't remember. We cruised around a floating city where more than 200,000 people lived on wooden junks and sampans. Families shared their boats with pigs and chickens, and there were floating stores and floating schools as well. Boys dove from the high poops of their junks into the harbor poop to retrieve the coins that were tossed to them from our ship high above them. A caring mother in an open sampan, carrying her baby on her back, cooked a meal over an open fire, all the while trying to catch our offerings with a butterfly-catching net which had a very long handle.

Thousands of refugees from Red China also lived on the hillsides in squalor under scraps of tin and cardboard. They enjoyed the same luxury that I had savored only eight years before in my tideland shack. Many had no toilets either. However destitute, these people with little education were striving to improve their lot through hope, vision and hard work. Their poverty gave them incentive; they were not paid to sit and mope and pout. And the fruits of their labors were not stolen through excessive taxation.

Even though Hong Kong has essentially no natural resources, it was a wealth-creation haven for two major reasons: low taxes and "cheap" labor of thousands of immigrants. The highest income tax rate there was only fifteen, now seventeen percent, which was paid by only the wealthiest. Average families paid no income taxes at all. Consequently many Hong Kong middle class families would become multi-millionaires in spite of accommodating tens of thousands of impoverished refugees over a period of many years.

I can hear it again, "Yeah, but they have cheap…but they shouldn't…but I had a bad childhood…but…" I'm only the messenger of these facts.

◆   ◆   ◆

Near the Celebes, we levitated peacefully in a lifeless space through the hot, still air over the glass-smooth Banda Sea. The pale-blue sea merged with the pale-blue hazy sky at an indistinguishable horizon. The empty sea joined the empty sky and became one. In the far distance the vague image of a blue cone of a volcano floated into nothingness.

Our peaceful glide continued uninterrupted for more than two weeks, as the "Oronsay" steamed south with the east coast of Australia on the starboard side and the Great Barrier Reef portside for one thousand and two hundred miles. Lounging on deck chairs and basking in the sun, Linda and I observed crewmembers dump oblong sailcloth bags overboard and wondered if these contained bodies of erstwhile people. We had heard that the thrill of the typhoon had triggered heart attacks in some passengers. If they had died it was no use to keep them onboard because they had a better place to visit.

In December, summertime in Australia, we visited Sydney, Melbourne, Adelaide, Perth and Fremantle. The Sydney Opera House by the harbor was still under construction and would be an inspiring landmark. Its design represented a cluster of billowing sails built of concrete and covered with snow-white tiles. Its final costs would far exceed the initial estimates, but it would be worth it, for it will be enjoyed for generations to come, and few will ask how much it cost but many will appreciate its function and beauty.

The harbor of Melbourne was open and unprotected. As the "Oronsay" approached it, a stiff breeze was blowing from the sea pushing her toward the dock. To prevent a collision, two tugboats guided her there to moor broadside. To resist the force of the wind, they pulled our ship seaward under full power with arm-thick hawsers tied to her bow and stern. When we neared the dock these snapped in quick succession, and the wind and waves pushed our huge ship into it, thus adding additional dents to her sides and to her pride.

◆   ◆   ◆

Sailing across another broad expanse of ocean, the Indian Ocean, we visited the ports of Durban and Capetown, South Africa, and later to Dakar, Senegal, on the west coast of the African continent. We anchored outside the Capetown harbor for most of the afternoon before going ashore. While waiting, we lounged on deck watching the bustle in the harbor. Capetown is located at the southern tip of the continent, where its high plateau terminates abruptly at a barren vertical cliff called Table Mountain. The sky was cloudless except for one fascinating cloud. It was the "cloth" on the Table, a flat, white cloud that spread thinly over its flat summit. It formed from the moist, warm air that rose from the sea to condense as fog at the top because it was cooler there. This thin layer of fog then slowly slid back down over the edge of the table, draping itself down the cliff like a cloth, like a dissipating slow-motion waterfall, dissolving again in the warmer air at the lower elevations.

At night we visited the top of Devil's Peak outside the city. From there we admired the Table Mountain cliff again. Illuminated by floodlights, it hung like a surrealistic luminous curtain from the starlit sky over the sparkling lights of the city.

Apartheid, separation, in this case mostly blacks from whites, was still enforced in South Africa. While traveling there, I made it a point to sit on benches marked for "Non-whites Only" and purchased food at "Non-Europeans Only" counters. I was more brown than white, and I was not European anymore. However, the race police did not seem to pay any attention to me. I could have been mistaken for a colored, or a civilized wild man, because I was tanned by the sun and the sea and sported a mane that was tousled by stiff ocean breezes.

We visited a Zulu village with huts built of whips and reeds. My eyes popped out while seriously studying comparative anatomy of the half-bare women going about their business. Balancing urns and baskets on their heads, they walked as regally as any queen, and when we asked them to dance for us, they did and their children as well.

◆   ◆   ◆

After visiting Dakar, and sailing through yet another storm, the "Oronsay" arrived in Lisbon, Portugal, on New Year's Eve Day. There we boarded a train towards Rheinfelden to visit Ma, whom I still prefer to call Linda's mother-in-law or Siggi's mother. We tried to sleep on the train while traveling across Spain but were awakened by Spaniards serenading in the New Year. Even though we were very tired from the stormy night before, we greatly enjoyed their fiery spirit and boisterous singing.

After crossing the Pyrenees we arrived in Périgueux, Southern France. Here we were supposed to change to an express train to continue to Basel, Switzerland, but nobody had told us that, or we had not understood our instructions in a foreign language. Since we were exhausted, we did not pay attention to our itinerary and arrived late at night in Paris instead. Because we had missed our transfer, we ended up in a place hundreds of kilometers from where we wanted to be.

While Linda guarded our many suitcases in a freezing snowstorm, I went to the railroad ticket office and tried to convince the agents there that we should be able to travel to Basel without having to pay for our detour around France. After a lengthy discussion in French, which strained my brain, they agreed that we could do so. We boarded an express and fell asleep but were later awakened by a conductor who insisted that we had no valid tickets. *Sacre bleu.* I could not stimulate my French brain cells enough to explain to him that we had permission from Paris to travel without fare, and therefore we had to pay him on the spot for our unintended journey.

We arrived in Basel early in the morning and were so tired that we did not want to change to another train for the last sixteen kilometers to Rheinfelden where Ma was still living. Instead, we checked into a hotel for a few hours to rest and bathe before commencing the short final leg of our long migration.

Although Ma had two bedrooms and had insisted that we stay with her, we were unable to do so. Her apartment was brimming with junk which was powdered with ancient dust. Therefore, while in the city of my birth, Linda and I resided at a nearby hotel, *Die Saengerhalle,* the same hotel where Siggi and I had practiced in the dance hall with the orchestra. This was also the hotel where Pa had resided between WWII and the official start of the Progenitors' War and had almost succeeded in killing himself during a three-day drunken stupor. Fortunately, or unfortunately, his friend, Dr. Lupfer, had found him stark naked and had revived him. This was now the base to which we returned inter-mittently during our travels around Europe via Eurailpasses. At those times we would also visit Ma, but only for an hour or two at a time, because that was all the motherly love and heart-warming home décor that I could withstand.

She was still living in the apartment where Siggi and I had lived before our exportation to the States. Her collection filled every room. One day while Linda and I were visiting in her cocoon, we heard a knock at its entrance. Ma clambered through her dark vestibule to answer the door, and I heard her talk to someone in a low voice. She returned without mentioning this visitor, so I inquired as to who had been there. "Oh, nobody," she replied with downcast eyes.

When we ended our visit sometime later, we bid her farewell on the stair landing outside her apartment. There was a door which closed off the stairs up to the attic. I received Ma's brain waves and asked her casually if I could open that door.

She squealed: "No, please don't open that door. Please Ami, don't!"

Now that I was enlightened, I made it a point to disobey her because I suffered a short bout of delayed and suppressed teenage rebel-lion. Very slowly, to create and stretch tension, to rattle the skeletons in her attic, I nerve-wrackingly slowly pushed down the door handle and mind-twistingly slowly opened the door. On the bottom steps of the dark stairway stood a gentleman dressed in a black power suit, holding a black briefcase, brazenly tipping his black bowler hat with a smile. It must have been the only such hat in Germany because I had never seen them before in this land. He greeted us with a graceful bow, *"Guten Tag,"* good day, and exhibited no embarrassment whatsoever. Linda and I said not a word and descended the stairs.

What's the name of her business? Katje's Nest? Lawyers' Heaven?
Special Today: Time-Share Condom?

◆   ◆   ◆

While Ma continued to live in her own world at Werderstrasse 3, Pa and Teufi had moved to Weil-on-the-Rhine, apparently at a time when they still liked each other. Again, the architect's office was in the basement of the new multi-family house that they had built with the help of our money, Siggi's and mine. On impulse Linda and I stopped there to visit. We rang the doorbell and seconds later the electric lock returned a buzz. Upstairs, Teufi greeted us at the lead glass doors to the vestibule of the apartment and seemed embarrassed and somewhat frightened when she recognized me. Would I harm her? Would I stuff my second mother deep into the precious possessions of my first mother where no one would ever find her?

Her chubby cheeks flushed as I remembered them from before, and she graciously announced that Pa did not live there anymore. A new door had been cut into the clay tile sidewall from the staircase, next to the lead glass entrance. The irony of what goes around, comes around, was that Pa resided now in one room by himself because his sweetheart had thrown him out, but only after she had cleaned him out. As Ma had written to me, "he lives on the edge of a bed," meaning that his bed was now the center of **his** existence, as it had been for the three of us in the prison in our previous mansion and our subsequent attic.

This mystery may remain forever unsolved: How did our second mother receive everything we owned with one or two court processes, while our first mother had not even been able to extract a meager living for the three of us with twenty such cases? Was it because our first mother wore homespun knit stockings and our second mother wore lipstick and false eyelashes? Was it because Ma had gray hair and massaged everyone with brutal truth, while Teufi oozed a gooey demeanor? Was it because Teufi soothed lawyers standing at stud? Had she promised a judge an orchard or a forest if he would help steal from us? Or was it simply that people who decided the fates of children were ignorant or inhumane?

Teufi invited us into her apartment and retrieved Pa from his mattress to join us. With its dark wood paneling, her apartment was even more luxurious than the one in Rheinfelden. Since I felt no animosity towards anyone, not even towards my father or his Teufi, another defect in my personality, the four of us had a congenial visit. Teufi served us liqueur, and I never thought that she might have enhanced my drink until after I downed it. Then I remembered that she and Pa had wanted to render the three of us stiff, had talked about poisoning us, when we were cold, hungry and forgotten in our Hardtstrasse prison.

We had a warm reunion.

Often Linda and I had no plans for our travels and had told them that we had Eurailpasses, and that we would probably travel the next day to Spain. Frequently we boarded the first express to a city or country where we hadn't been before and found of interest. When we arrived at the station, however, we did not want to wait so long for a train to Spain; instead we boarded one to visit some cousins in nearby Kandern. While there, savoring Rhine wine and homemade plum cake, Pa walked in and was very astonished to see us. I felt that he was not so much surprised that we didn't travel to Spain, but that we might have complained to our relatives about his treatment of us. If he indeed thought this, he was wrong because I never had, nor very rarely ever would, complain to other people about Teufi, Ma or Pa until I wrote this memoir.

"*Na, da schauts her,* look at that, I thought you went to Spain."

"We had to wait too long for that train. So we came here instead."

Linda and I were so independent and without plans that not even we knew what country we would be in on any one day. To us it did not matter where we were headed because all of Europe was a playground, rich in history and overwhelming culture. If the first train departed to Austria where we had not been before, we boarded it. That is how we crisscrossed Europe for three months. To manage to do so, we slept often on the trains and subsisted mostly on cheese, French bread, Cokes, oranges and chocolate bars. Occasionally we ate warm meals and took baths while recuperating in hotels or bed and breakfast establishments.

While my architecture classmates were busily preparing for their state examinations, I was blissfully traveling around Europe with my beautiful bride. Others were crawling around the jungles of Vietnam and for what reasons I did not know.

During our worldwide travels we tasted a broad spectrum of many natural wonders, societies and cultures, and to describe this would fill volumes. We toured up the mountains in Japan and cruised down rivers in Australia. We visited palaces and castles, took in Renaissance paintings and admired Roman sculptures. We felt the spirits of the ancient Druids at Stonehenge and lingered in enormous Gothic cathedrals, such as in Cologne and Paris. We suffered concentration camps and museums filled with medieval torture devices. We dwelled in old villages and vibrant cities; we dined royally in castles and slept occasionally, unwittingly, in houses of prostitution.

Our experiences were as varied as the types of toilet paper that we came in contact with. Because we could not afford any during our early years, I was quite interested in this item while traveling hither and yon, so much so that we collected samples. These ranged from double-ought sandpaper to slick magazine types. This valuable commodity was even rationed in the restrooms of an Italian railroad station. A woman sat at the doorway and dispensed several sheets to each customer on his or her way in, and there was no more to be had later, unless one were skilled enough to negotiate very complicated, multilingual, international transactions with one's pants down!

◆   ◆   ◆

We looked for Nessie in the loch and listened to bagpipes in the land of Linda's ancestors. We traveled from Sweden to Sicily, from Lisbon to Salzburg. We browsed the Louvre and the buildings designed by Le Corbusier, we wandered in the streets of Paris, Lyon, and Marseilles, as well as many others. We took a photo of the little bronze *Mannekinpis* going full bore in Brussels. Since we were on a very tight budget, we often slept on trains in first class compartments that were our real mobile homes. We could fall asleep in one country and wake up in another. We were mostly by ourselves and our infrequent companions were other Americans doing the same. We moved around so much that in our travels we met by chance two Canadian girls, three different times, in different countries.

On the rocky island of Capri off the coast of Naples, we climbed down a cliff to the Blue Grotto and passed by a lonely girl sitting on a rock. We said "Hi" because she appeared to be another American, and she returned our greeting. From Naples we traveled to the toe of Italy and wondered why so many people were heading north, while our train was nearly empty. These travelers also carried lots of luggage and resembled the refugees with whom Ma, Siggi and I had traveled after World War II so long ago.

From the toe of Italy we sailed between The Devil and The Deep Blue Sea to Sicily. We saw only a few people there, and they advised us to leave again as soon as possible because earthquakes had been devastating this area. These islanders made us nervous because they eyed us suspiciously. They must have been wondering why two obvious Yankees arrived here during the tremors, when most everyone else was fleeing. Although we wanted to wait for a calmer sea, we returned on the next ship, to sail again past the Devil, because we did want to suffer his fury in this land.

Returning northward again, we stopped in Venice and checked into a hotel. We washed our socks in the bidet, even though people normally used it for something else. Then we rested. Later we strolled along the canals, always curious, always camera ready. Headless, naked rabbits and chickens were hanging in a butcher shop window, where the door stood open and a cat had sneaked in. While it was pawing at the choicest rabbit, I recorded this on film. This was the perfect picture of the cat and the rabbit that I wanted to present to Ma as a possible title picture for her new cookbook, should she be inspired by it to write one for people who were homeless.

In Venice we also visited the Doges' Palace and other sights on Saint Mark's Square. Among the many life-size marble statues was one of great intrigue. One naked wrestler held another one upside down around the waist, who in turn firmly gripped him by his forty-carat jewels. As with poems, there must be a deeper meaning represented in this sculpture.

We traveled high through the Swiss Alps and looked down from heaven at twinkling villages drifting dreamlike far below in the pale blue moonlight on the snow. Linda was frightened that our train might fall off the sheer cliffs, and I wondered about the same but told her that we were in heaven. We traveled overnight from Oslo to Bergen through miles of snow tunnels. High up on the steep sides of deep fjords, our train raced through such heavy snow that, at times, we could see only a white sheet in front of our window.

In Stockholm we visited Skansen Park where it was so cold that squirrels climbed up my pants with needle-sharp claws, begging me to feed them.

Back in Basel, we visited museums to admire everything from solid gold sculptures from Europe to woodcarvings from Africa.

Not finding a trail because of fog and deep snow, we hiked through a forest up a steep mountain to the Neuschwanstein Castle in the Bavarian Alps. After an arduous climb we arrived at the gate on the opposite side and discovered a road leading up to it. We toured this castle and admired the many treasures, one of which was King Ludwig's bed. Its canopy sprouted dozens of replicas of ornate cathedral spires that were carved from wood by two artisans over a period of two years.

On a subsequent trip to Europe we rode up to this same castle in a horse-drawn carriage. It was obvious that Neuschwanstein had been the inspiration for the Disneyland fantasy castle. We visited two other palaces of King Ludwig as well, Hohenschwangau and Linderhof. Numerous fountains in manicured gardens surrounded this small but very lavishly adorned chateau. Inside were many rooms with carved and gilded walls, mirrors and dozens of treasures. There was a chandelier of intricately carved ivory like no other in the world. In spite of this concentrated wealth, there were no visible guards or obvious signs of security measures other than glass cases and doors with locks.

◆　　　◆　　　◆

In Amsterdam we lugged our suitcases from the train to find a hotel. Buildings in various interesting architectural styles bordered the streets and the canals. Within a short distance from the railroad station a sign advertised *Rooms* and we checked in. Our matronly hostess led us to a room on the second floor, and I asked her where we could board a boat to tour around the many canals. As she gave me directions, I leaned out of the window to survey the scene below but was distracted by the image of a girl in a mirror next door. Naively I assumed nothing. At nightfall, and after eating our usual rations in our room, we went for a walk. Not far away a girl was sitting in a window, but she was wearing surprisingly little. Linda and I continued our stroll and observed numerous scantily dressed girls tanning in the moonlight. Men were standing in line on the sidewalk outside of these parlors, extremely patiently, waiting their turns to get tanned, tuned, or toned down. *Was the bowler-hat man the only one in Ma's attic?*

We witnessed a fascinating scene through one of these moon-tanning windows: a sitting maiden with long, bare legs and big boobs ballooning out of a tiny top. My eyes bugged out and I became confused; Linda pushed them back into their sockets. I felt the closeness of my wife and reached for her hand as we continued our walk through this ancient culture of the second oldest profession.

My eyes popped out again when I saw this woman a second time, smiling mysteriously and wiggling her legs and the contents of her brassiere for me. I wished her bubbles to fall out and was disappointed when they didn't. On our stroll we spied many more girls in various places, in various poses, in different settings. Some were in dark doorways, some in mirrors and others were lit by candlelight behind sheer drapes that were screening the mysteries of this international city.

After our cultural veneration, Linda and I returned to our room and spent a restful night in what we finally realized was an *adult entertainment* club. Together.

Were these adults *mothers? Did their mothers know they bore* adults*? These Dutch people were not like the ones in Uncle Fullo's church who didn't drink, dance, play cards, or watch movies.*

◆   ◆   ◆

Our experience in Amsterdam was so enlightening that fate provided an encore not long thereafter. When we arrived in Frankfurt one evening, we discovered an illuminated display in the railroad station which listed the many hotels in the city. It also informed us that there was not a single room vacancy. Since we could not afford to hire a taxi to cruise around to find accommodations, and since we were limited as to how far we could walk with our heavy luggage, we walked down the most promising-looking street. We entered the first hotel that we came to and the female clerk at the reception desk said:

"Yes, we have rooms and I will take care of him," while pointing directly at me. I did not know what she meant by this because she never took care of me.

Linda and I lugged our suitcases up the dark stairs, down the dark hall, into a dreary room with a single light bulb dangling from the ceiling. We did not like this place but we were tired and relieved to find a room at all. After we deposited our stuff we went back out to find something to eat. Two American girls happened to walk by and appeared to be as lost as we had been a short time before. We informed them about the hotel vacancies and invited them to stay with us. But like us, they felt uncertain and therefore declined our offer.

By the time we finished our dinner, the automobile traffic had not diminished as is normal after working hours in the center of big cities. It was actually increasing. Again we went window-shopping as we had done in Amsterdam. When we looked into what we thought to be a store window, my eyes popped out again, and this was a persistent problem for me on this voyage. Color photos advertised what was being sold here. They showed naked women, with men…

As in Amsterdam, we had unwittingly stayed again in a red light district. A fortyish woman approached men on the sidewalk to drum up some kind of business. When we passed her, she did not try to enlist me, as it was obvious that I was with my wife.

After absorbing this high culture, Linda and I returned to our room. Since I was a hero, I had the courage to go to the bathroom first. I tiptoed down a dank and dark hallway and around a scary corner. Dirt caked to walls, floors and ceilings. I summoned intense willpower to levitate myself into the room because I did not want to get stuck to the grimy floor or to the throne connected to a sewer pipe.

When it was Linda's turn, I guarded her zealously outside the door. Afterwards we washed in the sink in our room, and when we threw back the covers of our bed, we discovered that it had been slept in the night before. Or a few hours before, a few weeks or many times before. *Do the guests here need protection?*

To protect ourselves, we slept in our clothes and put clean "cases" on our pillows, two of my tee shirts. We left them there when we split again from this five-star rated establishment because we did not want to get polluted. We spent a fitful night rolling around because the traffic roar did not die down until about four o'clock in the morning. I studied the proletarian wisdom scratched on the wall next to our bed. It was in English and spelled correctly. The mysterious Kilroy who seemed to have preceded us everywhere in the world had left a note that he had been here also.

We rose in mid-morning and I surveyed the street below. There she was again and still drumming up some kind of business. She caught one, a customer, a male in his forties who was unbuttoning his overcoat as he followed a few steps behind her. They entered the building across the street, probably a type of hotel like the one in which we were staying. I looked at my watch and observed the entrance. Ten and one-half minutes later this man came back out by himself, buttoning up his coat, obviously having drummed his business.

◆   ◆   ◆

On our cruise back to the United States we steamed through the Panama Canal and returned to San Francisco. Several years later we would cruise partway into this canal again, have a party on Lake Gatun, and return back out to admire the Cuna Indians on the San Blas Islands. When our ship anchored offshore of these small islands, beautifully dressed women met us in their wooden dugout canoes. One caring mother kept her very young, stark naked baby with her in her rocking little boat. She had stained it, the baby, with a black dye-like substance to protect it from the fireball in the sky, and to keep it cool she intermittently splashed it with seawater. Judging by my rooftop tanning experiences, that blackened little baby was tougher than this sun-fried baby had ever been.

The Cuna tribe lived in huts on tiny islands, coral peaks daylighting from reefs below, and in a lifestyle that I had only dreamed about as a youth. These little people were hardy because they had no electricity, except for a few car batteries, and collected the rain that flowed from their huts into their canoes parked beside them. All the females wore brightly colored molas, dresses sewn together in intricate cloth patchworks of unique geometric designs. Supposedly these Indians used to paint these designs on their bodies but were prompted by a missionary to get dressed. *Did the Cunas ask the missionary to go naked and paint clothes on his or her body?*

We met a little mola-dressed girl who had two of the saddest eyes that I had ever seen. They were so big, and so deep, that I could see the shadows in her soul. Around her delicate bare neck she wore a necklace of unprotected double-sided razor blades.

◆　　◆　　◆

After our initial half-year long adventure, Linda and I returned to the Seattle area to find new jobs. For the next few years, I worked with several architectural firms, which included a three-man office, as well as the largest one in Washington. Over the years I realized that architects belonged to an unstable profession. Many lost their jobs frequently, thus forcing them to move from office to office, depending on the booms and busts in the construction industry. An affirmation of this was that only three alumni from my architecture class attended our twenty-year college reunion, and they all worked for state transportation departments.

Not long after we returned from our trip around the world, another ghost began to haunt me, and for the first time. The midnight ghost. It reared its ugly presence probably because I must have suffered from an unrecognized depression, having to return from our careless lifetime adventure back to the workers' rats' race paradise. My first visit to the land of my birth must have torn open old wounds in my soul and up to this time, I didn't know that this ghost existed. It was the meanest one by far, the persistent and punctual midnight ghost. It woke me frequently, and strangely, almost always at the same time, within fifteen minutes of one hour after midnight. *What terrors created my midnight ghost so long ago?*

Once this ghost woke me, it would ruin my following day, even if I had been awake for only a short time. My head would hurt, and I would be totally exhausted. I always worried that my co-workers would guess that I was a wreck, and that I would perform my job poorly. But I did not complain to anyone because this could be a good reason to be fired. And I often wondered when I would make a big mistake, such as placing a column in a doorway or not allowing enough headroom for some mechanical equipment. Fortunately I never made such mistakes, always received excellent performance reviews and was never fired or laid off from any position that I ever held during my career in architecture.

My midnight ghost was almost always controlled by the alarm clock. It usually zapped me when this inanimate object dictated my schedule. I usually slept soundly Friday and Saturday nights and during vacations. Since I have become self-employed, and I set the alarm clock only when absolutely necessary, my midnight ghost bothers me only occasionally and mostly during the dreary winter months.

◆   ◆   ◆

When Linda and I returned another time to Europe, we naturally stopped again in Rheinfelden to visit her mother-in-law who was such an attraction. She claimed that this time she was ready to accommodate her loving children. Previously we had spent a lot of money for a hotel only several blocks from her because her apartment was a garbage dump. With great anticipation, she wrote us that she had asked Siggi what she could do to make us feel at home. He had told her that there were only two conditions, to clean a room for us and not to badger us with advice.

We arrived at her apartment at ten o'clock at night to find that Ma could not break her old tradition.

Nothing had changed. Nothing was ready.

Even though Linda and I were exhausted from jetlag, we had to rearrange junk until midnight to clear a place in her wilderness. Instead of resting, we wrestled with our mattress, which caused our nerves to become wired, while our lungs vacuumed the valuable microscopic and larger particles which covered everything, even though we were careful not to stir them up during our attempt to establish a campsite. But after a few hours of restless bouncing around our bivouac, we were too exhausted to rest, so we rose to play cards until six-thirty in the morning, after which we caught the first train out of town to somewhere. Anywhere.

Ma twittered that her stuff couldn't possibly hurt us, but if we wanted to avoid her generous hospitality when we returned again to our home base, Pa, like a devoted father, would pay for our stay at a new bed and breakfast that he had designed in Loerrach. When we returned from an excursion, we moved there as she had suggested. Pa confirmed that he would pay, and I can't remember if I believed him. As we prepared to depart again some days later, and it was time to pay for our stay, Pa conveniently suffered a heart attack and stayed in a hospital. We did not visit him there because spending two or three days every decade with one's father had already been excessive. Ma gave us almost three hundred marks to pay for what Pa had promised to pay. She retrieved it from a secret place in her nesting material and said that she would recover it from Papa. Ha, ha, ha! Since I had served for years as her object of catharsis, and she had sent me into unexpected slavery, I accepted her offer. Letting her pay for our room was by far my most extreme act of purposeful unkindness toward anybody.

At some point a man must lose his patience.

◆   ◆   ◆

Before Linda and I had left on this particular trip to Europe, we had made reservations for our hotel rooms while traveling through the Communist dictatorships of Czechoslovakia, Hungary and Yugoslavia. We had to pass through these countries to get back and forth to Greece where we had arranged for a Mediterranean cruise. We rented a car in Germany and drove eastward to Czechoslovakia where important men with grim faces, carrying efficient killing devices, guarded its border. To keep people in. One of them opened our luggage and searched only through our travel literature and did not seem to be interested in our camera equipment or anything else.

I wanted to take a photo of a flying squirrel gliding from tree to tree near the customs house, but an official "No Picture Taking" sign forbade anyone to do so. Reluctantly I complied because I did not want to tempt the sub-machine guns. In this country we found many such signs forbidding people to photograph important installations such as railroad stations, power substations and bridges.

We arrived at the Karlstein castle, parked our car and hiked up a narrow road to the top of the hill while the faint fanfare of trumpets grew ever louder. After a final turn, we squarely faced the entrance to this imposing castle. Its drawbridge was down and four men wearing colorful medieval costumes stood in the openings of the battlements above. We imagined that they were blowing their long bugles that were festooned with medieval banners just for us, because we were the only visitors here, and therefore they gave us a hero's welcome.

We strolled around Prague, the city of spires, to its numerous steeples, carvings and sculptures. These adorned everything: bridges, sidewalks, buildings and parks. But strangely, much of this beauty was coated with black soot. The socialistic dogma inspired no one to maintain the treasures of their foremothers and forefathers, and sadly, since we in America can't wait for the soot of ages to accumulate on our heritage, we decorate much of our landscape with garbage.

In Bratislava we were lost. Using gestures, we tried to ask two peasant women for directions while pointing to our map. When they seemed to indicate that they were also heading our way, we invited them to ride with us and after many miles they asked us to stop to let them out. It took us a while to realize that we were far from where we wanted to be, and that they were probably at their destination.

On our way to Pezinok we thumped along a single lane road that was built with pre-cast concrete planks, laid side by side. Therefore we could not drive very fast, and while traveling through a dark forest, we met a black car full of cigar-smoking macho men. They stopped us and asked us, "*Wohin?* Where to?"

"Pezinok."

We had a definite feeling that they were monitoring our progress through their country. It took us most of one day to travel only a short distance through Czechoslovakia, mainly because we were often stuck in an unending line of slow-moving diesel trucks, puffing huge clouds of black exhaust. This made it difficult for us to see ahead to pass them. We rolled our windows up and down at intervals, up to keep out the fumes, down to catch a breeze to cool off. Our routine was determined by the intensity of the fumes and heat that we could suffer inside our small car. Our endless processions passed through many villages, which were spaced a few kilometers apart, generously blessing their populace with noise, soot and carbon monoxide.

In Pezinok we drove to the hotel where we had made reservations through the Czechoslovakian state travel office. No one spoke English, French, High or Low German, or so it seemed. Even though we presented our official reservation papers for this hotel, the clerk indicated that he had no room for us. Later that day we realized that he probably wanted a bribe from us, especially since we saw no other guests there. Since we offered him nothing and kept saying something like *Cedok,* the name of the state travel office, he finally assigned us a room.

After checking in, we ordered dinner in the empty hotel restaurant. I drooled over the menu and ordered Steak Tartar, since I always go for the wildest, the mostest, the fastest, and the weirdest. When my steak arrived I was truly grateful because it looked like it had been tenderized in the old tradition, under a bareback pony rider while galloping across the steppes of Asia. Although this raw meat was pale, tender and very delicious, I worried about the seat. But my concern was unfounded because I had the stamina of a great Tartar and suffered no uncomfortable aftereffects.

While crossing the Czech-Hungarian border, we had to drive through a depression filled with some kind of fluid. I asked the hitch-hiker who traveled with us about the purpose of this wheel wash. He explained that it was to disinfect the vehicles coming from the neighboring country; that was the official explanation, he said, but the real reason was to insult the neighboring country. He also told us that he had waited all night at this border crossing to get permission to leave, and that only "trusted" people were allowed to do so.

After sightseeing in Budapest, we had dinner with wine by a window open to the still, warm summer night, while our souls were soothed with melodies from live Hungarian violins.

This was life. This was heaven.

At the border crossing into Yugoslavia, a customs official came down our line of waiting cars and asked us if we were Americans. Of course we were, therefore he barely looked at our passports and waved us ahead, so we could continue our journey without delay. As Americans it was easy to get into Marshal Tito's country, some of which is now called Bosnia. To his countrymen we looked so much like Yankees that when I bought some postcards, without saying a word, the clerk told me in English how much they would cost. This also happened in Germany when I addressed strangers in German, and they would answer me in English.

While driving to Belgrade, we stopped in the town of Niš and found a historical monument, a tower of bleached human skulls. These human skulls were all cemented together, their dark eye sockets silently gazing eerily through the glass coffin that mirrored the stained glass windows of the sheltering outer tower. During the fourteenth century, armies had come from the east, killing millions of sons and daughters, brothers and sisters, fathers and mothers. The killers then erected towers of the skulls of these brothers and sisters as reminders as to whose god was in control. We learned on our travels that the people who created the most cadavers were too often in control.

> *"Out of the mirror they stare,*
> *Imperialism's face*
> *And the international wrong."*

◆   ◆   ◆

We drove into Greece to Thessaloniki and continued through the Larisa Plain, to the Valley of the Meteora. These meteora were huge individual precipitous rocks that rose from the broad valley floor. During the time when invaders from the East had built skull towers such as the one in Niš, Greek monks had built monasteries on top of some two dozen of these stone pinnacles to isolate themselves. At one time they were only accessible by means of a rope and basket or a series of retractable ladders. Now only six of these cloisters remain. They are quite well preserved, and one of them covers the entire peak of a monolith like a crown.

Not far away from this area, one of these giant rocks had a cavity halfway up its smooth side that was big enough for a house. A house stuck in the belly button of a mountain that even now could only be accessed with a rope ladder. There was also a clothesline but no fence to keep people from falling from this lofty perch so high up above.

In Athens Linda and I visited the Acropolis to meet Zeus, chief god of the ancient Greeks, but he was not home. In the young night we sat in his temple ruins under a half moon to sense its history, to admire its culture, to visit its people. We walked to the edge of the cliff and looked down into an ancient amphitheater that had been built into the side of the rock. It was brightly lit and a cast of characters, wearing long white robes, practiced a play about the people from so long ago.

The next morning we waited for the right light to photograph the Acropolis from a distance, and what a spectacular picture we caught.

The Greeks were very friendly to us. When we could not decipher the restaurant menus, they sometimes invited us into their kitchens to let us taste the different foods simmering there. Once a cook came out and retrieved a bare leg of lamb from under a café chair where it had been stored. We also saw such a naked leg, strapped crossways, catching a ride, on the back of a motorbike travelling through the city.

From Athens we cruised to the islands of Rhodes, Crete, Santorini, Mykonos and Delos. We anchored beneath the barren cliffs of Santorini, one of the places where Atlantis might have disappeared into the sea. We rode donkeys up a steep narrow path to the top of the black rock cliff where snow-white cubes of houses huddled together. They all seemed to have been freshly whitewashed, many of the narrow paths between them as well, and at the end of the day the setting sun changed them to orange and pink.

We sailed through the Sea of Marmara to Istanbul, whose skyline sprouted hundreds of domes and minarets. We visited a mosque where men washed their feet at the spigots on an outside wall before entering to worship. In this bustling city many big, old American cars mingled with men and beasts that were loaded with burden, while numerous merchants were hawking their wares. We strolled through the Grand Bazaar where hundreds of shops offered everything from goatskins to brass housewares. At the Topkapi Palace we admired the collection of royal treasures which ranged from an ornate gold cradle to a fist-sized diamond.

◆　　◆　　◆

After we returned from our cruise, we retrieved our rental car and drove from the Greek mainland to the peninsula over a high bridge. Had we not looked aside, we would have missed it because we did not know that it existed. It was the Corinth Canal, a deep vertical cut into the sandstone up to two hundred-sixty feet deep and almost four miles long.

We visited the Oracle of Delphi, where a stout woman in a peasant dress was leaning into a rope and pulling a carved stone on rollers, to help rebuild a column of an ancient ruin. Here our spirits soared with the eagles that circled above. We learned that life is a journey into the unknown, and there is much to be discovered. Set free your imagination and unyieldingly follow your goals because even a slave can eventually soar with eagles.

We traveled back to Yugoslavia through Kotor and northward up the Dalmatian coast to the ancient city of Dubrovnik on the Adriatic Sea. Twice we walked around this old city along the top of its meters-thick solid rock wall. It was so high that we could overlook the red tile roofs of the multistory dwellings that bordered the narrow alleys below. Its main plaza was paved with light-colored cobblestones that were shimmering as if they had just been polished.

From Dubrovnik we hiked out into the country. When we returned in the evening, we were puzzled about an ever-louder murmur that eventually became discernable as voices as we re-entered this city. Multitudes of people were crowding sidewalks, leaning from windows, standing in doorways, and were all engrossed in conversations. Even though we could not understand a word, we greatly enjoyed their visitation frenzy. Later we learned that their nightly tradition is called *korzo. So what were they talking about day after day?* I've attended annual company picnics where most everyone quietly stared at each other, and into space, as if to search for the magnificent insignificance of being there.

◆   ◆   ◆

With uncontrollable joy and overwhelming anticipation, back in the city where I was born, we dropped in again at Linda's mother-in-law's. She had a visitor sitting in her nest. Pa! That's right, our father sat in the nest of our mother. Ma and Pa were happily nestled together in eclectic garbage. And they were not even beating each other with two-by-fours or lawyers; they had no black eyes, cuts or bruises. Only empty pockets. This was the first time in my life that I ever saw my parents congenially together and having a light-hearted conversation. It seemed that under our circumstances I had had an extremely long life, having survived half of the thousand-year *Reich,* and then some. *What is going on here? Did a black hole pass through our solar system and warp everything? Do empty pocket books foster congeniality in parents?*

Pa was jovial and as rotund as ever. He wore a snow-white shirt with very long sleeves, as well as fine suit pants that were also far too long. He still looked like a banker, albeit, a shrunken one. Maybe he planned to grow some more so that he could be as tall as Siggi and I. Now Pa was the centerpiece in our asylum and was totally out of place, like all the other objects that surrounded him.

When Ma is gone, I will sculpt an interpretive center *from the contents of our sanctuary. It will be two stories high and two blocks long. It will be named: "The Summation of the Tortures and Pleasures of Ami and Siggi."*

Pa nursed a bottle of wine that he had brought with him. The wine was for him, not for us, so he could drink to our well-being. He wanted us to be well in spite of his being. Ma was still pure and did not drink; she will always be pure regarding alcohol, or so I think. After fighting each other all of our lives, Siggi's and mine, our parents were now the best of friends. They were each other's only friends, companions in suffering. He had a minor problem in that he could not decide whether to love us or to kill us. Teufi had treated him as he had treated us, when she took his fortune and discarded him as he had discarded us. This led to the expression: "What is good enough for the goose, and her little goslings, is good enough for the gander." *Is there still room for him in the attic?*

They told us that Ma had found a girlfriend for Pa from a lonely-hearts column in a national magazine. Ma found boyfriends in attics. Pa was now living with the lady of Ma's choice, and her name was Hella. They lived together in her home near Munich and were enjoying a luxurious life, even though he owned nothing. Even the suit he was currently wearing had belonged to Hella's husband who had long since died. Graciously, Pa invited Linda and me to visit them at Lake Starnberg, and we set a date to stay with him for a few days.

When we arrived there, there was a surprise visitor, half-brother Oliver, son of Linda's father-in-law and Teufi. He was tall, had long hair and was a rock musician with a see-through electric guitar. Oliver was much younger than I, and we did not have much to say to each other.

That evening I drove him home to Munich and went with him up to his apartment. Sadly, Teufi, my other mama, was not there or was hiding in a closet. Her apartment oozed wealth with its glass and chrome furniture, and a real tiger skin with a head, tail and paws clawed the wall. After Teufi had sold our house and architect's office, after she had legally gotten rid of Pa, she invested a lot of her loot with two American shysters, Bobby and Bernie, who then robbed her of part of our inheritance. What went around, came around; the irony for our Teufi. *Should we be sad about this or should we be glad, Siggi and I?*

After dark I said good-bye to Oliver and returned to Hella's house. It occurred to me that I could have robbed Teufi of my tiger, but I did not think of it at the time. While I was thinking of this, and was about to curse myself, something appeared in my headlights. A lonely, long-legged tigress was leaning against her car, and I would have stopped to help, had she not wanted to help me. To help me she waved the most beautiful leg that I had ever seen in my lights on a dark highway. In good conscience I ignored her call but was sure that my chivalrous father would have helped her. I was confused, still, or again. *Did she need help? Or did I?*

◆   ◆   ◆

Hella served us a delicious dinner and afterwards we nursed from a big bottle of wine. She asked Linda and me to drink to our friendship, and we did so with interlocking arms. She was a lady. Linda and Hella were ladies. Now we could address Hella with the informal German *Du,* instead of the formal *Sie.*

Later that evening, Pa cried a few tears about his mother, who had died of cancer, but Siggi and I never knew this because she had departed long before we were born. No one had ever talked about her, nor about any of our relatives who had died before we were old enough to know that children had relatives. German and family history must be kept secret; it could be detrimental to our psyches. Even old family photos that we would find over the years had family members cut or torn away. Now I stroked Pa's shoulders to dry his tears. I knew how tough it could be for a man to lose his mother. These were my thoughts and these were my actions toward my father, my Buskohl, during this joyful night, and, as Dave Barry is wont to say…

Linda and I stayed in the guesthouse that Hella had built to accommodate refugees after World War II. It was a requirement of the *Lastenausgleich,* equalization of burden, law. This law required people who had not lost their dwellings during the war to shelter the homeless, either in one's home if one was lucky enough to still have one, or to build a new one to help accommodate them. Hella could afford to do so because she owned a factory, as well as a villa by Lake Geneva in Switzerland.

On an early Monday afternoon Pa and I drove with Hella's new BMW to the Munich *Oktoberfest* which seemed to be the oldest, biggest, loudest and longest recurring party in the history of mankind. Linda stayed behind to read a book; she could not visit much with Hella, because they did not speak a common language. When we arrived there, this Fest was already revving up for another week with rivers of beer and mountains of food disappearing into thousands of bellies. We sat in the tent erected by Lowenbrau, one of the more than three hundred breweries in the state of Bavaria. Steer number fifty-six was skewering, to be devoured by the barbarians sitting at long, heavy, wooden tables. Father and I emptied giant glass steins and also helped make the steer disappear. He showed off his son to the revelers around us and lied to them with a smirking face:

"This is my son from America. He is a reporter for *Time* magazine."

"Oooh, ahhh," they smiled their replies.

In all the tents oompah bands played oompah, and before long all the bodies bobbed and howled with the oompah. The pressure of downed beer sent us weaving out of the oompah and towards the *pissoir*. In the men's department, Pa parted his coat, humbly bowed his head, opened his fly and splashed into the trough. I took his picture, because one always takes pictures at family reunions, especially during moments to be remembered. At this moment my father was getting a hold of himself, with hands that painted beautiful pictures and played melodious music, with hands that also beat wives and fondled stray buttocks.

Afterwards we strolled among the tents, the crowds and the food booths. We took in the smells of hundreds of barbecued chickens, trout and the sounds of dozens of bands, and when Pa was all partied out we returned home again. During this visit with my father, one of the longest ever, we never talked about our good old days, about what he had done for us all of our lives to help mold strong characters, Siggi's and mine. We had never talked about it before and would never do so in the future.

◆   ◆   ◆

Linda and I returned to Rheinfelden for a reunion with another shred of our runted and stunted family. We took Ma for a drive around the Black Forest. Little white-haired Ma, who had shrunk a few centimeters since the peak of her career because she had sent too much of her calcium down the drain, sat by herself in the backseat. Advising as always.

At the monastery in St. Blasien she insisted that I take a picture of the domed church. I had hundreds of slides of magnificent structures, great and small, from around the world and did not want this one. Or I succumbed again to a long-suppressed teenage rebellion and therefore did not record this church on film. Once I gave my socks an additional twist to defy Ma, when she had told me that people would think that I had crooked legs if the knitted grooves did not align properly. Her fashion requirements had to be resisted from the start, otherwise before I knew it, she'd require me to dangle a stylish whip from my belt to defend myself against lawyers.

After admiring the monastery, we continued our tour until I screeched to a stop. There was a commotion at a Black Forest house-barn, somewhat like the one Siggi and I had witnessed in Simonswolde so many years before. On top of the obligatory manure pile beside the street, and in front of a farmhouse, were two people wrestling, this time not a pig, but valuable memories. I was squealing with delight, the man and wife were grunting. I clambered for my camera to record an important event. Here was a paramount activity of liberation, or hopefully not of enslavement, or of the family togetherness that I always so craved.

A husband and wife together on top of a pile. A picture poster of the exploited masses of the world, heaving kakadoodoopoopoo with pitch-forks onto a wagon. The idyllic picture of how a family should always work closely together through thick and thin. She was wearing a plaid dress that fell to below her knees. He was wearing a pair of pants. And both wore rubber boots like Aunt Houwke and I used to wear in cowboy country. From a safe distance I snapped a picture as they flung wads onto the wagon, and I noticed that German *nutrient* hung together much better than its American counterpart, probably because it was precisely engineered and reinforced with a lot of straw which was used for bedding in the *nutrient* production barns.

I heard Ma mumble in the backseat, in deep thought, trying to solve the mystery of her nutrient-obsessed son:

"My son won't take pictures of beautiful churches. He takes photos of manure piles."

I thought that this picture could document a family building together, or slaves building a nation, or how women's lib was progressing in Germany.

◆   ◆   ◆

After Linda and I returned to our home in the United States, I forgot my parents. It was easy because I had had a lot of practice. Siggi seemed to have a more difficult time with this, probably because he was still struggling financially to finish his Ph.D. In a letter to Ma that he wrote in the beginning of the seventies and without the usual greeting he said:

"I have to say that the resentment is now really cooking in me. I have spent nearly 100,000 Deutsche marks for my education and it will surely cost another 20-30,000 marks until I am finished. And for that one receives silly letters, which entices one to send silly letters in return. Always to be a tool of your power-political battles.

"Now B (Buskohl) has developed the first diplomatic chess move. Teufi doesn't fight for her child support anymore because he has hung a lure under hers and Oliver's noses. Yesterday I received a letter from B. It was without any content. Only that he is so terribly poor that we should come to visit. Nothing about marrying or the like. He does not dare to make us false promises. That would be too much. Vis-a-vis you, he still plays the old harp aggressively, and as expected we hear this song ever more beautifully.

"If something concrete does not happen very soon, I am liable to take the matter into my own hands, to make contact with Hella, naturally in private, to explore the matter and to confirm the things that I hear from you. If I have been lied to, then I will tell her how her fiancée plays power politics with her property. So he himself will suffer the consequences of any allusions and temptations. I am angry that I have written him for his birthday, a forced letter without any content but which he can again use to secure his existence.

"Damn it, now again I am expected to waste my hard-earned money to serve as ornamentation for my 'parents' (pardon, the biological parents), and hopefully also take a position over there to serve as a productive family member for parents of whom one can only be a party boy. And the other one is not able to straighten up a twenty-year old junk apartment."

It's always so stifling.

"Go to Tirana, Albania. You will be rather well received, surely handed a shovel and ordered to work the land. On top of this you will learn to keep your stall clean and in order. And now you are astonished at what I have to say. Maybe you can also learn there to work on a production line or to do dishes.

"…The dam in the form of your mania for dictatorship and justification has been torn away and…He had the piggish inclination to tell me that in the summer of sixty-eight Ami and I have abandoned our father. This is a terrible statement.(?)"

Siggi and I abandoned our father?

"You seem to handle money matters very miserably. First of all you seem to have nothing left from the December payments and besides you have an enormous, fantastic urge to waste money on a lot of useless things until I could just barf. Can you not fathom the effects and anticipate when we in the last twenty years always tried to criticize your junky apartment, even though this would not be allowed and was always prevented through your dictator-like inclination and other talk? Such stuff accumulates and comes to light as soon as enough power is behind it. How often have you said that we could say anything, only not to criticize the junky apartment?"

Ma had forwarded this letter to me, probably because she had wanted sympathy and had written the following note on it:

"Here starts the letter. (<u>He</u> has studied psychology.)"

Siggi included me in his apparent threats and demands. *Could a son who so suffered from his parents threaten or blackmail them?* He tried to force them to live up to their promises that we'd be blessed with a third mother who was wealthy, and that her wealth would rub off on us. I tried to remain detached from this warm familial interaction and was ignorant about his correspondence with our parents.

◆   ◆   ◆

Over the years Ma had often tried to entice us to return to Germany. Her bribes were usually brilliant proposals, such as that we could live with her; or that she knew an old lady who had to go into a nursing home, and we might inherit her house. Now it was the wealth of Hella, and Pa also joined her efforts, even before his Teufi had evicted him from his room in her house. During this time period Pa wrote me a few short letters, and as far as I can remember, his first letters ever to me after we had moved away from Simonswolde. He said that he could find work for me in Switzerland that would pay about fifteen hundred Swiss francs a month. I desired to work there because I yearned to return to my roots and gain outstanding experience in my profession. But after paying for our living expenses there'd not be much left, especially since Pa was probably puffing up my potential salary. He had proved to be a simple, but expert, puffer.

Ma wrote me that Hella was quite wealthy, was in her mid-seventies, and had only one relative, a brother in New York. In other words, she could check out of this lonely world any day now. She implied that Pa and Hella were engaged to marry, and that we could inherit great wealth, Siggi and I. She wrote me that Siggi would receive the mansion on Lake Geneva but did not specify as to how I would be blessed. But as always I ignored her bait. To catch fish, the fish have to be hungry and you need the right bait. This fish was hungry but as always before, she used the wrong bait.

◆   ◆   ◆

Linda and I traveled extensively. During the later years I always wrestled with a strong approach-avoidance conflict about visiting Germany again, because my homeland was filled with too much beauty and too much pain. Even so, Linda and I would visit there again long after Pa's ashes were buried in the cemetery in Wollbach.

After he died of a heart attack caused by self-inflicted hedonism, which might someday be classified as a sue-able *disease*, he was cremated and must have burned vigorously. But he was not immediately interred, and no memorial services were held for many months. Could it have been that our relatives were waiting for us to come from the States to attend to these things? They had notified us that he had died, and Uncle Fritz also had sent us an official form to fill out so we could apply to get our potential inheritance. I did not do this and will never learn what I may have thrown out with it.

Like all German cemeteries, this Wollbach graveyard was more like a park. It had many polished, black headstones that were all inscribed with shiny gold letters, as if everyone had died only yesterday. There were many Neumans under these stones, because this clan had originated here in Wollbach. Its history book mentioned that at the time of our father's birth, almost half the families in this area had our surname. The families of the deceased maintained these gravesites which were flaming with flowers, just like many of their homes, where window boxes blossomed throughout much of the year.

We were as overwhelmed by these flowers as we are with the litter along our highways in America. I have walked many miles of them, doing surveys and picking up trash. This garbage is a mother lode of material to study for dissertations for Ph.D. degrees. I have found pre-owned diapers, plastic bottles with yellow liquids, gun clips and holsters, money and mirrors, as well as poisons for minds and for bodies. But I never found a Wall Street Journal or Scientific American, and I am certain that the garbage along our highways screams bloody murder. There was no garbage along the highways that we traveled in Europe. But there had to be garbage. Everyone produces garbage. *Was it all in Ma's apartment? Or was it hidden in thousands of court files across the land?*

We walked around the Wollbach cemetery to search out Linda's underground father-in-law. Aunt Mathilde had told us that he had no headstone and for strange reasons, Siggi and I had not erected one for him. She told us that we would find him under a patch of quackgrass, and therefore we found his plot quickly because his was the only gravesite so decorated.

I had to pee. For old times sake.

"Where shall I pee?" I asked my wife. We've always made major decisions together.

"Go wherever you want," she said to me.

I knew that she was a little disgusted with my incivility, because she had said, "wherever you want." She always let me make my own decisions whenever I annoyed her. I just wanted to relieve my frustrations, and the devil tempted me to pee on the quackgrass, but I was stronger than he.

We visited a lot of our relatives and people who had been friends of our parents during or before WW II, in and around the Black Forest, and greatly enjoyed them. I had never really known them before, and they were all exceedingly friendly and hospitable. All of them fed us big dinners and home-baked desserts, even though they didn't even know that I was fixated in the oral stage, that I liked to wolf down food like my father. Only now did I really learn how kind they were. Linda and I stayed with our Aunt Mathilde and Uncle Hermann several times, some of which we spent in bed with severe flu because we were exhausted from our prolonged travels.

A cousin in Switzerland took us up to the Schilthorn peak, and we rode four different cable gondolas to get there. After silently drifting high over idyllic farms with steep, green meadows and fields of snow, we arrived at Piz Gloria, a rotating restaurant offering a breathtaking view of the Alps. Part of the James Bond movie, *On Her Majesty's Secret Service,* had been filmed here. While we stood in the sky to admire the mountains across the deep valley before us, we heard a sudden thunder. Agent 007 zipped by in a military jet, following the course of the valley and coming so close that we could see the Swiss white cross in its red field on the side of his plane. I reacted quickly and caught this on film.

◆   ◆   ◆

Siggi has spent many a summer in Germany, to visit and to do research, sometimes taking his family with him. For him the rich culture and beauty of his homeland overcame his pain from our past. Maybe if I went more often and stayed there longer, the pleasing culture and friendly relatives would crowd out the sad portion of my memories. Siggi always stayed in hotels and never with his mother; she had no room and being with mother brings together the critical mass that can lead to explosions. The only way to prevent this, and still enjoy motherhood, was to tape mother's mouth shut. Or plug up our ears. I could not think of any other solution. *Can heroes deal with mothers? Can mothers deal with heroes? Is Mother not our heroine?*

8

THE VISIT

Which home is He giving **us**?

◆   ◆   ◆

Ma wrote me from Switzerland that she wanted me to visit her
before she died. She also wanted me to feel her skull. She said that
three men had whacked it, and it felt like corrugated metal. *Why had
she never told this to Siggi and me?* Of course not one of these *heroes* was
ever officially pampered, counseled or rehabilitated for their deeds. Or
sent to trial or to jail. Ma had also taped her will to a wall requesting
that her cadaver be sent to the medical school in Basel, with the
instructions to photograph her skull before the students cut up her
corpse.

She wrote me:

"For one year I will remain in a basin filled with formaldehyde,
together with people who come from the penitentiary, who have no
next of kin to take care of their graves. My skeleton will then be sent to

a school in Switzerland. I will ask the Department of Anatomy to take pictures of my skull or send you the address where it will be displayed."

Naked, stiff and shriveled mother floating with stinky criminals in a stinky chemical pool? Mother's lonely rippled skull resting on a pedestal?

Enticing attractions for Siggi and me to visit her **before** we would have to find her in a more gruesome state of being. If she died before we saw her again, she wanted us to study her in her advanced state, and after she would be wasted, her pictures. *Does she think that her skull configuration would be a testimony to her life and help justify how she had dealt with it?*

For many years Ma had lived with Franz in the village of Moehlin, Switzerland. Since she talked incessantly, we concluded that he must be deaf or nearly so. They were not married and were now in their mid-eighties. She also wrote that she was living in "hell" because one of his children was pushing to evict them both from his old house so he could remodel and rent it.

She also wrote that Franz had lost control over his body. Therefore she did not have time to answer the many questions about our family in writing that I had asked her recently. She had to change his bag several times a day and wash him as well. If we visited her, she would be able to tell me our family history. She still had an excellent memory and had always wanted to write a memoir to tell the world about what men had done to her. I thought that her memory was another lure to catch me so I'd come back to Europe. She had even more time than she had junk and she tried to reel me in. She said that she would answer my questions in person and invited Siggi and me to stay upstairs in Franz' house. I was sure that even if she literally removed one ton of her stuff to make room for us in her apartment in Rheinfelden, we could not reside there. No one dwells in hell voluntarily, even if it were polished, and I didn't know if Franz had allowed her hellish décor in his house.

I read Ma's many letters to me again only to write this memoir, and much of their content was new to me, because I had forgotten, or repressed, so much of the heroic counter-cheerful advice and admonitions that interfered with my objective thinking. But now that I was writing, I was eager to learn what she would have to tell me about our past, and especially about her personal experiences in the horrible world that she had lived in before, during and after the infamous Nazi era. I decided that if I wanted this information from her, I would have to talk to her face-to-face, because judging from her letters, she could not stay focused on any one subject long enough to elaborate about it in a meaningful manner.

Ma was extremely gregarious, but because of a quirk in her personality she had few friends, and her nearest relatives lived hundreds of kilometers away. Over the years Ma had lured us with the material things that she had accumulated since our father had evicted us over forty years ago. She had offered us used furs, violins, accordions and tons of clothes. She was still very poor, and I wondered how she acquired some of these seemingly expensive items. But I was not interested in her material bribes, because they would only be unpleasant reminders cluttering up our home and minds.

Ma threw me a morsel of what I could learn from her in a letter to my wife Linda:

"…My dear grandfather had a sister who was a widow and had a beautiful farm near the railroad in Loppersum, two villages from Emden. She asked an attorney to visit her to draw up her last will and testament. When the good aunt died it was discovered that she was very much taken in. She probably did not understand what she signed. Her beautiful villa and the farm suddenly belonged to this <u>abominable</u> (Ma's emphasis) attorney. He moved into the villa right away and my dear grandfather got the short end of the deal."

Already so long ago?

"…Dear Ami should quit his job, because what is in my memory will earn him more. It would be very interesting for a movie firm to film the attic with the bats where we lived, and the jail in Saeckingen where I had to stay because of my homelessness. This is unique in the world.

"Don't wait until I can be viewed in the Anatomy Department of the university, dear Ami. Franz isn't going to live much longer, he breathes heavily every time he moves, and then we will lose our domicile in Moehlin. One can say dark clouds are on the horizon. Another thing, I can help a little with the money. So prepare for the trip. It will be very interesting with your Ma, who has loved you more than any other person."

Now you tell me that you love me.

◆   ◆   ◆

Even though our mother was living in Switzerland, she still kept an apartment in Germany. Its rent was probably paid by the German taxpayers, because some official apparently thought that she actually still lived there. She wrote me that she could not access it now because someone had inserted an object into the lock of its only entrance door. *Was it her landlord, an official? Or was it yet another one of Ma's lonely cries?*

As much as wanting to see our mother again, probably for the last time, I also wanted to find the court documents that she assured me were still in her possession. I was curious about how it had been possible for our parents to shred our family for so long and with such intensity. *Were there no referees to call for a stop of their insane behavior?* I wanted to learn how the laws could be twisted to favor liars and crooks. Siggi and I had learned from outstanding personal experiences that the weaker you are, the more abused you are, and the more exploited you will be. At least this had certainly been true in our case, and I now had a strong desire to inform everyone about our erstwhile plight. I rarely have mentioned anything about our fine background to anyone but my wife. I had learned that if I dropped a tiny hint about it to other people, they did not seem to care or understand and for example would merely say, "When I grew up, we had nothing to eat but beans and potatoes," thereby taking the wind out of the sails of my story.

At one time we would have dug into real doodoo for beans and potatoes. Most people could not fathom anything worse than having to survive on them, such wonderful food. I could never understand their disinterest or lack of sympathy, until I learned that it was a quirk in human nature to avoid or repress unpleasant situations and associated emotions, and I figured that collectively this could get us into big trouble. For many years I had been too ashamed or too troubled to think about the skeletons in our closet, but now that I am wiser, I am proud of all my wheel-spinning accomplishments to stay alive and forge ahead in life.

Without sacrificing our bodies.

Without losing our minds.

Ma's court documents and her tales would be a great help to me. I had counted the names of the many lawyers and judges whom she had referred to in her letters, who had helped dissolve, torment and impoverish our "family" in an unending war filled with schemes, lies and threats of murder. Since Ma had referred to the lawyers only in passing, I was sure that more could be added to this already substantial list, and I wanted to learn especially about the absurdities of the German judicial system. I also wanted to find out if it were our unsettled lifestyle that this system had forced upon us that caused, at least in part, my caustic humor and blunt honesty? Or was it mainly Ma's whip, such an effective and powerful tool? Siggi and I make some people quiver when we confront them with unpleasant truth, and we do this to *win friends and influence people.* Sadly, too often they have seemed to go into denial, even before understanding what we tried to explain to them.

Siggi has published dozens of articles, and his observations on many issues are unique and out of the mainstream. He wrote a twelve-page abstract called *Reflections On Conventional Versus Non-conventional Trade Development* to advise on how to boost the economic performance of his state. Another one of his articles was *To Liberate Women, Depoliticize Men.*

◆   ◆   ◆

I wanted to return to the land of my birth, hoping to find the missing pieces in my life. But after returning to my adopted country from previous visits to Europe, weeks would pass before my gloom would lift. I wanted to live in both places, hoping to strengthen my roots by cementing together those that had grown in worlds so far apart.

I weighed the pros and cons of this trip for many months. I wanted to see my mother; I was concerned about her mental and physical health. Would we be able to deal with her aberrant behavior? Would she be able to deal with our foreign behavior? Long ago she had requested me to send her a few toothbrushes, such and such brand and hardness. Recently she wrote that she had ever made only one request of me, to send her toothbrushes. I never did. But later she wrote that she had found a good source of them at the old age home across the street from her. When somebody died in this undertaker's waiting room, his or her useless belongings were thrown out, and she collected these from its garbage.

Now Ma had accumulated a good supply of brushes. I mentioned this to Siggi and he informed me that when he had visited her during the previous summer, he had found bundles of them rubber-banded together under the bumpy blanket covering her sofa. He had said to her:

"I suppose you saved the one I left here in eighty-six."

"*Ja,* naturally," and she had produced more of them.

"Did you also save the toothpicks that I've used."

"You know I never throw anything away."

She retrieved the world's finest used-toothpick collection, while saying:

"I have lived through two world wars, hyperinflation, two depressions and a long divorce. I have lost my children. I cannot throw anything away. You can criticize anything about me, but I forbid you to attack me about my stuff. I know *Ich hab' einen Vogel,* I have a bird, I am crazy, and nobody can change that."

Over the years Siggi had attacked Ma about her hoard, verbally and in writing. I understood her emotional craving for her collection of fine garbage and could forgive her. Twice during her lifetime the German currency had been destroyed and survival had depended on bartering. Her subconscious was afraid that this might become necessary again, thereby causing her to accumulate everything. But Siggi could not accept that. He accused her of valuing her junk more than her family. This was very true. This was very untrue. Whatever the case, Ma could never change.

I understood Siggi's frustrations and yearnings; they were the same as mine. He boiled in quiet desperation that they could not be resolved. He wanted to find comfort in the home of his mother. And in his mind.

Siggi was going to travel to Europe and would meet me there if I decided to go also. But I had many doubts about the trip: Would we get along together near our former hell? Now Ma was requesting us to come to help her clean her apartment so she could die in peace. We were not sure how to search out the mementos that we might want from there. Something in us craved for them; but we were also pained by them. Should we haul her stuff to the dump? Should we give it away? Would there be anything useful? We'd find childhood memorabilia in schoolbooks and toys that we had crafted. We knew that all of these would still be there, buried in deep clutter, as had been the memories of them in my soul. What would we do with our frail mother? What if she died from the excitement or torment of our visit? Should we bury her or carry her corpse in a suitcase to the university in Basel and deliver her "To Whom It May Concern?" Was Ma's request her final attempt to gain sympathy from someone, anyone? Would I be emotionally strong enough to be able to inspect her skull? What other secrets did she keep? Did I even want to know? Had she suppressed them, because they had been too painful? Could I find the loose screws in her head?

My questions and doubts could only be resolved if I returned; therefore I decided to make this trip. This would be the first time that our mother, my brother and I would be together in thirty-five years, and we would have a fine time. We were a closely-knit family; we were a blown up family. When I had received the announcement of my father's death in the seventies, my only comment at that time had been, "Well, the old bastard finally croaked." I went into the bedroom and closed the door. Then I cried. But I do not know if I cried for myself or for my father.

◆   ◆   ◆

Siggi picked me up at the Zurich airport, where he had rented a car, and we drove to Rheinfelden, Germany, to stay at a bed and breakfast. It was the middle of summer and central Europe was suffering from a hundred-year heat wave. In addition, there was almost no air conditioning or insect window screening, and I wondered how the walls of my room had gotten so bloody. To keep cool, I had to keep my window open at night, and I soon figured out that no one had been murdered here. During my nightly mosquito hunts, I also added to the décor of my room with Type A negative blood splatter.

The day following my arrival, while still suffering jetlag, we drove to Switzerland to visit our mother. Without previous announcement we walked into her "living room," where she and Franz were sitting in immense disorder watching television. She was wearing two pairs of glasses, on top of each other, so she could see better and removed one pair so she could see us even better, as her face momentarily lit up before turning to a frown. Her body was frail with a slight dowager's hump that mismatched her much younger face which had surprisingly few wrinkles and no "age spots."

"Ami!"

A bubble of joy momentarily rose in her soul. We did not exchange greetings, did not hug, even though I had resolved to do so. Ma's mouth kicked into action, not with advice as before, but with subtle excuses and reasons for her past behavior. Thoughts burst forth rapidly, skipping from subject to subject. Pointing to a photo of her young father hanging on the wall, she said:

"He hanged himself. When I was small, I prayed: Dear God, I wish my father were dead. Amen."

Then why are you an atheist, Mama?

I interrupted her: "Ma, how are you?" wanting to bring our conversation to a more soothing level. But this was not possible. Years of brooding kept pouring from her soul and Siggi and I could not stop her.

She presented me with a strap, holding it as if to sell me a tie.

"See this. This is what I used to spank you with."

To show me that it is harmless? Does she feel guilty for spanking me so hard? Or is she proud of it?

"No," I said, "I don't remember it but I remember two others. They were made of rubber and wire." I did not know why I said that because I did not feel any animosity towards her, only sadness. I thought it to be a miracle that she had lived this long, physically intact, and apparently suffering only a form of *organic brain syndrome*. I'm not a doctor, but it seems reasonable that a dented brain could be the physical cause of her behavioral abnormality.

Before too long Siggi rushed out of the room. *The pain?*

"I'll wait for you in the car, Neuman," he said to me on his way out.

Not long thereafter I followed him out. The pain! My fourth visit with our mother in thirty-five years ended in twenty-five to thirty-five minutes. Numbly, we drove back across the Rhine River to cruise aimlessly around the city of my birth, speaking little as we passed through our old neighborhoods. Everything was so prosperous, clean and well maintained even though Rheinfelden was still mostly a factory town. The German middle class had greatly expanded, and had grown a lot wealthier as well, while many areas in America had stagnated or declined, twisted statistics notwithstanding. This also caused me pain.

Two days later we made another courageous charge on Franz's house and immediately asked Ma for the key to her German apartment.

"You cannot go there alone. I will go with you," Ma insisted.

"But why? We want to go there alone," I said.

"No, I will go with you!"

Siggi and I did not want her along, because she would add to our homesickness, or whatever our complex, convoluted emotions could be called. She'd cackle with advice and draw the attention of her neighbors. As older children we had not wanted to be with her in public because of her incessant advising and instructing. Although she had a sweet, beautiful face, it contradicted her overbearing personality and irrational behavior. For years her neighbors must have wondered about the things that she had dragged into her home. Therefore we wanted to sneak in now and take a quiet survey of her German nest. But she insisted on going also. Since she could crash stone walls with her delicate bullhead, we relented, and the three of us drove to her apartment, while heat and gloom filled our car, and we spoke little. We walked up one flight of stairs, where Ma fumbled for the right key among a messy bundle of strings, keys and safety pins. *Hurry up, someone might see us.*

She finally found the right one, opened the door, and I noticed that there was no obstruction in the lock as she had claimed. A wave of repugnant, intensely antique odor rolled over us from the dark vestibule. Without a word, Siggi pushed Ma inside to escape the neighbors' prying eyes. I held my breath, because it was hard to breathe in hell, and Siggi cussed, stepping back out. He had always treated his body with care; more so than I. It was much easier to soothe your body than it was to soothe your soul.

"Open the windows," he exclaimed.

I groped for a light switch and flipped it on, but the power had been shut off years ago. This was the first time that I had been here, because Ma had moved to this apartment after my last visit. In the sweltering darkness I tried to push open the door to the next cell in hell.

What I saw was worse than I had anticipated. The entire cell was a tangled sculpture created by a tormented mind. It was the core of a frozen tornado. Clutter hurled against the walls, vortexing up to the ceilings. Boxes, bike wheels, lamps, newspapers and clothing. There were hundreds of objects, all crammed, mangled and pickled in a tomb-like atmosphere. I climbed through the vortex, bored my way to the window that was hidden on the far side and covered with a moth-eaten blanket. I opened it as far as I could. Barely breathing, I struggled to the next compartment to open another hole to the world. Though sweating, I was unaware of my physical discomfort, because the heat, the mustiness and the motherly creations had temporarily numbed my mind.

As I groped around, I realized that she had not lived here for many years, because all of the kitchen and bathroom fixtures were totally buried as well. I looked for artifacts from my youth: drawings, toys, school papers and books, anything from my previous life. Of the thousands of objects in Ma's shrine I recognized only the rounded top corner of an imbedded old wardrobe. Two mattresses were stacked on top of it, wedged between it and the ceiling. *Who lifted them? Who knows about this shrine?*

The long-forgotten feeling of shame and disgust anguished me again. Once more I had that sinking feeling in my heart and belly. As I stumbled back out of the apartment, Siggi came back up the staircase. I exhaled and inhaled deeply.

"Did you open some windows?" he asked me.

"Two of them, but not very far. Too much junk in the way," I responded.

"You better let this place air out before you get sick," Siggi admonished me. Then he said, "What is causing that stink?"

"Smells like mothballs, mouse seasoning and mother's armpits to me," I responded.

Ma had always been worried about moths. They destroyed; therefore they had to be destroyed. Courageously, I ventured back in to explore our catacombs. Siggi followed. Ma was wedged in the tangle of her dominion, lost in thought, scrutinizing some papers and was unaware of us. Her face was serious, the way I remembered it from my childhood.

Ma, why do you look so sad?

Little bird, I will explain when you're older.

What is she looking for? What is she hiding? She hides men in her attic.

"Where are the court documents?" I startled her.

"In that cupboard," she responded, pointing to one side.

I moved clutter to get to the doors of a dining room cabinet. Carelessly I tossed things aside, causing dust to rise to enhance hell's miasma. I moved more cautiously. Its first compartment contained only plastic flowers. I thought this to be odd because I had never seen such in this land before. There was no plastic on the graves or in the flower boxes; there was little plastic anywhere. I worked open doors and drawers but all were filled with old newspapers, to be read again some day, to refresh the ammunition for Ma's admonitions.

I lost hope that I would find what I came here for. It would take days of hard work to lift, throw, bore and search through this mess, or to move most of everything to the outside to get down to the mother lode, to discover the items that were deposited there so long ago. Like archeologists, we would have to remove the surface layers to get to the fossils that we were searching for. We could heave stuff out of the window into dumpsters while hiding inside. But Ma would not permit this and scream hysterically, besides it was muggy and hot, and there was no power to run a fan to cool us. *Would her neighbors send for the police when violins and sitz baths were flying out of a second-story window?*

Would we have to buy beer to bribe a policeman? But Siggi and I were too honest to bribe anyone; we would just get arrested. Besides I did not have the heart to sever Ma from her precious collection. It belonged to her. It belonged to me.

Quietly the three of us riffled through separate graves where we could stand up only at the doorways. I was curious and venturesome and crawled around the top of Ma's belongings, often stooping to clear the ceiling. This was a new experience for me because like a daring circus performer, I had to balance on broom handles, coffeepots and many other unusual objects of support. I found something worthwhile, a bundle of new toothbrushes, still in their original wrappings, and put them in my pocket. When Ma came to the entrance of my tomb I tossed them to her.

"Here, you wanted some toothbrushes," I said.

She dismissed me with a disgruntled wave and did not pick them up.

The heat of hell soon drove Siggi and me back out. We told Ma that we had had enough, locked up and went back to our rental car. On the way, I instinctively scanned the windows around us. I had forgotten this feeling, this demeanor from so long ago, my feeling of shame and my desire to be invisible. Now I willed myself to be invisible again. I knew that all of the world's eyes were upon us because I could feel their mockery: There is that crazy old woman again. Those must be her sons. *I'm not her son. I'm not even German.*

Because I could not have a focused conversation with Ma, it was all the more important for me to find the court documents. After our unsuccessful exploratory expedition, I tried to dispel my gloom with objective thoughts, while the three of us silently returned to Moehlin, where we left Ma with Franz without a goodbye.

*When I get back home I'll have In*sensitivity Training.

◆   ◆   ◆

The hot, muggy days passed while Siggi and I drove around in the villages near where we were born. We had come to tour and sightsee, as well as to visit relatives in Germany and Switzerland. But we could not leave the place that oppressed us, the grave of our souls.

This is my home! There has to be a mother, there has to be a father! Maybe we could be reborn. We stopped to visit many churches, to find relief inside from the humid heat and to admire their treasures. Many of them were unlocked and unattended every day and this impressed me.

"In America it would not be possible to keep the churches unlocked," Siggi said to me. "They would be destroyed within hours or days," he continued.

"Why would they do that? You and I never even thought of deliberately destroying anything. Many of the experts might agree that we could be justified to rape, pillage and murder," I said.

"Yea, shall we start right now? With our ol' lawyers?" Siggi replied.

"Then if we get caught, we can say *we made mistakes*," I continued, "and be pampered and rehabilitated. The only thing I ever destroyed intentionally was the antenna on your father's car. I was mad at him and took a swipe at it. Broke it off. Even felt guilty then."

The churches had been very expensive to build, like all of the houses, and I had seen few such in America. The interiors were decorated with bright colors and intricate carvings; even the ones built since World War II were adorned with large colorful frescoes and had lofts with huge pipe organs. But I was almost apathetic about their outstanding quality, craftsmanship and great beauty and would simply snap a picture or two and go back outside. The gloom would not lift from my soul.

Even though, or because, Western Germany had been building and renovating more churches after WWII than it had at any time in its history, we discovered that they were almost empty, even on Sundays. There were few worshippers, and we wondered why so much had been spent to build so many churches when so few people attended them. *Worthwhile or not, can a tax remain in place indefinitely? No free market balancing supply and demand? Historical guilt and shame?*

For dinner Siggi and I often returned to the same restaurant in the Black Forest because it was cooler there, with less air and noise pollution. We needed peace. Often we had to wait a long time to be served, for a good meal can take a long time to prepare. Sometimes we spoke little and at other times we discussed our past at great length. We even joked about it. We had the weirdest and funniest parents on earth; two fools who should have been born two days earlier, on April Fool's day.

"What shall we do about your mother's junk?" I questioned Siggi.

"That's not my problem. I've come to realize that for most of my life your parents have burdened me. And this junk of your mother. I've told her many times that she valued it more than her children. Therefore I have no responsibility to clean it up," Siggi answered.

"We don't have parents. We are only by-products of their encounters," I responded. "There are a few things I want from her apartment."

"Ma said that she had three thousand marks in there," Siggi returned.

"Could we rent a dumpster, park it below the window, and just throw her stuff into it?"

"We could. But can you?"

"I am not sure, it would be too depressing. And it is so hot and stinky in there."

We could not throw out the treasures of our mother. We could not throw out the presently biggest burden in our lives.

"The *Sozialamt* provided her this apartment. They helped with her creation. Let them clean it out," suggested Siggi.

"Yeah, but the shame. All I want is those court documents. Otherwise, why did I travel so far? I cannot stand to visit Ma even though I want to. I even want to hug her to help heal pain. You don't want to drive very far because of all the traffic. Even these beautiful villages are depressing. I will have to return to the States and look at trailer huts. I read that in my state as many as one out of eight people live in *mobile homes*."

"So far we have not seen a single trailer house. Some of these houses are hundreds of years old. And still look new. Even the new ones will last that long," Siggi responded.

As far as we could tell, the land of our birth was changing, and for the better. Judging by the homes and yards, it was difficult to distinguish between the rich and the poor neighborhoods. Even to view only the entrance doors to these homes was like visiting an art museum. Most of them appeared to have been handcrafted. Many were custom-made of hammered or cast bronze, iron, oak or stained glass.

There were few signs cluttering the landscape. For example, a veterinarian simply advertised with a cast-metal sculpture of stylized cats and dogs in the front of his building, and the entrance door was of the same design and forged of the same metal as well. There were no written words such as "Veterinarian."

During his visits here over the years, Siggi had taken many pictures of cemeteries, houses and restaurants. He had photographed some of them repeatedly because of the great improvements being made to them between his visits. A restaurant might have the simple words, *Café Sonne,* Café of the Sun, which in later years would have been replaced by a gilded iron sun hanging from an ornate, black wrought iron bracket from the side of the building. We inspected a door to a village restaurant that was made of a one-inch thick tempered glass panel set behind a heavy, hand-forged, ornamental wrought iron grille. In all my travels around the world I had never seen so much consistent and widespread quality, combined with such man-made beauty, as in this country and some other European countries as well.

I noticed that the seemingly oversized rain gutters and downspouts on the houses were made of copper. This prompted me to find the cheapest ones, so we kept looking for them as we drove around. We thought that we had finally found them on a house, and after we stopped for a closer look, we discovered that these downspouts were not made of plastic, iron or aluminum but of welded stainless steel.

"These people have pride. They build everything to last a thousand years," Siggi said to me.

"But in America we have Desert Sky Mobile Home Estates, with flags flying. Here there are no estates," I replied sarcastically. "But things are not so rosy here either."

"What do you mean? Look around you. Where can you find so much beauty in America?"

"Mostly with the rich, mostly in nature, but remember what got us to America," I said to him.

Siggi could not acknowledge the problems in Germany, and his temper rose instantly. Every morning at breakfast we read the newspapers about dioxin-polluted eggs, dying forests, and the pollution theme was constant in the news media. We had looked at a polluted area in Rheinfelden that was located next to the house of our former friend, Juergen, where Siggi and I had camped in his backyard as children. This half-block was now cordoned off, and no one was allowed to enter. Its soil was contaminated with dioxin to a depth of more than one hundred eighty feet and would be very expensive to remove and process.

Juergen's backyard was also the place where someone had stolen our new tent in the middle of the night. I remember it well. We had pitched our small new tent there; it was to be our haven away from our hot attic during the warm summer nights. We had kept our bedding and our beebee gun in it, along with a few other things. Late one night we had heard the cracking of the tiny grenades that children threw during celebrations. Wrapped in paper, these blew up on impact. Crack. Crack. We had crawled out of our tent with our gun and had found no one outside, but I had yelled, "Shoot whoever is hiding out there." I had wanted to intimidate whoever was there, so that he would leave us in peace.

The next night it had rained, so we had stayed in our batty attic and had left our tent in place. During that night Juergen's mother thought that she had heard the firecrackers again, and the following morning our tent and its content was gone. The thief had wanted to wake us, to check if we were sleeping in it, to determine if he could steal our home away from home. We hadn't been paranoid enough to anticipate such a clever robbery scheme.

This very area next to Juergen's house was now identified as the most dioxin-polluted site in the world. During the reconstruction after WWII, the bomb craters around Rheinfelden had been filled with the toxic waste from the factories as well. Later I learned from a website in Switzerland, that that waste had also been used to remodel this entire townscape until well into the seventies. Someone had bargained with the devil, and only now was this evil deed being publicized. I would have to be paid at least fifteen dollars before I'd pollute the earth in such a fashion! *Who was punished for this? Who was rewarded for this? Who might suffer from this? Who will be sued?*

We also read that the trees were dying in the Black Forest, so we drove to the higher elevations to verify this and found it to be the case. They would be dead forever. There might never be trees here again, at least not certain kinds. Billboards explained the cycle of pollution, the nitrogen and heavy metals that fell from the sky and were taken up by the soil and the trees. *How can such poisons ever be cleaned from mountains and streams?*

◆   ◆   ◆

As we waited for our meals to arrive, we studied the menu of our favorite village restaurant. It was always quiet here. It was quiet in all of the restaurants that we visited, except when there was a big crowd. I made the observation that there was never any background *music* playing in stores, restaurants and other such public places, and I was able to converse more easily. I wondered why the difference between here and the noisier equivalent locales in America. I could only guess as to the difference and have not yet learned why this was so. *Were deaf, acoustically-challenged people not included in the extensive handicap laws?*

"Look at all these entrees," Siggi said to me.

We counted the drinks listed on the menu of this country inn. There were one hundred forty-two different beverages, everything from dozens of brands of beer and wine to various undiluted fruit juices and many different mixtures made from them.

After we enjoyed a delicious dinner I said to my brother, "I am going to find those divorce documents."

We had kept Ma's keys from our first safari to her apartment. They were a messy collection of every type ever invented, including ancient skeleton keys. It took Siggi and me several days to regain our nerves to return there and did so several more times during our sojourn. We dug around in her helter-skelter but only for short periods each time. Reaching into crannies, to search for files, I found a plastic bag containing glossy porno magazines. I scanned the naked couples in wonderfully interlocking and contorted positions...*Did Ma find these in her garbage mines?*

I pulled out an egg carton filled with black, shriveled fruit from under a cupboard. It was garnished with mouse droppings, the inescapable spicing from my slavery days. There was a half-liter carton of unopened, ancient orange juice and many other exotic delicacies. Finally I discovered a foot-thick bundle wrapped in newspapers, tied securely with string. I pulled it from its crypt and noted that its date of publication was 1952, about the time of the divorce of our parents. So many years ago. I tore open a corner, determined that these could be some of the files that I wanted and placed them into a bright-yellow *Elmer Citro* brand backpack that happened to be nearby.

"Siggi, I found something. Let's go." Documentation of our disaster.

We locked up Ma's secret warehouse and drove into a forest, parked our car, and opened the rucksack to inspect our find. A musty odor escaped from the file folders which mostly contained letters that were written by our parents, including a few from relatives and some official documents. It was obvious that these files were prepared as evidence for the court. One of them contained only love letters that our father had written to our mother before they were married. Saving letters was in our genes because I had also done so all of my life and Siggi probably as well. Quietly we studied our newly found bundle of garbage, our new treasure, in the darkening forest. We hardly knew our father and were anxious to learn more about him.

I was disappointed that most of the official papers were not in this bundle. There would have to be hundreds of documents generated during the subsequent fourteen, fifteen or more years of court activities. We discovered that this bundle was only for the initial divorce process between our father and our first mother. Therefore we made a few more attempts to find more court files, but by the time we had to return to America, we could not find any others. The biggest reason for this was that we could not bring ourselves to dwell in Ma's warehouse long enough to search for them. Like workers handling hazardous materials, we limited our exposure to keep within reasonable health guidelines.

Siggi and I never threw out one single one of Ma's items, leaving it all behind in forgotten silence.

◆   ◆   ◆

Before we flew back to America, we returned Ma's keys to her. We arrived at her place in Moehlin at about eleven fifteen. Siggi stayed in our car, as he could not face his mother again. A long lost son could not face his brain-whacked mother anymore. I still wanted to talk with her at great length, and also assure her that I was not bitter about what she, Pa and so many countrymen had done for us. At one time Ma had written that, "What we will never forgive is that the police never helped us when our 'father' wanted to kill us. Poor Ami has required years to overcome the consequences of this terrible intimidation." Had she never realized that this had been only one tiny incident in my seemingly unending intimidation, and that my most painful and intense one, aside from our wonderful WW II experiences, had always been her whip? Oddly, I have always felt differently about forgiveness than Ma. As I have never suffered from envy, I also feel blessed that I have never felt bitter about our parents because such bitterness would probably have destroyed me long ago. Instead of bitterness I suffered sadness, but I have always attempted to live my life at its fullest. I also wanted to tell Ma that I did not blame her for anything.

With a mixture of bravado and trepidation, I entered Ma's living room. Within minutes of my arrival, she realized that it was nearly eleven-thirty, lunchtime at the old age home.

Without any greetings, Ma accused me: "You came just during lunchtime so you would not have to stay very long."

"I did not realize that your lunch starts this early," I replied dumb-foundedly.

"I have to go now, or the *Altersheim* will get mad with me because I've reserved lunch for today," Ma continued. "I could tell you many interesting stories. And you come just before lunch. Don't you have a heart? Forty-two people who have tormented me are now dead, or very ill. Remember that, Ami."

My mother threatened me with a grim, sad look. A familiar emotional bomb from our past hit me again. Like so many times before, it destroyed all of my objective thoughts. I did not say, "Dear Mama, don't worry, we'll tell the *Altersheim* you won't eat there today. Or maybe I could eat there also."

Instead I said, "I'm leaving. Good bye."

"Will you take this to the city hall in Rheinfelden?" she asked me, while handing me a sheet of paper. It appeared to be a form that she had filled out for the *Sozialamt,* to reserve a place for herself in a German *Altersheim.*

"No I won't take it, but I will mail it for you and pay the postage."

Ma followed me out of the house, insisting that I take her form, but I obstinately refused. Her stubbornness further shut down my objectivity. With a final wave of rejection, paper in hand, she shuffle-jogged down the sidewalk to her lunch. Her long white hair was fluttering about her battered skull. Sadly, I watched her; she never looked back and disappeared around the corner of a building. I resisted my urge to run after her. And hug her. But I was not even man enough to yell out that I loved her.

I will never see her again. Maybe only her skull. Maybe in heaven.

◆   ◆   ◆

Siggi and I flew back to America on different flights. On my way from Zurich to New York, I visited with a young man from Oman who sat next to me. While waiting for our next flights, we continued our talk and he insisted on buying me a drink. During my next stop, O'Hare Airport, I waited in a deserted hall for another connecting flight, while admiring a man gracefully floating though the motions of T'ai Chi Chuan by a high glass wall.

"What is he doing?" I heard someone say behind me.

I turned to discover a man who was wearing a long, threadbare coat. I explained to him what little I knew about this ancient Chinese exercise. Then he told me that he had been robbed on the subway and had lost his wallet. He showed me his injured wrist, where the thief had torn off his watch as well. His old-fashioned, horn-rimmed glasses, which had broken during the shuffle, were held together with cellophane tape. But I was suspicious of his story because his clothes looked a little shabby, like the ones I always used to wear.

"I have to get to Virginia and need some money," he said to me.

"How would you get there?"

"I would take the bus," he responded.

"How much will it cost?" I asked him.

"I need twenty dollars."

We had a long discussion; he was intelligent and well read and this impressed me. He told me that his wife was from Joburg, Johannesburg, and that they now lived in Israel. He said that if I gave him this amount, he would send me a copy of a book that he'd written. I told him that I would like to read it, but that I might not be able to understand its contents. Regardless, I gave him the money because his book would be a fascinating souvenir.

In our many travels we had found people who had been very friendly and helpful to us. In Australia, Linda and I had bought something, and the clerk had insisted that we did not have to pay for our purchase. In France, a traveler had bought us sandwiches, while at another time, we had returned a like favor to a lady on a train in Italy. I liked Italians. They had fiery spirits and fit my liking of the wildest, the mostest, the fastest, the... Linda and I had observed two dark-eyed women arguing with each other. They had gestured vivaciously and shouted melodiously, as if acting out an opera scene, and their language was music to my ear.

And we also had met a few people who were not so kind to us. I had let an older German gentleman step onto the train ahead of me because we had a lot of luggage with us. He entered the doorway and lingered there as if no one else wanted to get in behind him. Forgetting what I had been taught so long ago, to have respect for my elders, and without saying a word, I placed our biggest suitcase on his foot. He moved forward and said nothing as if he hadn't felt a thing.

I remembered other *Sauerkraut* that I could have done without. After Linda and I had visited Aunt Adele on her farm in East Frisia, we took a taxi to the city of Emden. We had told the driver in English to take us to a hotel and did not let him know that I could understand German. I was an American and played the role. He told us that he knew of a good hotel and would take us there. But before we arrived in Emden, we asked him to take us to a hotel near the railroad station instead, so we would be able to walk there in the morning and save a taxi fare. But he insisted on taking us to **his** hotel. When we arrived there, he hurried into it, closing the door behind him, even though we had not paid him or gotten our suitcases out of his trunk. I rushed after him and heard him say to the clerk *"Dies sind Amerikaner, verstehen Sie,* these are Americans, do you understand?"

When I then heard this clerk repeat, *"Dies sind Amerikaner, verstehen Sie?"* to the porter, I remembered little firecrackers in the night. Crack. Crack. I knew that someone would try to take advantage of us, but I did not yet know when and how and would have to be vigilant. The porter led us to our room in a house next door, and I found that its lock was broken. Knowing that this was highly unusual in this land, since Germans always build things that are difficult to break, window hardware being up to ten times as massive as its American counterpart, I told Linda "I'll bet the window won't lock either." This was the case, and it appeared that it had been intentionally disabled.

We blocked our door with a chair and went to bed. But I could not sleep. At about four in the morning, I heard someone tinkering outside our door. I cleared my throat to let them know that I was awake and heard the would-be thief run away. That's when I finally fell asleep. When we checked out of this joint late that morning, the clerk asked me if we had slept well.

"Yes," I forced the lie.

After I paid for our room, he asked me again: "Did you really sleep well?"

Linda and I did meet kind German strangers as well. We had landed very early one morning at the Frankfurt airport and took a taxi to a hotel in this city. There was yet very little traffic, and our driver was in such a hurry that he drove across two, and three, lanes through some curves. Linda again left finger marks in her seat. When we checked into the hotel and told the clerk about our exhilarating ride, he offered us a free hotel room for the remainder of that night.

Another kind stranger that we met in this land was at the ruins of the Roetteln castle. While we were paying to visit it, I casually mentioned to the ticket agent that the German middle class appeared to be getting a lot richer than its American counterpart. This prompted him to let us visit these ruins free of charge.

◆　　　◆　　　◆

On my long flight back I wondered why I had taken this trip. I had found only a very small portion of the files that I wanted from Ma and had visited only a few relatives after Siggi already had returned to the States. For one long month we had been immersed in stifling heat and gloom from our past, and our visit with our mother had been a disaster. Again. She had written us for help to clean out her apartment, so she "could die in peace." When we arrived there, she did not ask us to do so, and we had left it as we had found it. *Would she not now be able to die in peace?*

Had her request to clean up only been another bait to lure us to visit her? Or did she not ask us to help because it would be too great a trauma to part with her material collection that she had acquired as an emotional anchor? Why could she not exchange her junk pile, her treasure, for the great pleasure of having two sons that she so longed for? To always be together with the two heroes that she had created? Did we not want...

**"Not universal love
But to be loved alone."?**

Epilogue

There are two kinds of injustice. The first is found in those who do an injury, the second in those who fail to protect another from injury when they can.

—*Cicero*

If Cicero's statement is true, is everyone guilty of injustice?

◆　　　◆　　　◆

Along with the papers that I brought back from Ma was a recently-dated notice from a social worker who wanted to see her about her housekeeping. A few weeks after Siggi and I returned from our European visit, Ma wrote me that she had lost her apartment, and everything that she had accumulated had been removed. Someone had taken her home, and she did not know what happened to her treasures.

Was Ma's collection, her paradox, preserved as a shrine?

Or did it become someone's garbage?

Either way, for this philanthropic service Ma had to pay about 2000 dollars. That's inflation. Our Christmas eviction from our luxurious home in the Hardtstrasse 45 had not cost us anything, in terms of money.

Maybe Ma could have hired a merry band of lawyers to recover this huge sum.

During the last few years she lived in an *Altersheim* in Rheinfelden, Germany, where she again had decorated her room in her motherly motif, but in an international style. Several times a month she toured with other old people around Southern Germany, Switzerland and

France. They frequently stopped at wholesale outlets where free, or nearly free, product samples were given to *seniors*.

Ma did not give up by the age of fifty, sixty, seventy, eighty or ninety, and I doubt if she ever took more than a few aspirins to ease her pain in all of her life. After attending a party at her *Altersheim*, she recently died in her sleep at the age of ninety-three. All partied out.

◆   ◆   ◆

Pa, Teufi and Oliver. Well, I rarely think of them.

◆   ◆   ◆

Aunt Adele visited Linda and me in the States in the nineteen-seventies. Yellowish, bumpy blotches decorated both of her upper eyelids. Was it the good or the bad kind of cholesterol that she stored there? She is now in her eighties in spite of the gruesome cholesterol in her eyelids.

◆   ◆   ◆

Uncle Deepo died of prostate cancer.

◆   ◆   ◆

Shortly after Uncle Fullo retired from the mill, he suffered a stroke and was confined to a wheel chair for several years before he died. *Did he take it all with him?*

◆   ◆   ◆

Maxo went slowly. In addition to other illnesses, he had suffered bladder cancer, and during his last few years, he wore disposable diapers which he hung up to dry around his home and his car. *A new kind of air freshener?*

A couple of years before Maxo departed, he visited Linda and me and told her that he would leave us something because we had come to the United States on his behest, Siggi and I. Now I knew why we had come; we came on his behest. That's the word he used, "behest." It is defined in my dictionary as "a command, an order, a direction or injunction." Maybe that's why his final will stated that Siggi, his wife and son were to receive the largest share of his estate; and I was also to benefit somewhat.

Over the years, several different *law* firms had prepared multiple wills for him, but I did not know this until he died. His final will appointed Siggi as the executor of his estate and it stated:

"1.3 Friend. I have one friend in whom I have great confidence **who is related to me by marriage** whose name is Siggi Neuman who resides at…"

Another paragraph was as follows:

"4.7 Disinherison. I specifically make no provision in this Will for Willem Schitzma and Mrs. Willem Schitzma, son and daughter-in-law of my brother Deepo. I also make no specific provision for my nephew Raichel Timmermann in this Will."

For a long time after he died, Siggi, with a lot of excellent assistance from his wife, was in the process of executing Maxo's final will in the spirit of his wishes and to the letter of the law. When suddenly…

Hallelujah!

…suddenly, unexpectedly, virtuously, there they were again, another merry band.

At the court hearing, the main lawyer for our relatives came into the courtroom with a dolly loaded full of boxes, full of documents, and big posters diagramming the Schitzma lineage. Very impressive. The stack of boxes, not necessarily the lineage. Our lawyer entered the courtroom with a briefcase containing Maxo's wills and copies of depositions.

Should I have continued Ma's tradition of carrying a whip? To help me untangle our jurisprudence?

During the proceedings I was called to the witness stand to present the silver sugar and creamer set, that was engraved and signed "Uncle Maxo," to show the judge that my deceased benefactor also considered me to be his relative.

Siggi testified that we had been the Schitzmas' slaves. Through the earphone that the court clerk had provided for me, I heard their collective gasps. *Were our former masters shocked about the truth? Or were they shocked because they thought that they had helped us greatly, and we did not appreciate it?*

More than one year after Maxo died, our cousins' lawyer convinced the judge that Siggi was not qualified to continue as the executor of his estate. Furthermore, they claimed that since we were not relatives by blood, we should not receive a large portion of it. Even though more than half of Maxo's many beneficiaries sent affidavits to this judge contesting his ruling, he removed Siggi anyway, and never even mentioned Maxo's specifically named alternate executor, his accountant. No one claimed that Siggi had been negligent, incompetent or fraudulent. Nevertheless, the judge replaced him with a trust officer from a bank where some of the Schitzmas appeared to do business. *Was this because the judge thought that Siggi and I were merely boat people that happened to drift ashore? Or was this so because we did not live in the judge's voting district?*

This judge also awarded substantial shares to the three **specifically disinherited** people. The lawyer and his secretary who had prepared Maxo's final will had to give depositions ahead of the court hearing. When they then testified before the judge, both of them had poor memories and contradicted themselves, and each other, so often that afterwards the lawyers for the opposing parties stated, off the record, that they were "not impressed with their competencies." *If contracts and laws are only pieces of paper, should not everyone be allowed to partic-*

*ipate in merry anarchy? In spite, or because, of thousands of laws, how far
have we advanced towards such?*

Poof! Poof! Poof!

◆　　◆　　◆

Do you think that Siggi and I are sour, bitter, suffering *victims*?

Ha! We never said "uncle!"

We are Americans do you understand? Old-time and self-made. We
live in the land of unlimited opportunities and have fine-tuned our
mindsets to benefit from them. Siggi was a Senior Fulbright Scholar. I
have more zest and enthusiasm at sixty-something than some people
have at sixteen! I enjoy the smallest, biggest, fastest, weirdest and the
wildest. I've climbed Mt. Rainier and floated the Colorado River. I
love to eat and feel like a deer when I run in races. At least after I get
my second wind. As long as possible, Linda and I will continue to
delight in exploring both ordinary and exotic places.

I have traveled many lands and have read thousands of publications.
This has convinced me that there has been no greater land than America. America allowed Siggi and me to wrench ourselves from bondage
and thrive through our own individual efforts. These struggles obviously required a great deal of patience and self-discipline. Not blind
obedience, but a brute stubbornness to do right, even at the risk of
offending others.

◆　　◆　　◆

**"Negation and despair,
Show an affirming flame."**

Candlelight!

Are we blessed, Siggi and I?

Printed in the United States
92944LV00003B/1-48/A

9 780595 223145